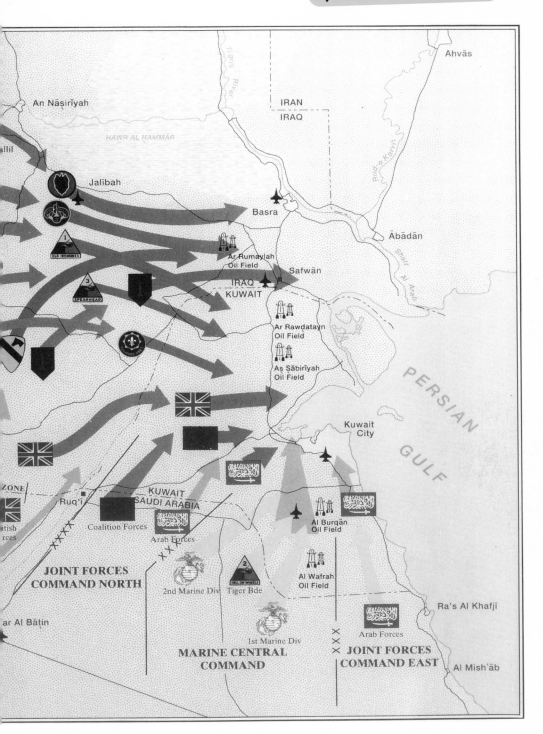

LIGHTNING

Also by Lt. Gen. Edward M. Flanagan, Jr.

Before the Battle (1985)

The Los Banos Raid (1986)

Corregidor: The Rock Force Assault, 1945 (1988)

The Angels: A History of the 11th Airborne Division (1989)

Battle for Panama: Inside Operation Just Cause (1993)

An AUSA Book

LIGHTNING

The 101st in the Gulf War

Lt. Gen. Edward M. Flanagan, Jr., USA (Ret.)

BRASSEY'S, INC.
Washington • London

Brassey's, Inc.	
Editorial Offices	*Order Department*
Brassey's, Inc.	Brassey's Book Orders
8000 Westpark Drive	c/o Macmillan Publishing Co.
First Floor	100 Front Street, Box 500
McLean, Virginia 22102	Riverside, New Jersey 08075

Brassey's books are available at special discounts for bulk purchases for sales promotions, premiums, fund-raising, or educational use through the Special Sales Director, Macmillan Publishing Company, 866 Third Avenue, New York, New York 10022.

Library of Congress Cataloging-in-Publication Data

Flanagan, E. M.
    Lightning: the 101st in the Gulf War/Edward Flanagan, Jr.
        p. cm.—(AUSA Institute of Land Warfare book)
    Includes bibliographical references and index.
    ISBN 0-02-881095-3
    1. United States. Army. Airborne Division, 101st—History—Persian Gulf War, 1991. 2. Persian Gulf War, 1991—Division history—United States. 3. United States. Army—History—Persian Gulf War, 1991. I. Title. II. Series.
DS79.724.U6F555 1994
956.7044'2—dc20

All photographs and maps are courtesy of the U.S. Army

10 9 8 7 6 5 4 3 2 1

To the courageous troopers who put the
"lightning in the Storm"

An AUSA Book

The Association of the United States Army, or AUSA, was founded in 1950 as a not-for-profit organization dedicated to education concerning the role of the U.S. Army, to providing material for military professional development, and to the promotion of proper recognition and appreciation of the profession of arms. Its constituencies include those who serve in the Army today, including Army National Guard, Army Reserve, and Army civilians, and the retirees and veterans who have served in the past, and all their families. A large number of public-minded citizens and business leaders are also an important constituency. The Association seeks to educate the public, elected and appointed officials, and leaders of the defense industry on crucial issues involving the adequacy of our national defense, particularly those issues affecting land warfare.

In 1988 the AUSA established within its existing organization a new entity known as the Institute of Land Warfare. Its purpose is to extend the educational work of the AUSA by sponsoring scholarly publications, to include books, monographs, and essays on key defense issues, as well as workshops and symposia. Among the volumes chosen for designation as "An AUSA Institute of Land Warfare Book" are both new texts and reprints of titles of enduring value that are no longer in print. Topics include history, policy issues, strategy, and tactics. Publication as an AUSA Book does not indicate that the Association of the United States Army and the publisher agree with everything in the book, but does suggest that the AUSA and the publisher believe this book will stimulate the thinking of AUSA members and others concerned about important issues.

Contents

Preface

One Saturday night in late April of 1991, I attended an Airborne Awards dinner in Atlanta. Seated next to me was Maj. Gen. (at the time) Binnie Peay. He had given a briefing that afternoon on the part played by the division he commanded in the Gulf War, the 101st Airborne Division (Air Assault). My old airborne mind (dating from my four years of service with the 11th Airborne Division during and after World War II) was most impressed by the 101st's superb implementation of the air mobility concept, a radical combat tactical maneuver never before launched and completed on such a large scale.

During the dinner, I talked to General Peay in more detail about the 101st in Operations Desert Shield and Desert Storm. He mentioned that if he had had the time, he would write a book about the 101st in the war. He had even selected a title: *North to the Euphrates.* After some additional conversation, I told him that I had just written *Battle for Panama: Inside Operation Just Cause* and that I would like to take on the challenge of writing about the 101st in Desert Shield/Desert Storm. He readily agreed and said that he would cooperate fully.

My thirty-five-plus years in the U.S. Army (starting upon graduation from West Point with the WWII class of January 1943 until my retirement on July 1, 1978) included service in three wars. I saw the U.S. Army swell to unprecedented size and quality and, after World War II, contract with unimagined and almost uncontrolled haste to a hollow shell of its former power. My generation also saw the army implode upon itself and almost disintegrate in the aftermath of the Vietnam experience and wondered if it could ever regain even a semblance of its former stature and credibility.

In the late 1980s, we began to hear army generals and junior officers boast about the fact that "today's Army was the best that we have ever had." We older types listened with interest and a great deal of skepticism. To see if some of the bragging was in fact warranted, I decided to investigate and to write about Operation Just Cause in Panama. After a great deal of research and many interviews, I came to the conclusion that, yes, this was a superb new army, whose ranks were filled with disciplined, smart, and well-trained soldiers and imaginative, self-confident leaders. This new army, I found, was equipped, during the Ronald Reagan and George Bush presidencies, with the most modern weapons and equipment that a heavily funded research and development program could produce. I also found that the top leaders of the country were willing to give the military forces a clearly defined mission and the means with which to accomplish that mission, and then to stay out of the micromanagment business.

Operations Desert Shield and Desert Storm proved again that the branches of the U.S. armed forces were, in fact, smoothly operating components of a top-flight military machine both commanded by officers who understood military tactics and manned by soldiers, airmen, marines, and sailors who understood their jobs and were willing, even eager, to carry them out in combat.

Lightning will, I trust, demonstrate that the 101st Airborne Division (Air Assault) was a superbly trained outfit that completed its unique tactical missions with skill, initiative, and courage.

Acknowledgments

A book of this sort, the military history of a division in combat, could never have been completed with some degree of accuracy without the active and full cooperation of many officers and soldiers who were a part of the action. I will undoubtedly and inadvertently neglect to mention some of the troops who were so helpful to me in compiling the necessary data, records, and statistics.

At any rate, I must thank Gen. J. H. Binford Peay III, now the vice chief of staff of the U.S. Army, for his inspiration, interviews, letters, manuscript review, and encouragement; Lt. Gen. Henry H. ("Hugh") Shelton, now the commander of XVIII Airborne Corps, for his interviews, letters, manuscript review, and tapes; Maj. Gen. Edison E. Scholes, then the chief of staff of XVIII Airborne Corps, for his letters, personal interviews, and encouragement; Lt. Gen. Jack V. Mackmull, U.S. Army, retired, a pioneer in the development of the air mobility concept, for his clear explanation of some of the tests that led to today's air mobility tactics; Lt. Col. Thomas J. Costello for an absorbing narrative of his experiences in the Gulf War; Maj. Steven A. Chester for a most interesting letter explaining his observations of events during and after the 3d Brigade's helicopter assault into Area of Operations Eagle along the Euphrates; Lt. Col. Terry M. Peck, a staff officer of XVIII Airborne Corps, for his interviews and letters that clarified the part played by the "Jedi Knights" in the genesis and evolution of the overall tactics of the Gulf War; Lt. Col. Dick Cody for his help in reconstructing the initial air strikes of the war by his AH-64 Apaches and his review of and comments on the chapter detailing those first strikes; Lt. Col. Charles G. Thomas for acting as my liaison officer with the staff and commanders of the 101st, for sending me after-action reports, briefings, and charts outlining the actions of the 101st in the Gulf War, and for answering many of my telephoned questions on details; Maj. Richard P. DiSilvio for gathering and sending me photos depicting the 101st's units, actions, and camps in Saudi Arabia and Iraq, and for answering hundreds of telephoned questions; Tom Donnelly, of *Army Times,* for loaning me more than a score of taped interviews with commanders in the 101st; Capt. Ida M. McGrath, the 101st Division historian, for her personal history of the initial commitment of the 101st to Saudi Arabia; Col. Emmitt Gibson for a detailed account of the part played by his Europe-based 12th Aviation Brigade in the war; Lt. Col. William Bryan, commander of the 2d Battalion of the 229th Aviation Regiment, for his after-action reports, telephone conversations, and tapes detailing the widely dispersed actions of his Apache battalion, attached to the 101st; Lt. Col. Peter C. Kinney for a detailed letter outlining the actions of the 3d Brigade, the Rakkasans; Lt. Col. Rhonda Cornum for reviewing chapter 19 and correcting details of which she was intimately and painfully aware.

I would be remiss if I did not at least allude to the help of many commanders in the 101st who were taped by the staff of *Army Times* and whose comments provided details and helped flesh out the book.

I must also thank two Brassey's, Inc., professionals: Don McKeon, the associate director of publishing, for his patience and expert guidance in many letters and phone conversations; and Vicki Chamlee, copy editor, for her discerning comments, questions, and corrections to the original manuscript.

Acronyms

AA	Assembly area
AAA	Antiaircraft artillery
AASLT	Air assault
ABN	Airborne
ACL	Allowable cargo load
ACP	Assault command post
ACR	Armored cavalry regiment
ADA	Air defense artillery
ADATS	Air defense, antitank system
ADC (O)	Assistant division commander for operations
ADC (S)	Assistant division commander for support
ADVON	Advance party
AFN	Armed Forces Network
AH-1S	Attack helicopter (Cobra)
AH-64	Attack helicopter (Apache)
AHO	Above the highest obstacle
ALCE	Airlift control element
ANVIS	Aviation night vision goggles
AO	Area of operations
APC	Armored personnel carrier
APO	Army post office
APR-39	Radar warning receiver
ARCENT	Army Forces Central Command
ARTEP	Army Training and Evaluation Program
ARVN	Army of the Republic of Vietnam
AVSCOM	Aviation Systems Command
AWACS	Airborne warning and control system
BDA	Bomb damage assessment

BM	*Boevaya mashina* (Russian command vehicle)
BMP	*Boevaya mashina pekhoty* (Russian tracked APC)
BP	Battle position
BRDM	*Boyevaya razved yuale-1'naya dozornaya mashina* (Russian LAV)
BRO	"Big Red One," or the 1st Infantry Division
CA	Civil affairs
CAB	Civil affairs battalion
CARF	Commercial Aircraft Reserve Fleet
CAS	Close air support
CBAC	Cavalry brigade air combat
CE II	Camp Eagle II
CENTCOM	Central Command (General Schwarzkopf's command)
CEWI	Communications, electronic warfare, intelligence
CFA	Covering force area
CG	Commanding general
CH-47	Cargo helicopter (Chinook)
CIA	Central Intelligence Agency
CINC	Commander in chief
C&C	Command and control
CNN	Cable News Network
CO	Commanding officer
CONEX	Container express
COSCOM	Corps Support Command
CPG	Copilot/gunner
CPX	Command post exercise
CRAF	Civil Reserve Air Fleet
CSAR	Combat search and rescue
CUVC	Commercial utility and cargo vehicle
DCU	Desert camouflage uniform
DIA	Defense Intelligence Agency
DISCOM	Division Support Command
DPICM	Dual-purpose improved conventional ammunition
DRB	Division ready brigade
DRF-9	Division Ready Force 9 (last-priority infantry battalion)
DS	Direct support
DSA	Division support area
DTO	Division transportation officer
DZ	Drop zone
EA	Engagement area
EDRE	Emergency deployment and readiness exercise
EENT	End of evening nautical twilight
EIB	Expert infantry badge
EOC	Emergency Operations Center
EPAC	Eastern Province Area Command

EPW	Enemy prisoner of war
ESSS	External stores subsystem
ETO	European theater of operations
EW	Electronic warfare (when used separately)
EW/GCI	Early warning/ground control intercept
FA	Field artillery
FAARP	Forward area arming and refuel point
FARP	Forward arming and refuel point
FASCO/FASSE	Forward Area Support Command/Forward Service Support Element
FAST	Forward area support team
FDC	Fire direction center
FFAR	Folding fin aerial rocket
FLIR	Forward-looking infrared
FLOT	Forward line of own troops
FOB	Forward operating base
FORSCOM	Forces Command
FOV	Field of view
FRAGO	Fragmented order
FSO	Fire support officer
FTX	Field training exercise
G-1	Personnel officer
G-2	Intelligence officer
G-3	Operations officer
G-4	Logistics officer
GCI	Ground control intercept
GPS	Global positioning system
HARS	Heading attitude reference system
HEDP	High-explosive dual-purpose
HEI	High-explosive incendiary
HEMTT	Heavy expanded mobility tactical truck
HET	Heavy equipment transport
HE/VT	High-explosive/variable time
HHC	Headquarters and headquarters company
HMMWV	High-mobility, multipurpose, wheeled vehicle, or Humvee, the successor to the jeep
ID	Infantry division
IHFR	Intermediate high-frequency radio
INS	Inertial navigation system
IP	Initial point
IPB	Intelligence preparation of the battlefield
IV	Intravenous fluid
JAG	Judge Advocate General
JCS	Joint Chiefs of Staff

JLAB	Joint logistics assault base
JOA	Joint operations area
JOTC	Jungle Operations Training Center
JRTC	Joint Readiness Training Center
KFIA	King Fahd International Airport
KKMC	King Khalid Military City
KTAS	Knots air speed
KTO	Kuwaiti theater of operations
LAB	Logistics assault base
LAW	Light antiarmor weapon
LBE	Load bearing equipment
LD	Line of departure
LOB	Logistics assault base
LOD	Line of departure
LOS-FH	Line of sight–forward heavy
LRSD	Long-range security detachment
LZ	Landing zone
MAB	Marine amphibious brigade
MAC	Military Airlift Command
MARCENT	Marine Central Command
MCC	Movement control center
MCF	Multinational Coalition Forces
METT-T	Mission, enemy, troops, terrain, time
MFO	Multinational Force and Observers
MHE	Materiel-handling equipment (forklifts)
MI	Military Intelligence
MKU	Mobile kitchen unit
MLRS	Multiple-launch rocket system
MOPP	Mission-oriented protective posture
MOUT	Military operations in urban terrain
MP	Military Police
MPS	Maritime pre-positioned squadron
MRE	Meal, ready to eat
MSR	Main supply route
MTMC	Military Traffic Management Command
MTO&E	Modified table of organization and equipment
NBC	Nuclear, biological, chemical
NCA	National Command Authority
NCO	Noncommissioned officer
NOE	Nap of the earth
NSC	National Security Council
NTC	National Training Center
NVG	Night vision goggles
OH-58	Observation helicopter (Kiowa; Scout)

OP	Observation post
OPCON	Operational control
OPEC	Organization of Petroleum-Exporting Countries
OPLAN	Operations plan
OPLAN 90-3	Theater Operations Plan for Defense of Saudi Arabia
PADS	Position azimuth determining system
PB	Pyridostigmine bromide (nerve agent pretreatment pill)
PIC	Pilot in command
PJ	U.S. Air Force Para-rescue Jumper
PL	Phase line
PNVS	Pilot night vision system
POE	Port of embarkation
POR	Preparation for overseas replacement
POV	Privately owned vehicle
POW	Prisoner of war
PSC	Personnel service company
PX	Post exchange
PZ	Pickup zone
QM	Quartermaster
RATT	Radio and teletype
RCT	Regimental combat team
RGFC	Republican Guard Forces Corps
ROAD	Reorganization of the army division
RORO	Roll-on roll-off
RP	Release point
RPG	Rocket-propelled grenade
R&R	Rest and relaxation
RRP	Rapid refuel point
S-2	Intelligence officer at battalion or regimental level
SAAFR	Standard Use Army Aviation Flight Route
SAMS	School of Advanced Military Studies
SANG	Saudi Arabian National Guard
SAR	Search and rescue
SFC	Sergeant first class
SITREP	Situation report
SOAR	Special Operations Aviation Regiment
SOCCENT	Special Operations Command, Central Command
SOF	Special Operations Force
SOP	Standard operating procedure
SOS	Special Operations squadron
SPOD	Sea port of debarkation
SUPCOM	Support Command
SWA	Southwest Asia
TAA	Tactical assembly area

TAAC	Theater army area command
TACON	Tactical control
TACSAT	Tactical satellite
TADS	Target acquisition designation system
TA-50	Table of allowances 50 (personal, government-issued equipment)
TF	Task force
TFW	Tactical fighter wing
TOC	Tactical operations center
TO&E	Table of organization and equipment
TOW	Tube-launched, optically controlled, wire-guided missile
TPFDL	Time-phased force deployment list
UH-1H	Utility helicopter (Iroquois but commonly known as the Huey)
UH-60	Utility helicopter (Black Hawk)
UN	United Nations
USAF	U.S. Air Force
USAREUR	U.S. Army, Europe
USO	United Service Organization
VMI	Virginia Military Institute

LIGHTNING

UH-1Hs fly in formation in northern Saudi Arabia.

1 | The U.S. Path to Battle

"This will not stand. This will not stand, this aggression against Kuwait."[1] The president of the United States was adamant, forceful, stubborn, and specific. On Sunday afternoon, August 5, 1990, three days after Saddam Hussein's tanks and armored personnel carriers had rolled almost unchallenged and untouched into a virtually defenseless Kuwait on August 2, 1990, President George Bush voiced his feelings. He had just stepped down from his helicopter on the White House lawn and walked to the inevitable phalanx of photographers and reporters armed with handheld recorders, microphones, and cameras, ready to record on tape and film his every word, nuance, facial expression, and tenor. Simply listening to him, one could almost see him pounding his fist into his open hand as he vowed to stand up to Saddam Hussein and throw the world's current bully out of Kuwait.

Who does this guy think he is? the president must have thought, just before his helicopter lowered onto the landing pad, and he knew that as soon as he stepped off the helicopter he would be asked about Saddam Hussein. Doesn't he know that the UN (United Nations) had ordered him to withdraw from Kuwait the day he invaded? Does he think that the United States is simply going to ignore the invasion, redraw its atlases, and give him Kuwait? How can he possibly think that the free nations of the world will rubber-stamp his blatant disregard for international law and order?

In late July of 1990, President Bush's thoughts, readings, briefings, and discussions with the key people in his administration were not focused on Saddam Hussein and his activities. The president had a host of other things on his mind, momentous events that were almost miraculously transforming, for the better, a world that had been in the throes of a mega-billion-dollar cold war since the end of World War II. In a microsecond of recorded history, the piecemeal disintegration

1

of the Communist Empire—or, as President Reagan called it, the "Evil Empire"—raced from one former USSR satellite to the next. Germany was reuniting, with the Berlin Wall tumbling down on November 9; Eastern Europe, nation by nation, was throwing off the binding shackles of communism; Lithuania, Latvia, and Estonia were increasingly impatient for their independence fifty years after Joseph Stalin and Adolf Hitler had conspired to steal their freedom; almost half of the republics in the Soviet Union were voting to secede or change radically their relationship to the central government in Moscow; and Mikhail Gorbachev was rethinking perestroika for the homeland. Historians, to keep pace with the almost daily transformations in what used to be the Soviet Union, had to rewrite history with the help of fax machines. Ordinary citizens could keep up with the rapidly changing world stage only by watching it unfold on the Cable News Network (CNN). Weekly newsmagazines were outdated as soon as they hit the stands.

Saddam Hussein's buildup along the Kuwaiti border in late July, however, had not gone undetected. Shortly before Saddam's invasion, a U.S. KH-11 spy satellite had tracked the massing of his armor almost tank by tank, but apparently no high-level intelligence analyst had deduced Saddam's intention of blitzing into Kuwait. If one did, his anxiety had not reached the top levels in the Bush administration. In a few days just prior to his attack, Saddam had tripled his forces on the Kuwaiti border to more than one hundred thousand men. Satellite photos picked up his logistics trains to the rear of the frontline forces, inevitably suggesting that an attack was imminent. But given the prevailing conditions in the Middle East, many U.S. intelligence agencies concluded that Saddam was bluffing.[2]

Moving his Republican Guard armored forces to Kuwait's border was not a sudden, unpremeditated whim on Saddam's part. Iraq's eight-year war with Iran (1980–88) had severely depleted Hussein's supply of cash. He desperately needed more money to pay off his $80 billion in war debts. As he had so often in the past, he saw his super-rich, minuscule neighbor to the southeast as easy prey and a way out of his financial problems. And after claiming that country's oil, there were the vast pools of oil in a poorly defended Saudi Arabia right next door, waiting to be sucked out of the ground by Saddam's machines.

For almost a year prior to the invasion, Saddam's pointed rhetoric against Kuwait had filled the desert airways. At a meeting of the Arab Cooperation Council in Amman on February 24, 1990, he alleged that the United States was the culprit in the problems of the region: the United States wanted to dominate the gulf, build up Israel, and humiliate the Arabs, who could no longer look to the decaying Soviet Union for backing. He ranted and raved in a hotheaded, impassioned speech against the U.S. naval forces in the gulf and called on his Arab cohorts to weaken the pro-Israeli American influence.

Saddam thought that "putting down" the United States might not be easy but that it was attainable. "We saw that the U.S. as a superpower departed Lebanon immediately when some Marines were killed, the very men who are considered to be the most prominent symbol of its arrogance," he reasoned, to his later regret. "The whole U.S. Administration would have been called into question if the forces that conquered Panama had continued to be engaged by the Panamanian armed forces," he argued, apparently without having been briefed honestly by his subservient minions on the facts of Operation Just Cause and its results. "The U.S. has been defeated in some combat arenas," he continued, no doubt thinking of Vietnam, "despite all the forces it possesses, and it has displayed signs of fatigue, frustration and hesitation when committing aggression on other peoples' rights and acting from motives of arrogance and hegemony."[3]

Saddam summoned U.S. Ambassador April Glaspie to a surprise meeting early in the morning of July 25. Glaspie had been in Baghdad for two years, but this would be her first meeting with Saddam. In 1984, he had claimed that he was "too busy" to meet with any resident foreign envoys except those of the Soviet Union. At the meeting with Ambassador Glaspie, Saddam claimed that the Central Intelligence Agency (CIA) and the State Department were plotting against him and that the United States was scheming with the Kuwaitis to keep oil prices low and wreck Iraq's financial future. He also sneered at the unwillingness of the United States to get involved in foreign wars. "Yours is a society," he told Glaspie, "that cannot accept 10,000 dead in one battle." (Big losses in battle were not new to Saddam. In the last major battle of the Iraq-Iran War, the Iranians lost 65,000 soldiers.) He told her that if the United States brought pressure on him, he would respond with terrorism.[4]

Throughout the months prior to his invasion of Kuwait, Saddam continued his tongue-lashing of the Kuwaitis, who sat regally and autocratically on the world's third largest stock of proven oil reserves (Iraq is in second place). He ranted that Kuwait had dug slanting oil well shafts into his Rumaila oil field from Kuwaiti territory and had thereby stolen $2.5 billion worth of Iraqi oil. He demanded repayment and an additional $13 billion to $15 billion in reparations because Kuwait had driven down world oil prices by exceeding its OPEC (Organization of Petroleum Exporting Countries) quotas. He accused Kuwait of advancing its border 45 miles into Iraqi territory while Saddam was preoccupied with the war with Iran. He pressed Kuwait to forgive Iraq's debt of $10 billion that he had borrowed during the Iran-Iraq War. (And in a twist of logic that only he could conjure up, he reasoned that the rest of the Arab world, to whom he owed approximately $40 billion, should cancel Iraq's debt because he had fought the Iranian fundamentalists on behalf of all Arabs.) He insisted that Kuwait relinquish its corner of the Rumaila oil fields and cede him a long-term lease on the Kuwaiti mudflat islands of Warbah and Bubiyan, a move that would have provided him with an essential deepwater seaport and would have expanded his coastline on the Persian Gulf from a minuscule 18 miles, most of which was blocked by Bubiyan, to 225 miles. He fought with Kuwait and OPEC over oil prices and production quotas, claiming that Kuwait's ruling emir, Sheikh Jabir al-Ahmad al-Jabir al-Sabah, was keeping oil prices too low and, as a result, was reducing Iraq's oil revenues. Saddam also purported that for every dollar drop in the price of a barrel of oil, he lost $1 billion per year. Oil accounted for 95 percent of Iraq's export revenues.[5]

OPEC held a meeting in Geneva in July 1990, one aim of which was to settle the oil price and production quotas. To emphasize his demands and his resolve, Saddam moved some thirty thousand troops of his theoretically elite Republican Guard to the Kuwaiti border. Kuwait and the United Arab Emirates understood the meaning of the troop movement, and they did agree to cut production. OPEC also raised oil prices for the first time in four years, but these minor concessions did not satisfy Saddam or mollify his barrage of complaints. He knew that if oil went up to $30 a barrel, he could net $60 billion a year and pay off his huge war debt in four years. To emphasize his dissatisfaction with the oil situation and to bully Kuwait, he moved an additional seventy thousand troops to the Kuwaiti border in late July.

The July 1990 movements of Iraqi troops to the Kuwaiti border was not the first show of Iraqi force in recent decades. For years, especially since he took over control of Iraq in 1979, Saddam believed the old Baghdad claim that Kuwait belonged to Iraq anyway. Under the Ottoman Empire, Kuwait was part of the province of Basra, and Iraq had never acknowledged the sovereignty of Kuwait. In earlier times, Britain had maintained a protectorate over Kuwait and finally granted the small country its independence in 1961. When the British left, Iraq threatened to invade and restore Kuwait to its territory. To block Iraq's move, the British sent in troops that were later replaced by Arab League forces. In 1973 and again in 1976, Iraq tried to invade Kuwait without success.

With one hundred thousand Iraqi troops on Kuwait's border, Washington was still not convinced that an invasion was either imminent or probable. The administration was distracted by the events in Europe and the Soviet Union, but that was not the only reason it was surprised by the events of August 2, 1990. Just days before the invasion, President Bush had talked to President Hosni Mubarak of Egypt and to King Hussein of Jordan about Iraq's intentions. The king had assured Bush that Iraq would not invade.[6] The president of Egypt also told President Bush that Saddam had promised him personally that Saddam would negotiate with—not invade—Kuwait. And during the Iran-Iraq War, the United States publicly espoused neutrality but in reality favored Iraq because Saddam could provide a counterbalance to Iran, a revolutionary country whose possible ascendancy to power in the region "horrified" Washington. In April 1980, Zbigniew Brzezinski, President Jimmy Carter's national security adviser, claimed that "we see no fundamental incompatibility of interests between the U.S. and Iraq."[7]

In 1981, after Ronald Reagan became president, Washington's support of Saddam increased, and, in 1984, diplomatic relations with Baghdad were restored. A CIA station, "slipped" into Baghdad, had a mission to supply intelligence to Saddam, not to spy on him. In 1986, when Iran and Iraq were deadlocked in their war, the United States began to pass intelligence to Baghdad about Iranian troop movements. In 1987, the Reagan administration became more involved in the area and reflagged and escorted Kuwaiti tankers in the gulf, making Iran's ability to attack more difficult. Even an Iraqi warplane's "accidental" attack on the USS *Stark* with an Exocet missile, killing thirty-seven American sailors, did not divert U.S. efforts from helping Saddam defeat Iran. Neither did Iraq's 1988 slaughter of thousands of Kurdish civilians with chemical weapons nor its flagrant and despicable human rights violations deter U.S. efforts to reason with and to cultivate Saddam Hussein.

4

"It is better to be talking to this man than isolating him," said Ambassador Glaspie. The U.S. Senate did pass a bill condemning the gas attack, but its attempts to initiate economic sanctions against Iraq did not pass after successful lobbying by U.S. agricultural and industrial interests.[8]

The Bush administration set up normal trade relations with Iraq, and, in 1989, nearly $1.2 billion in sales flowed to Iraq from the United States. Iraq became the biggest foreign consumer of U.S. rice and one of the top purchasers of corn and wheat. Other nations followed the lead of the United States in supporting Iraq by supplying it with consumer goods.

By the spring of 1990, Saddam's ravings had reached a new level of intensity, and his actions mirrored his words. In Britain, British security agents arrested Iraqis trying to smuggle out triggering devices for nuclear weapons. The British also seized parts for a mammoth, long-range artillery weapon bound for Iraq. Gerald Bull, the Canadian who had designed the gun, was assassinated in Brussels on March 22, 1990. In its turn, Iraq arrested and executed Iranian-born Farzad Bazoft, a British journalist, for alleged spying.[9]

On April 2, Saddam raised his warrior talk to a new level of ferocity. He said he had chemical weapons, and he was prepared to use them. "I swear to God we will let our fire eat half of Israel if it tries to wage anything against Iraq," he threatened. To reinforce his words, he moved Scud missiles to western Iraq near the border with Jordan and within striking distance of Israel. The U.S. administration's reaction was muted.[10]

On April 12, a group of U.S. senators took a fact-finding trip to Baghdad.[11] Robert Dole of Kansas told Saddam that the president of the United States would veto any attempts by pro-Israeli congressmen to impose sanctions on Iraq and that "we in Congress [will] also try to exert our utmost efforts in that direction." After additional soothing words from the senators (they also condemned Israel's 1981 bombing of Iraq's Osirak reactor), Saddam could only conclude that the U.S. administration was attempting to avoid a conflict with him. During the spring and summer of 1990, Saddam's threats and complaints against Kuwait became more intense, with him railing about oil prices, quota violations, slanted oil wells, territorial disputes, and the "yellow streak" of the U.S. administration and the American people.

Saddam had another indication of the reluctance of the United States to get involved in his affairs. At her July 25 meeting with Saddam, Ambassador Glaspie had informed Saddam that "I have direct instruction from the President to seek better relations with Iraq," and "we have no opinion on the Arab-Arab conflicts like your border disagreement with Kuwait."

Later, the ambassador asked Saddam, "in the spirit of friendship," about his intentions regarding Kuwait. Saddam replied that, through consultation with the president of Egypt (reinforcing President Mubarak's report to President Bush), he had agreed to meet with and talk to the Kuwaitis. The ambassador told him that that was good news and congratulated him. She also told him that she could now take a planned trip to the United States that she had thought of postponing. For the next few days, Saddam kept his word.[12]

5

Soldiers of 1-502d Infantry, 101st Airborne Division (Air Assault), wait in an aircraft hanger at Fort Campbell, Kentucky, on the way to Saudi Arabia.

2 | Iraq's Invasion of Kuwait

Wednesday, August 1, 1990, was a hot and steamy day in Washington, D.C. In the deserts of the Middle East, the temperature was probably 35 degrees higher, but the humidity in Washington hovered around 95 percent. By that evening, Saddam had finished massing one hundred thousand of his men, tanks, armored personnel carriers (APCs), artillery, logistics, and communications on the border with Kuwait. Saddam's forces outnumbered the Kuwaitis about five to one.

Walter P. ("Pat") Lang, Jr., a fifty-year-old retired army colonel, worked for the Defense Intelligence Agency (DIA) as the national intelligence officer for the Middle East and South Asia.[1] He reported directly to the head of the agency, Lt. Gen. Harry E. Royster. Lang examined raw intelligence data—satellite photos and communications intercepts are primary sources—and developed intelligence summaries for the secretary of defense and the chairman of the Joint Chiefs of Staff (JCS). Prior to his job in the Pentagon, Lang had been the defense attaché in Saudi Arabia for three years in the early 1980s and had been to Iraq numerous times. He was intimately familiar with the area and the personalities of its key figures. He had been carefully plotting the movements of Saddam's forces from the beginning of the Iraqi buildup on its southern border.

On Monday, July 30, he had reported to General Royster that Iraqi artillery, aircraft, and logistics were on the move. He added, somewhat ominously, "I do not believe he is bluffing. I have looked at his personality profile. He doesn't know how to bluff. It is not in his past pattern of behavior. . . . Saddam Hussein has moved a force disproportionate to the task at hand, if it is to bluff. Then there is only one answer: he intends to use it."[2]

On August 1, when Lang arrived at his office at about 6:00 A.M., his staff showed him the latest pictures of the Iraqi troop movements on the Kuwaiti border. What he saw was a portrait of a corps-sized armored force deployed for an attack. Three Iraqi armored divisions had spread out in an offensive posture and had moved to within 3 miles of the Kuwaiti border. The Hammurabi and In God We Trust armored divisions had moved near the main six-lane highway—built by Kuwait in the days when Iraq and Kuwait were on friendlier terms—leading directly into Kuwait City about 37 miles away. The tanks were deployed on line some 50 yards to 75 yards apart. The Medina Luminous Division had positioned itself on the western side of Kuwait. The tanks in all the divisions were spread out for miles, with the command elements positioned behind the center of the battle formations. Some eighty helicopters were poised close to the border. Lang flashed his top-secret assessment up his chain of command: the Iraqis will attack on the night of August 1 or early the next morning.[3]

Because Saddam had massed his forces without camouflaging their movements, other U.S. intelligence specialists concluded that Saddam was using a show of force to bluff the Kuwaitis into paying him one more time to solve his debt dilemma. For many reasons, including the fact that the United States was still trying to court Saddam, the CIA, the DIA, and the State Department's Bureau of Intelligence and Research had been predicting that (a) Saddam was bluffing, or (b) if he did attack, he would seize only the islands of Warbah and Bubiyan and a part of the disputed Rumaila oil field that abuts Iraq and Kuwait and then withdraw the bulk of his forces.

Iraqi Ambassador Mohammad Sadiq al-Mashat met with John Kelly, assistant secretary of state for Near Eastern and South Asian affairs, in Kelly's sixth-floor office of the U.S. State Department on the afternoon of August 1. Kelly was visibly excited. Without any of the diplomatic niceties of such a meeting, Kelly glared at the ambassador and told him specifically and directly that the United States was greatly disturbed about the buildup of Iraqi forces on the Kuwaiti border. With the positioning of the logistics train, the battle-ready deployment of tanks, and the activities of the Iraqi Air Force, Kelly continued, it seemed perfectly clear to any reasonable observer that Iraq was about to invade Kuwait. Kelly demanded that the Iraqis pull back. The Iraqi ambassador replied that Iraq had a complete right to move its forces anywhere it wanted to in its own territory. He indicated that the press was not reporting correctly Iraq's recent oil negotiations with Kuwait. "You don't need to worry," al-Mashat said, trying to calm Kelly. "We are not going to move against anybody."[4]

Later that day, about 5:00 P.M., Kelly met with representatives of the White House, the Pentagon, and the CIA in Secretary of State James Baker's conference room. Secretary Baker was in Siberia, meeting with Soviet Foreign Minister Eduard Shevardnadze. Baker had discussed the Iraqi-Kuwaiti situation with the Soviet foreign minister and asked him, in the spirit of the new cooperation between the United States and the USSR, if the Soviets would try to restrain Saddam from an invasion. Shevardnadze thought that the Iraqis would not invade and replied that a warning to Saddam would not be necessary.

CIA Deputy Director Richard Kerr was also at the meeting with Kelly. He had been reviewing the satellite photos and radio intercepts and had come to the conclusion that the Iraqis would invade within six to twelve hours. None of the other men at the meeting was so positive.

In the Pentagon that morning, Pat Lang's flash warning of an impending attack reached top officials such as JCS Chairman Colin Powell, who also read a CIA assessment that predicted an invasion. Gen. H. Norman Schwarzkopf was also in the building at the time. Schwarzkopf was the commander in chief of U.S. Central Command (CENTCOM), the joint military agency based at MacDill Air Force Base in Florida that was created to "look after" the situation in the Middle East and to develop contingency plans for possible emergencies there. During peacetime, CENTCOM was a joint planning staff of some seven hundred personnel; until an emergency arose, Schwarzkopf commanded no actual forces. But in a Middle East crisis, he would command troop units from all the U.S. services to accomplish whatever mission the command authority assigned him.

That afternoon, Schwarzkopf briefed the Joint Chiefs and Secretary of Defense Richard Cheney in the "Tank," the Joint Chiefs' secure briefing and conference room in the Pentagon. In his briefing, he concluded that Saddam's one hundred thousand troops were so positioned to allow Saddam several possible courses of action, one of which was, of course, to invade Kuwait. However, Schwarzkopf did not predict this.

Schwarzkopf also discussed, in summary, his contingency plan for a crisis in the area—his Operations Plan 90-1002, loosely referred to as "ten-oh-two" by those staffers at CENTCOM and the JCS who were familiar with it. "Ten-oh-two" was developed in the early 1980s. It depended on a thirty-day advance warning, after which troops would begin to move. The plan called for the deployment of a tactical F-15 Eagle fighter unit on day 1 and the arrival of the the ready brigade of the 82d Airborne Division on day 7. By day 17, marines would arrive and join up with their gear, which would have been transported on a squadron of five MPS-2 (maritime pre-positioned squadron) cargo ships from Diego Garcia, 2,500 miles away. The cargo could support 16,500 U.S. Marines for thirty days of combat. It was not until day 27 that tanks would begin to move into the theater. "Ten-oh-two" would take three to four months to move about one hundred thousand troops and equipment into the area.[5]

The meeting ended without reaching a consensus. Secretary Cheney and Chairman Powell felt that Saddam obviously had the option either to bluff or to invade. General Powell, however, was leaning toward the invasion option and felt that some positive steps were necessary on the part of the administration. His suggestion, however, was not carried out.

Saddam's forces overran all of Kuwait in less than a day. At 2:00 A.M. local time in Kuwait on August 2, Republican Guard tanks roared across the border, past the customs buildings and a gas station at Abdaly, and headed down the six-lane highway toward Kuwait City, 80 road miles away. At the southeastern corner of Kuwait Bay near Al Jahrah, the tank columns turned east and raced toward Kuwait City. Along the route and in Kuwait City, Kuwaitis were awakened by the ominous thunder of artillery and mortar barrages, the rumble of tank engines, the rattle of machine guns, the penetrating noise of jet fighters, and the whumps of attack helicopter blades swarming through the darkness of the night. Kuwaitis in their ultramodern high-rises in Kuwait City could look out their windows and see the flash of air-to-ground missiles and hear the rockets crash into the Dasman Palace of Emir al-Sabah.

At 5:15 A.M., Emir al-Sabah telephoned the U.S. Embassy for help but asked that the conversation not be made "public." An hour later he called again officially to request American help, and he did not care who knew it. Kuwait was in serious trouble. But all that the United States had "in-country" at the time was a small detachment of U.S. Marine guards at the embassy. Kuwait would have to wait for U.S. military help.

In three and a half hours, Iraq's tanks were in Kuwait City. As the tanks circled the palace, the emir loaded his family onto a helicopter and flew off in the morning turmoil to a safe haven in Saudi Arabia. For two hours, his soldiers had resisted an intensive artillery barrage around the palace, but it was the traditional problem of "too little and too late."

As the emir flew out, he could witness the devastation in Kuwait City caused by the artillery and tank fire and could see some of the three hundred Iraqi tanks that rumbled and blasted their way through the city. One force had encircled the central bank building. Other Iraqis laid seige to the Ministry of Information, the home of Kuwait's state television and radio broadcasting facilities. The last message from the radio station was a plaintive plea for help. "O Arabs, Kuwait's blood and honor are being violated," an emotional voice cried over the radio. "Rush to its rescue. The children, the women, the old men of Kuwait are calling on you. Hurry to our aid!"[6]

By nightfall of August 2, all of the emirate of Kuwait and its 2 million people were under the control of Iraq's armed forces. The civilized world had a new menace on its hands, one whose atrocities in the past dwarfed the likes of Lt. Col. Mengistu Haile-Mariam of Ethiopia, Fidel Castro of Cuba, or Manuel Noriega of Panama. It was now definitely up to the free world and the United Nations to combat Saddam. And President Bush took the initiative.

An AH-64 Apache is prepared for loading onto a C-5A transport bound for Saudi Arabia.

3 | A Line in the Sand

On Wednesday evening, August 1, the Washington hot lines erupted. A series of phone calls alerted the power clique to what would be yet another surprise in a tumultuous year.

From the Pentagon, Rear Adm. Bill Owens, Secretary Cheney's military assistant, called Cheney at home to tell him that Iraqi tanks had crossed the Kuwaiti border and were probably on their way to Kuwait City. The senior staff duty officer in the Joint Chiefs' Crisis Situation Room alerted General Powell on the secure line at his home—Quarters 6 at Fort Myer, overlooking the Potomac River and downtown Washington—with the same message: Saddam had made his move. This was not a bluff. General Powell decided to stay home for the time being and get telephonic updates as the situation developed.[1]

Lt. Gen. Thomas W. Kelly, whose ruddy complexion properly reflected his Irish heritage, was General Powell's solid, literate, no-nonsense, and politically and militarily savvy director of operations.[2] Kelly got a call about 9:00 P.M. at his home, Quarters 23A at Fort Myer, and was in the Pentagon's Crisis Situation Room in less than half an hour. Alerted by the JCS duty officer, the vice chairman of the Joint Chiefs, Adm. David Jeremiah, checked into the Pentagon at about the same time.

The president's national security adviser, Lt. Gen. Brent Scowcroft (U.S. Air Force, retired), was at home in Bethesda, Maryland, when he got the word. He was surprised that Saddam had actually invaded Kuwait, having felt that Saddam's buildup was just more of his bluster and bluff to scare more millions of dollars out of his militarily weak, smaller neighbors. Scowcroft immediately went to his office in the White House and called President Bush, who was in the family quarters. Bush told Scowcroft that he "wanted something done right away."

Secretary of State Baker was flying from Irkutsk to Ulan Bator when he received the word. At first he told the reporters on his aircraft that the Iraqis had "seized a border town." A few minutes later he apprised them, "I don't want to mislead you. It appears that their objectives are greater than we thought."[3]

The two centers of the administration's power in Washington, the White House and the Pentagon, swung into emergency operation. Staff officers reported for duty not knowing when they would get home again. Bunk beds and cots transformed offices into dual-purpose rooms. Eighteen- and twenty-hour work days became the norm for a time. Hot lines were fully manned and operating at maximum capacity. The Pentagon's alerts streamed rapidly down the chain of command to those commanders with a "need to know."

Information flowed into the Crisis Situation Room from a number of intelligence agencies. For example, the Defense Intelligence Agency had sent Maj. John F. Feeley, Jr., an intelligence specialist, to the U.S. Embassy in Kuwait a few days before the invasion. He was able to keep the DIA abreast of the Iraqis' destruction and occupation of Kuwait City as the invasion developed. During this period, Feeley was actually assigned to Central Command.

That same night, General Scowcroft called a meeting of the deputies committee of the National Security Council (NSC) at the White House. That group drafted a statement denouncing Saddam's invasion and demanding the immediate and unconditional withdrawal of all Iraqi forces from Kuwait. Later, Scowcroft hand carried the statement to President Bush, who approved it on the spot. At 11:30 P.M., the statement was made public.

Scowcroft, legal counsel Boyden Gray, and Treasury Department representatives went back to work that evening. At this very first stage of the emergency, they needed to determine what the United States could do immediately to counteract Saddam's invasion and to alert the American people and the world that the Bush administration was concerned, alert, responsive, and in control. The most obvious and potentially damaging step that the United States could take at once would be to freeze Iraqi assets in the United States and to ban all U.S. business dealings with the Iraqis. Another step—one that assumed that Kuwait would be totally overrun—was to freeze Kuwaiti assets, which were estimated at $100 billion in investments worldwide. Scowcroft and his team drafted two executive orders, and at 5:00 A.M. Scowcroft was outside the president's bedroom door with the orders for him to sign. Thus, all Iraqi and Kuwaiti assets in the United States were frozen within hours of Iraq's invasion of Kuwait.

Half an hour later, President Bush and General Scowcroft were in the Oval Office discussing how to persuade allies to freeze Iraqi and Kuwaiti assets in their countries, how to encourage the Israelis to stay out of the rapidly developing emergency, and how to swing the Soviets to the U.S. side. Undoubtedly, also on their minds were how quickly and how much of the U.S. armed forces the United States could send to Saudi Arabia and how to persuade the Saudis that such help was in their national interest. Clearly the president and his national security adviser saw that the situation in the Middle East was grim: The Iraqis had completely overrun Kuwait's undermanned forces in less than a day and, in a matter of hours, could have armored divisions on Kuwait's southern border, poised and capable of invading and overwhelming Saudi Arabia's sixty-five-thousand-man force. If he gained control of Saudi Arabian oil fields, Saddam would dominate more than 45 percent of the world's known oil reserves. This crisis affected not only the United States but a number of nations, particularly Japan, which was almost totally dependent on Middle East oil. President Bush called for an NSC meeting at eight o'clock that morning, Thursday, August 2.

In the Pentagon's Crisis Situation Room, designed and manned around the clock specifically for the type of emergency now facing the United States, was a scene of controlled frenzy presided over by Gen. Tom Kelly. He sat at the center of a long table surrounded by his operational and intelligence specialists. Secure telephones connected the crisis staff to major U.S. military headquarters and to U.S. intelligence agencies at home and aboard. One of three large projection screens in Kelly's center plotted the minute-by-minute movements of the Iraqi forces and other key events as fast as the intelligence analysts could interpret the incoming data—both photographic and verbal. Another screen was tuned to CNN's around-the-clock broadcast so that the Pentagon knew what the American public and overseas viewers were seeing and hearing.

Just prior to the NSC's 8:00 A.M. meeting, President Bush told reporters that he had no plans to use American troops to resolve the crisis. He told the reporters that Iraq did not appear to be a threat to any other Middle Eastern countries, but it was his aim to "have the invasion reversed and have them [the Iraqis] get out of Kuwait." He also told them that "there will be a lot of frenzied diplomatic activity. I plan to participate in some of that myself."[4]

Schwarzkopf, who had just returned to his headquarters at MacDill Air Force Base, Florida, after his meeting with Powell the previous day, received a call from Tom Kelly at 2:30 Thursday morning. A very surprised Schwarzkopf heard that General Powell wanted him back in the Pentagon by 7:30 A.M. "This morning?" "Yes, sir, this morning." He made it. After a short conference in the Pentagon, Powell and Schwarzkopf headed for the White House.[5]

Also present at the NSC meeting were, among a number of others, Secretary of Defense Cheney and Robert Kimmitt, the under secretary for political affairs at the Department of State. Kimmitt was sitting in for Secretary of State Baker, who was in Siberia meeting with Soviet Foreign Minister Shevardnadze.

The Security Council discussed a wide variety of subjects. CIA Director William H. Webster gave an intelligence briefing in which he concluded that Saddam had used more than one hundred thousand troops to subdue Kuwait in an extravagant show of force. And Iraqi troops were now only 10 miles from Saudi Arabia's border and its vast oil fields. He concluded that the Saudi forces would be no match for the heavily armored and Soviet-trained Iraqi forces.

Next came discussions of diplomatic maneuvers, the viability of economic embargoes, the vulnerability of Iraq's system of moving oil via pipelines through Turkey and Saudi Arabia, possible economic sanctions, the possibility of China's support in the situation, UN actions, the oil profits that Saddam could amass by

15

selling Kuwaiti oil ($20 million per day), and the stranglehold Saddam would have on the oil market if he also controlled the Saudis' output.

Secretary Cheney led the talk to military options. He told the group that some KC-10 tanker refueling planes had been moved to Saudi Arabia. He also emphasized the threat posed by Iraq's million-man army and Saddam's control of 20 percent of the world's oil. General Powell then reported on the professionalism of Iraq's military maneuvers and that a U.S. attack air package, a squadron of F-15s, was on alert to go to Saudi Arabia if the Saudis gave their consent. General Schwarzkopf discussed a variety of possible military options including retaliatory air strikes and the defense of the Saudi Peninsula, an effort requiring upward of two hundred thousand troops from all the U.S. services.

The meeting was a forum for an exchange of views and a discussion of the effects of Saddam's actions nationally and internationally. President Bush seemed to sum up the meeting when he said at the end, "This must be reversed." He called the invasion a "naked aggression" and adjourned the meeting with only one course of action determined: Bush ordered three aircraft carriers to move to the gulf.[6]

That afternoon President Bush flew to Aspen, Colorado, to give a speech at the Aspen Institute. He also met for two hours with Great Britain's Prime Minister Margaret Thatcher, who, by chance, happened to be in the area and staying at the mountain guest house of the U.S. ambassador to Britain, Henry Catto. Referring to the invasion, Mrs. Thatcher declared that Saddam "must be stopped." She said that the only way to convince Saddam of the folly of his action would be to use military force and "to send troops immediately."

During her conversation with President Bush, Prime Minister Thatcher proved once again that she was known as the "Iron Lady" for good reason. She reminded Bush that in 1982 she had had to send armed forces to the British-administered Falkland Islands to drive out an Argentine invasion force. She also drew an analogy between Hitler and Saddam. And she clearly felt that there was no hope for an Arab political solution to the problem. She pointed out that Saddam had previously told a number of Arab leaders, including King Fahd of Saudi Arabia, King Hussein of Jordan, and President Mubarak of Egypt, that he had no intention of invading Kuwait—yet now he occupied the entire emirate and called it his nineteenth province. To him, it was a fait accompli.

Thatcher reminded Bush of the close and very special relationship Great Britain and the United States enjoyed. What was needed now, she said, was Western—read U.S.—leadership, and Thatcher was prepared to follow with troops if Bush decided to commit U.S. forces. She also told him that France would be willing to tie in with Western leadership. "Don't worry about France," she said. "When it gets difficult, you can count on her. She will be with you."[7]

During Bush's talk with Thatcher, King Fahd returned a phone call to Bush. King Fahd told the president that he was "astonished" at Saddam's invasion of Kuwait; Saddam had promised the king personally that that was not his intention.

16

Bush remarked that, with the Iraqi armored forces rapidly deploying along Kuwait's southern border, he thought that Saudi Arabia was in danger. He offered air, naval, and ground support. King Fahd then mused about whether the U.S. forces would stay long enough to defeat Saddam, whether the United States would withdraw its forces rapidly after the threat was over, and whether Washington would sell to the Saudis the advanced weaponry and aircraft necessary to defend themselves. Bush responded affirmatively to all three questions but drew nothing positive or specific from Fahd.[8]

Back in Washington the morning of August 3, President Bush again met with the NSC in the Cabinet Room in the White House. He asked the council two major questions: What are our interests, and what are our military options?

General Scowcroft started the discussion by saying that the council had to begin with the fact that Saddam's invasion of Kuwait was unacceptable but that "it's hard to do much. There are lots of reasons why we can't do things, but it's our job." He said that the United States could not tolerate the invasion; there was too much at stake. Satellite photos showed that the Iraqis had already moved through Kuwait City and were within 10 miles of the Saudi border. While the Saudis had the latest and best advanced fighters and airborne warning and control system (AWACS) reconnaissance planes, its sixty-five-thousand-man army could put up only a token ground fight against the armored might of Saddam's million-man force. In just a few days, if he so decided, Saddam could control the oil of Saudi Arabia.

Other members of the council voiced their concerns about U.S. interests: the West's oil supply was in danger; some nations' economies, especially of some Eastern European emerging nations, were in jeopardy; Israel's security was threatened; Saddam, who already had a chemical and biological capability, was within a few years, or less, of building a nuclear weapon; and other world leaders were watching the United States, whose credibility, as the sole surviving world power, was in question. In short, the national and international dangers were real, not imagined. The national interests of the United States were in peril. "What if we do nothing?" was clearly not a viable option. The result of "doing nothing" would be catastrophic, observed one adviser.

Cheney had been underwhelmed by the dearth of military options offered by the Joint Chiefs thus far. "Modest," someone had called them. So Cheney brought General Schwarzkopf to the meeting. The Pentagon and Schwarzkopf's CENT-COM staff had been working feverishly for the past thirty-six hours, dusting off old contingency plans and melding them into a new plan for the U.S. military forces—one that would be more than a surgical strike or a "one-shot" affair. General Schwarzkopf briefed the council on this revised plan, calling for the deployment to Saudi Arabia of two divisions plus a separate brigade, more than five hundred air force planes, a multicarrier navy battle group, plus a support naval task force of scores of logistics, operational, and command ships. Schwarzkopf said that his joint force would number about 150,000 troops.

Schwarzkopf's presentation seemed to shock some of those sitting around the large conference table in the Cabinet Room. But since an Arab solution to the invasion seemed remote—the Arab League could not even get a full vote to denounce the Iraqi invasion—a U.S. military effort appeared necessary. It was also clear to all participants that King Fahd would first have to give his consent to such a deployment of foreign forces on his soil. They also knew Saudi Arabia was a conservative Arab country, home of the key religious shrines at Mecca and Medina. To accept hundreds of thousands of U.S. and other foreign troops swarming all over his country, King Fahd must be persuaded that they were necessary to protect his country's interests.

During the meeting, President Bush had instructed Cheney and Chairman Powell to meet with Prince Bandar bin Sultan, Saudi Arabia's ambassador to the United States. They were to brief him on the details of the situation, the perceived danger to his country, the extent of Saddam's invasion, and the possible U.S. courses of military action.

Bandar, forty-two, had been Saudi Arabia's ambassador to the United States for almost ten years. He was well known around Washington, and he dealt personally with the upper echelons in the Department of State, CIA, and the White House. He spoke fluent English, knew American customs and mores, and had been a Saudi jet fighter pilot for seventeen years. Brash, swaggering, and personable, Bandar threw big parties, enjoyed ties with important people in other governments and the media, and had dealt closely, including lunches and fishing, with then-Vice President Bush during the Reagan years. He was the son of the Saudi defense minister, Prince Sultan bin Abdul Aziz, and had great influence on King Fahd.

That afternoon, Bandar met with Cheney and Powell in a Pentagon conference room. Bandar opened the meeting with what he sensed from his conversations with Saudi leaders: the House of Saud thought that the United States would not go all out to drive Saddam out of Kuwait. He reminded them of President Carter's token effort in a previous Mid-East flare-up, when he had sent only twelve unarmed F-15 fighters. Bandar told Cheney that the royal family could not reach a consensus about accepting U.S. military aid. The king did not want another token show of force, a gesture that he felt would only prod Saddam to more plundering and land-grabbing.

To emphasize the severity of Saudi Arabia's situation and to impress upon Bandar that the United States was earnestly intent upon a formidable commitment, Cheney did two things. First, at Bush's direction, Cheney showed Bandar classified, high-resolution satellite photos of the three Iraqi armored divisions that had led the attack on Kuwait. One division was now moving through Kuwait to its southern border with Saudi Arabia and was followed by other divisions massed in a formation similar to the one seen just before the Kuwaiti invasion. This formation appeared, in all likelihood, to be deploying for a thrust at the Saudi oil fields 200 miles to the south near Dhahran. Second, General Powell briefed the prince on classified military plans to deploy two divisions and one brigade plus substantial air and naval support, including three aircraft carriers. The president had not yet approved the deployment but was "leaning toward it," Cheney said. The prince seemed impressed, especially when General Powell told him that they were talking about one hundred thousand to two hundred thousand troops. Bandar promised to call King Fahd and said that he, Bandar, would be "an advocate for immediate American deployment."[9]

At 5:00 P.M., the president reconvened the NSC. CIA Director Webster strongly felt that the Iraqis intended to invade Saudi Arabia and go for the jugular—the Saudi oil fields in eastern Saudi Arabia—and that Saudi Arabia could not defend itself. Bush was convinced that Webster was right. The threat was real and clear. Besides that, mused Bush, Americans in Kuwait, Iraq, and Saudi Arabia were also in danger.

At this session of the NSC, the president appeared more forceful, decisive, and determined. General Powell, noting the president's apparent readiness to use U.S. military power, advised him to "draw a line in the sand." The United States needed to send enough troops, reasoned General Powell, to convince Saddam that "if he attacks Saudi Arabia, he attacks the United States." The president asked Powell to see him the following morning at Camp David to discuss the military options in more detail. At the end of the meeting, Bush said, "I believe we go."

The next morning, August 4, the president, Vice President Dan Quayle, Secretary of Defense Cheney, General Powell, General Schwarzkopf, Secretary of State Baker, and additional advisers met around a 25-foot-long table in the modern conference room of the Aspen Lodge at Camp David. The purpose of the meeting was to sort out the national interests and the extent to which Saddam had assaulted them and to decide on a course of action.

CIA Director Webster opened with an intelligence briefing that showed, ominously, the Iraqi armored forces massing near the Saudi border. Secretary of State Baker, who had hurried back from his meetings with Shevardnadze in the Soviet Union, reported that Moscow would readily support UN sanctions against Iraq but not the commitment of U.S. military forces. Baker also announced that he had persuaded Shevardnadze to cut off supplies of Russian weapons to Iraq and that they issued a communiqué condemning the "brutal and illegal" Iraqi invasion and calling all nations to join the arms embargo against Iraq. Baker then discussed prevailing on the United Nations to bolster its condemnation of the invasion by imposing economic restrictions and a naval embargo on Iraq.

He left the conference early to work with the United Nations on this last point; On August 6, the United Nations imposed trade sanctions, depriving Iraq of imports and earnings on its exports—primarily oil. By then President Bush had already imposed the naval blockade.

When Schwarzkopf was called upon to brief the conferees, he used two charts; one showed what it would take to defend Saudi Arabia and the other detailed the forces needed to liberate Kuwait. Schwarzkopf also gave a schedule of units and their possible deployability dates, the availability of air and sea transportation to ferry these units from their U.S. and European bases to the gulf area, the buildup timetable and the dates when troop units could be in Saudi Arabia, and the difficulties inherent in the plan. He made one point absolutely clear: ground troops would be essential for air and naval forces alone would not suffice.

At one point, the conferees discussed the possibility of having President Mubarak accomplish the mission with just Egyptian forces, but they quickly decided that Saddam would not be impressed. They were moving more and more to the realization that the only action that would grab Saddam's attention was American "boots in the sand."

During the session, President Bush received a phone call that shook the group. Calling from Cairo, President Mubarak reported that the Saudis had decided against accepting U.S. troops on their soil. Bush left the conference room to telephone King Fahd. Without mentioning Mubarak's call, Bush told the king that he was deeply concerned about an Iraqi invasion of Saudi Arabia, that he did not want to establish any permanent U.S. military bases in Saudia Arabia, and that he would withdraw U.S. forces as soon as the king thought the time propitious. He also proposed that Secretary of Defense Cheney should visit the king for more complete discussions so that the king himself might see the classified satellite photos that had so impressed Bandar the day before. The king was noncommital and even suggested that a lower-ranking team might be more appropriate "if anything went wrong."

Returning to the conference room, President Bush said he was convinced that sending a large force to Saudi Arabia was necessary. The key questions were, How much was enough to do what job? Was the mission to defend the Saudis or to drive Saddam out of Kuwait? Bush also wanted to avoid another conflict like Vietnam— a classic example of too little too late without a clear-cut objective or mission.

General Powell insisted that, whatever the mission, half measures would be disastrous; the United States had to send enough forces to do the job rapidly. To prove his point, Powell reviewed the experience of Operation Just Cause in Panama. In that operation, the United States had sent enough forces to overwhelm the Panama Defense Forces immediately with minimum casualties.

Bush then accepted Powell's and Schwarzkopf's plan of sending substantial air, naval, and ground forces to defend the Saudis, even though King Fahd had not yet consented to allowing U.S. ground forces into his country. A naval aviator in World War II, Bush knew that in the long run it might be necessary to throw Saddam out of Kuwait by military force, but that had not been decided upon at the Saturday session. For the immediate future, first the president seemed to want to try diplomacy and economic sanctions to free Kuwait.

With the Powell-Schwarzkopf unified plan, Bush had agreed to send what some termed "a trip-wire" force of the division ready brigade (DRB) of the 82d Airborne Division, a brigade that is on twenty-four-hour alert and ready to be in the air in eighteen hours; a 16,500-man marine amphibious brigade (MAB) armed with tanks and armored personnel carriers aboard pre-positioned ships; two squadrons of air force F-15s; and a number of B-52 bombers moved from the continental United States to Diego Garcia to go into action against Iraq in the event that Saddam headed for the Saudi oil fields. This force would be followed by the 101st Airborne Division (Air Assault) from Fort Campbell, Kentucky, and the 24th Infantry Division (Mechanized) from Fort Stewart, Georgia. Before ground forces could move into Saudi Arabia, Bush still needed King Fahd's permission, but the president readied plans to send upward of two hundred thousand troops to fight Saddam. His belligerency and determination were clear when Bush snapped to reporters on his return from the Camp David conference, "This will not stand, this aggression against Kuwait."[10]

The next day, the Saudi royalty was still dickering among themselves about permitting U.S. and other ground forces onto Saudi terrain. King Fahd, who had known Bush since he was the director of the CIA, tended to trust the president's assessment of the danger Saddam posed to Saudi Arabia. The king's brother, Crown Prince Abdullah, however, wanted an Arab solution with no outside help. About fourteen hours after Bush had suggested it, King Fahd agreed to a visit by a team headed by Secretary Cheney.

Cheney, General Schwarzkopf, and several others left Washington at 2:30 P.M. Sunday, August 5, for the sixteen-hour flight to Jidda. They arrived at 1:00 P.M., August 6, Saudi time. Cheney's CIA representative was armed with an array of satellite photos, maps, and intelligence estimates. Schwarzkopf brought along his top-secret plan, Operations Plan 90-1002, which included a deployment schedule for the U.S. ground, naval, and air forces.

At the conference with King Fahd, his brother, Prince Bandar, and other members of the Saudi government that evening in the king's private council room in the summer palace, Cheney began by repeating what President Bush had told the king on the phone. Moreover, in addition to asking for permission to bring in ground and air force units, Cheney requested that the king shut down the Iraqi oil pipeline that runs from Basra across Saudi Arabia to Yanbu al Bahr.

During the subsequent discussion, Schwarzkopf brought out top-secret photos that showed Iraqi tanks moving toward the Saudi border, tanks that belonged to one of the Republican Guard divisions. He also presented other information that verified the movement of two other armored divisions near or toward the Saudi border and the emplacement of seven Scud missiles outside Kuwait City and well within range of Saudi Arabia. Schwarzkopf then outlined the buildup of American forces. First he mentioned that the aircraft carrier USS *Independence* and several other warships were already in the area. Second, in the buildup, fighter squadrons would arrive next, followed almost immediately by light, air-transported army forces. He also presented the follow-on deployment schedule, week by week, and emphasized that by week 17, the U.S. forces, along with the Saudis' armed forces, would be strong enough to defeat anything Saddam could throw at them.

King Fahd and his brother then talked to one another in Arabic. Prince Bandar interpreted as best he could for Secretary of Defense Cheney. Prince Abdullah, still unconvinced that the Americans' plan could work, remained in favor of an Arab solution. "There is still a Kuwait," he pointed out. The king reminded him that Kuwait was all in the hotel rooms of Saudi Arabia, a reference to the exiled Kuwaiti leaders who were residing in a Sheraton hotel near Taif. Finally, King Fahd turned to Cheney and said that Saudi Arabia would go along with the American plan on two conditions: President Bush had to promise that U.S. forces would pull out as soon as the threat to Saudi Arabia was over and that the United States would not launch a war without King Fahd's approval. Cheney agreed and immediately called the White House. President Bush backed up Cheney and, in addition, gave him the approval to start moving U.S. forces.[11]

After the August 4 meeting at Camp David, General Powell had hurried back to the Pentagon to alert his staff and subordinate commanders to the decisions the president had just made. Shortly thereafter, fifty warships, including the aircraft carrier *Eisenhower,* steamed toward the gulf to join the *Independence* and other ships in enforcing the embargo. The next day, Sunday, General Powell telephoned Gen. Hansford T. Johnson, commander of the U.S. Air Force's Military Airlift Command (MAC). Powell alerted General Johnson that Washington was thinking about sending "the biggest, fastest, farthest military deployment in the country's history" to Saudi Arabia. Johnson and Powell knew that air transportation would play a major role in making the deployment the fastest.[12]

Thus, on August 6, the scenario for Operation Desert Shield began to take shape. First, King Fahd had finally, and apparently reluctantly, asked for U.S. troops to defend Saudi Arabia. Second, the United Nations authorized economic sanctions against Iraq. Finally, the Pentagon sent out orders alerting the first units for deployment. Two squadrons of F-15 Eagles, or forty-eight aircraft, from Langley Air Force Base in Hampton, Virginia, received orders to move to airfields near Riyadh and Dhahran, Saudi Arabia. The next afternoon, a traffic jam developed at Langley's West Gate as hundreds of locals, learning through the grapevine of the F-15s' departure time, arrived to watch the planes of the First Tactical Air Wing take off for Saudi Arabia. The air force commander was prepared to have his planes fight their way in to Saudi Arabia so he timed their arrival for dusk, when the Iraqi Air Force was known to be less than alert and courageous.

Arriving with the planes of the First Tactical Air Wing was the division ready brigade of the 82d Airborne Division. Maj. Gen. James H. Johnson, Jr., commanding general of the 82d Airborne Division, received orders on August 6 from the commanding general of the XVIII Airborne Corps, Lt. Gen. Gary E. Luck, to deploy by air his division ready brigade of some twenty-three hundred men. The brigade, plus staff from XVIII Airborne Corps, arrived on August 8 and 9, the first ground element in Saudi Arabia. The first U.S. soldier, a member of the 82d, was on the ground in Saudi Arabia within thirty-one hours of the initial alert order. Operation Desert Shield was under way.

101st Airborne soldiers load up into C-5A transports on the way to Desert Shield.

4 | Fort Campbell: Summer 1990

For the troops of the only air assault division, the 101st Airborne, summer 1990 was a period of intensified training at Fort Campbell, numerous off-base specialized training exercises, and multiple commitments for training the Reserves, the National Guard, and the cadets at West Point. From the commanding general, J. H. Binford ("Binnie") Peay III, to the newest private in the rear ranks, the 101st Airborne was busy.

Lt. Col. Gary Bridges, commander of the 3d Battalion of the 327th Infantry Regiment, which is part of the 101st Airborne's 1st Brigade, had a task force of some one thousand men at West Point's basic training site, Camp Natural Bridge, about 10 miles from the main West Point campus. Bridges and his men were training the cadets from the third class—sophomores, or "yearlings" in West Point lingo. This training focused on the basics of the army's combat arms: rifle marksmanship, infantry squad maneuvers, weapons' identification and functions, drills for artillery crews, patrolling, map reading, and general soldiering. It was the cadets' first serious introduction to the ways of the active army, an institution somewhat different from West Point and especially the plebe year that they had just finished.[1]

The 101st Airborne Division had a number of other diverse missions that summer, requiring some troops to move far from the home base at Fort Campbell. Lt. Col. Andy Berdy and his 2d Battalion of the 187th Infantry Regiment, for instance, trained at the Jungle Operations Training Center (JOTC) in Panama to learn how to operate in the heat and humidity of Panama's jungles. The battalion did not know that soon it would suffer and bear a different type of heat and terrain in the Saudi desert. Another division element, this one from the aviation brigade, had deployed to Honduras to support the U.S. Southern Command with Task Force Bravo. The 101st Airborne had sent another task force to Puerto Rico for Exercise Ocean Venture, demonstrating the division's capability to self-deploy. From the 101st Aviation Brigade, the 4th Battalion's UH-60 Black Hawk helicopters and the 7th Battalion's CH-47 Chinook helicopters made the trip to Puerto Rico without problems. In addition, the 101st Airborne Division moved equipment by barge to the Joint Readiness Training Center (JRTC) at Fort Chaffee, Arkansas, in the largest military movement of equipment on U.S. inland waterways since World War II.

A third battalion task force—Lt. Col. Joe Chesley's 2d Battalion of the 502d Infantry Regiment—was preparing to deploy to the Sinai as part of a UN peace-keeping force. According to the assistant division commander, Brig. Gen. Henry H. ("Hugh") Shelton, "It was a three- to five-month process getting everything prepared for that, . . . getting reorganized and trained for that mission."[2] Its assignment was slated to be a six-month tour of duty with the Multinational Force and Observers (MFO) in support of the U.S. commitment to the peace-keeping force established under the terms of the 1979 Israeli-Egyptian peace treaty. The 82d Airborne Division at Fort Bragg, North Carolina, and the 7th Infantry Division (Light) at Fort Ord, California, also rotated battalions through the Sinai. Pulling MFO duty was somewhat unusual in the annals of the modern army although training and deploying soldiers on peace-keeping and war-fighting missions were not new concepts, given the uses of military forces in various capacities, such as postwar occupation, over the ages.

In fulfilling other commitments, Lt. Col. Charles DeWitt had his air defense artillerymen from Company A and headquarters batteries of the 2d Battalion of the 44th Air Defense Artillery Battalion at Fort Knox, Kentucky, training other West Point cadets. A small group from Lt. Col. Mark Curran's 3d Battalion of the 101st Aviation Brigade was assisting a U.S. Reserve unit during its annual summer training at Gagetown, Canada—an outstanding training site, in the opinion of some U.S. officers, jointly used by U.S. and Canadian forces. D Company of the 1st Battalion of the 502d Infantry was on a field training exercise at the Greenville Wetlands, an off-post National Guard training site about 50 miles from Fort Campbell. C Company of the 326th Engineers sent a team to compete in a sapper competition at Fort Bragg, North Carolina. Another engineer unit, A Company of the 20th Engineers, was working on an on-the-job training site, helping to build a campground project at Piney Camp Ground, Land Between the Lakes, Tennessee. With all the commitments of his division around the world, General Peay must have wondered what troops he was going to use for the next assignment. Little did he know the 101st Airborne would shortly be engulfed with a mission that took his whole force and then some.

One of the 101st Airborne's most significant off-base training exercises that summer was a CENTCOM-sponsored command post exercise (CPX) at Fort

Bragg from July 23 to July 28. Developed and engineered by CENTCOM commander General Schwarzkopf and his staff, this CPX, dubbed Internal Look, was based on the fictitious scenario that a hostile Iraq had invaded Saudi Arabia.[3]

The XVIII Airborne Corps staff and the staffs of the 82d Airborne Division, the 101st Airborne Division (Air Assault), and the 7th Infantry Division (Light) deployed to Fort Bragg's training area and set up their tents, communications, and computers in the woods. The CENTCOM staff remained "hunched over their terminals at Eglin Air Force Base, Florida." The Third U.S. Army, playing its actual role of the army command in CENTCOM, and U.S. Navy, Marine, and Air Force units were also taking part.

While the CPX did not exactly foreshadow Saddam's invasion and pillage of Kuwait, it did help familiarize the 101st Airborne Division staff and other participants with the entire Persian Gulf region, particularly the geography and terrain of Saudi Arabia. And there were some uncanny and startling similarities between Internal Look and actuality. A CENTCOM colonel played the part of Saddam Hussein and, according to Tom Donnelly writing in *Army Times,* "was giving the American defenders fits. He was lobbing Scud missiles at the Saudi ports of Al Jubayl and Ad Dammam, the airfield at Dhahran, and the Saudi oil fields. He was massing his tanks for a two-pronged attack."

The only forces deployed on paper during this simulation had entered the country only two weeks earlier. These forces included simply the understrength 24th Infantry Division (Mechanized), the paratroopers of the 82d Airborne, and the light but mobile 101st Airborne Division (Air Assault) and a Marine contingent. In Internal Look, "Saddam" drove his forces down the highway along the Persian Gulf and was successful in beating a small marine force back into Al Jubayl. He also drove a second force into the desert of Saudi Arabia's Eastern Province. The understrength 24th Infantry could not handle both attacks. What could it do?

"We were down here playing the damned scenario . . . that in fact was being played out in reality," said Col. Bob Beddingfield, who was the operations officer for Third Army, the ranking army headquarters in the CPX.

"During the exercise, we received short, detailed briefings on the buildup of Iraqi forces on the Kuwaiti border," remembered Lt. Col. Mike Burke, a staffer for XVIII Airborne Corps. "At the time, the assessment was the Iraqis were saber-rattling to compel the Kuwaitis to settle the debt situation [from the Iran-Iraq] war." But by the time Internal Look was over on July 28, 1990, intelligence clearly indicated that "this is going to happen."

After Internal Look was completed, General Schwarzkopf reviewed the results. According to Lt. Col. Richard Rowe, another staffer from XVIII Airborne Corps, Internal Look had been played with a "force list (of units) very similar to what it had been a decade ago—the rapid deployment force for this area of responsibility." In those days, the area of responsibility was Iran, where light infantry might have blocked the mountain passes. "The key is the different ground," continued Rowe. "The difference between Iran and this area was that now we had a flat desert with very few roads. The planning throughout the entire time in Iran reflected the topography of Iran, which is very mountainous, so attacks became channelized." Colonel Beddington said, "We needed a heavier force because the threat was more heavy. And also a cav [cavalry] regiment, because you had a lot of screening to do here." The general consensus was that the troop roster had to be beefed up with at least one more heavy division and another cavalry regiment.[4]

Other factors General Schwarzkopf worried about were Iraq's Scud missiles and what countermeasures he could use. Col. Joseph Garrett, the commander of the 11th Air Defense Brigade at Fort Bliss, Texas, thought he had the answer—the Patriot air defense missile. After Schwarzkopf learned that the Patriot batteries would get early warning of Scud attacks and that they could provide a viable defense against Scuds, the general included the Patriot batteries in the revised troop list when he briefed the Joint Chiefs in the "Tank" on August 1.

After the 101st Airborne Division returned to Fort Campbell following Operation Desert Storm, General Peay talked about the value of Internal Look. "It was a CENTCOM exercise under General Schwarzkopf's control. We were just one of the many forces that played in that CPX. We played under XVIII Airborne Corps, our higher headquarters. We took the division's main CP [command post] and assault CP over there [to Fort Bragg] and participated in that particular map exercise, which as you now know had a Southwest Asia focus. . . . It had some actions from a map exercise perspective that correlated to what we pre-supposed would be similar kinds of enemy actions, but it was not exactly situated on the same land mass. . . . When the situation broke in Southwest Asia, it was still very fresh in the mind both from that standpoint and knowing exactly what you needed, or what you thought you needed to deploy rapidly, having just done that. . . . I think that clearly was helpful although our division had had a Southwest Asia focus as one of many war plans that we have. So over a number of years we have trained [for] the high intensity of Southwest Asia environment as well as the lower to mid-intensity of a Caribbean/Latin America focus. We've really trained across the spectrum now for a number of years."

Another exercise that benefited the division before and during Operations Desert Shield and Desert Storm was Slim Eagle. "It really wasn't an exercise in terms of a training exercise," General Peay recalled after the war. "It was a staff action that was designed to make the Division more relevant to the times and terms of its deployability. And so we started on that in 1989 by reviewing our fighting concept doctrinally both from the operational and from the tactical standpoint. It came about because General [Carl] Vuono, Army Chief of Staff, when he sent me down here to command, told me to get the division in a more deployable status because there were those in the Army that felt it took too many sorties for it to deploy.

"So we started a number of different things. We started looking at multiple ways of deploying, by rail, by convoy, by self-deployment of our helicopters, which we really practiced at long distances on the joint exercise approach and . . . a little bit later, by strategic air, by civilian reserve fleet and by ship and also we did some inland waterway barging that we felt had promise. We did that from here to Fort Chaffee as part of JRTC rotations, actually to get at the economic cost of the railroads to have some competition. But, secondly, we found that we could do some inland waterway with ocean going barges hauled away from close to Ft. Campbell here on the Cumberland River all the way to the Latin America area. It was an attempt to look at multiple ways of deploying so we could close the division more quickly into the theatre where we were being sent. And we looked at ways to cut down the number of sorties for the strategic work. So we started a project known as 'Slim Eagle,' reducing C-141 [Starlifter] and C-5 [Galaxy] sorties. We set as goals also to improve the tactical flexibility and increase the operational tempo of the division, make it more agile, through the optimization of the air assault structure. We also said that we wanted to retain the essential war-fighting capabilities of the Division.

"So that's what we did. We had every unit go through its TO and Es [tables of organization and equipment], its MTOEs [Modified Tables of Organization and Equipment], [and] looked at ways to downsize equipment, looked at ways to consolidate and cut out unnecessary equipment . . . very much like the program of the 9th Infantry Division, the high-tech test bed of some five, six, seven years earlier. . . . Bottom line, we reduced the sortie requirements but we increased the logistics flexibility and enhanced the operational tempo while reducing the number of C-141 sorties some 25 or 26% and reducing the C-5 sorties some 10%. And that was basically exercise 'Slim Eagle' that we started on in '89. We were just about to document it in '90 when were deployed."[5]

Also that summer some officers and men were away from Fort Campbell on individual assignments. Col. Tom Hill, the commander of the 1st Brigade of the 101st Airborne, for example, was at Camp Attebury, Indiana, evaluating an Indiana National Guard unit. But the units that were still at Fort Campbell were undergoing hard training. Most started the training day at 6:30 A.M. with a battalion run, scheduled for an hour. Headquarters company of the 3d Battalion of the 187th Infantry Regiment had a 25-mile road march scheduled for August 2. Other units were practicing tube-launched, optically controlled, wire-guided (TOW) missile gunnery; drownproofing by leaping into swimming pools with full combat gear; running through platoon ambushes; training nuclear, biological, chemical (NBC) warfare teams; parachuting onto the Corregidor drop zone (DZ); running through battle drills; training to load railroad cars; navigating over land; constructing bridges; learning how to build rafts from ponchos; training with demolitions; and qualifying on the ranges with the M-16 rifle, the M-10 antitank mine, the M-249 squad automatic weapon (SAW), and the M-72 light antiarmor weapon (LAW).

*   *   *

By the summer of 1990, the 101st Airborne Division (Air Assault) had been through a number of major battles and transformations since its birth as an airborne division on August 16, 1942, at Camp Clairborne, Louisiana. It gained fame in World War II with its initial entry into combat, parachuting behind Utah Beach for the Normandy invasion on June 6, 1944. Then, on September 17, 1944, it was a part of the largest airborne operation ever attempted, Operation Market-Garden. According to Cornelius Ryan's *A Bridge Too Far:*

> Shortly after 10 A.M. on Sunday, September 17, 1944, from airfields all over southern England the greatest armada of troop-carrying aircraft ever assembled for a single operation took to the air. . . . Market, the airborne phase of the operation, was monumental: it involved almost five thousand fighters, bombers, transports, and more than 2500 gliders. That Sunday afternoon, at exactly 1:30 P.M., in an unprecedented daylight assault, an entire Allied airborne army, complete with vehicles and equipment, began dropping behind the German lines. The target for this bold and historic invasion from the sky: Nazi-occupied Holland.[6]

The 101st Airborne Division was part of a three and a half airborne division assault and fought a bloody fight in Holland for seventy-two days of continuous action.

The division's third major World War II battle was its famous stand at the strategically important Belgian town of Bastogne in December 1944. On December 16, the Germans launched a surprise attack involving thirteen German armored and infantry divisions against the U.S. VIII Corps, which occupied a 40-mile front in the Ardennes. The U.S. front began to collapse in the face of the assault, and the entire northern wing of the Allied armies in the west was threatened. At 8:30 P.M. December 17, Brig. Gen. Anthony C. McAuliffe, the 101st Airborne's commander in Gen. Maxwell Taylor's absence, received orders to move the division's 11,840 soldiers from their rest area in France 107 miles north to Bastogne. General McAuliffe's first action was to send the 501st Parachute Infantry Regiment east in an attack that temporarily upset the German advance and gave the 101st Airborne time to set up the defenses of Bastogne at the hub of a highway network, tactically important to the Germans' plans. Before the Germans tightened the noose around Bastogne, Combat Command B of the 10th Armored Division, the 705th Tank Destroyer Battalion, and the 969th Field Artillery Battalion arrived and became a part of the division's defenses.

On December 20, the Germans seized the last road leading out of Bastogne, isolating the division. For the next few days, strong German armor and infantry forces from five divisions tried to break the 101st Airborne's hold on the town. Blood plasma and ammunition had to be air-dropped to the beleagured 101st.

Nevertheless, the division held. On December 22, Lt. Gen. Heinrich von Luttwitz, the German commander in the area, sent a team of officers under a white flag into the division's lines and demanded its surrender. General McAuliffe thought that he had the situation well in hand, despite the German forces deployed all around his troops, and was surprised by the Germans' arrogance. He thought for a few moments about what he should say. His G-3, or operations officer, Col. Harry Kinnard, reminded him that his first reaction would make a good reply and repeated it to him. McAuliffe agreed. Then he sent his now-famous message to General von Luttwitz: "To the German Commander: Nuts. The American Commander."[7]

Although surrounded, attacked constantly, and faced with the care of four hundred wounded soldiers and little medical help, the division continued to hold out. On December 26, the division received belated Christmas presents—the 4th U.S. Armored Division broke through the German line, and gliders brought in litter jeeps, medical supplies, aid men, and surgeons. On January 18, VIII Corps relieved the 101st Airborne. For its gallant stand at Bastogne, the division received the Distinguished Unit Citation, the first time that an entire U.S. Army division received the award.

At the end of March, the division went to the Ruhr River region of Germany without the 501st Parachute Infantry Regiment, which stayed behind for a proposed, but never executed, parachute assault to free Allied prisoners of war (POWs). Later the division went to southern Germany and, with the 3d Division, captured Hitler's vacation locale, Berchtesgaden. With some units in Austria, the division spent the remainder of the war in the German Alps. On August 1, 1945, the division moved to Auxerre, France, to stage and train for Operation Olympic, the planned but unnecessary invasion of Japan. The famous Screaming Eagles were inactivated at Auxerre on November 30, 1945.

World War II and the Korean War were over. The cold war was heating up in Europe. Nonetheless, some forward-looking thinkers in the Pentagon were urging the army to look for new ways to fight wars—wars that might not be fought with massive arrays of tanks, artillery, and hundreds of bombers on one mission. Even President John F. Kennedy (JFK), whose massive retaliation strategy was his answer to the Russians' continued military buildup, urged the army to search for a "new look."

In April 1962, Secretary of Defense Robert McNamara prodded the army to open its collective mind to innovation and break away from the tactics and equipment of the past. He directed the army to investigate enhanced "land warfare mobility" and to conduct its examination in an "open and free atmosphere." The army set up the U.S. Army Tactical Mobility Requirements Board and appointed one of its most open-mined generals—Lt. Gen. Hamilton H. Howze, commander of the XVIII Airborne Corps at Fort Bragg—as its president. The board secretary was Col. John Norton, the former G-3 of the 82d

Airborne Division when in combat under Gen. James Gavin. Both General Howze and Colonel Norton were army aviators. The board became known throughout the army as the "Howze Board." Looking to the future, the Pentagon told General Howze to determine the army's requirements and organization for the 1963 to 1975 period. The Pentagon did not know at the time that those would be the years of the buildup, fighting, and withdrawal from Vietnam.

The Howze Board reached out to the army, the air force, and industry for new ideas, equipment, organizations, and tactics. The Howze Board developed many recommendations using army helicopters and fixed-wing aircraft in close support roles, as battlefield transportation, and as tank killers. These recommendations were so extensive that the army decided to test them, unrelated to current organizations and tactics; therefore, it created an entirely new division to be the test bed. On February 7, 1963, the 11th Air Assault Division (Test) was activated at Fort Benning, Georgia, under the command of Major General Harry W. O. Kinnard, the veteran G-3 of the 101st Airborne Division. In theory, the 11th Air Assault Division was to be a "light" division capable of air movement by air force or army aircraft. The planners scrubbed previous TO&Es, made many imaginative changes, and kept the division as lean as possible.

In addition to the standard infantry, artillery, and support units, the division included an extra multibattalion aviation group. This group had enough aircraft to lift one-third of the division at one time. Another group, the 10th Air Transport Brigade, composed of several battalions of both fixed- and rotary-wing aircraft, was activated and attached to the 11th Division to provide an air line of communications to forward elements.

For more than two years, the 11th Air Assault Division's equipment, organization, and tactics were developed, tested, refined, and retested time and time again. The Air Force and the Army argued about whose role was close air support on the battlefield and tactical mobility.

Test sites were in Florida, Georgia, and the Carolinas. For the men participating in the tests, the times were exciting. One army aviator assigned to the division, Col. James Bradin, a captain at the time, wrote recently that "no scheme was too wild to be considered. Most of the flying, more often than not dangerous, kept pilots' adrenaline flowing. Lieutenants and captains found themselves making decisions that in other organizations would have been reserved for colonels. In hindsight, it was an early test of a decision process later known in the Army as the 'power down,' where decisions are made at the lowest appropriate level. What's more, those participating in the air assault tests enjoyed a hell of a lot of fun."

Large-scale air mobile operations eventually became commonplace in the Vietnam War. So did close air support and medevac by army helicopters. In Vietnam, the army used its organic aircraft—fixed and rotary wing—separate from and independent of the air force. As Colonel Bradin said, "In the end, the efforts of the 11th Air Assault Division cemented air mobile doctrine into the soul and fiber of the Army."[8]

The 101st Airborne Division (Air Assault) was the unit that profited by the imaginative innovations introduced and perfected by the 11th Air Assault Division.

Over the next eleven years, the division went through the reorganization convulsions peculiar to the army in those postwar and Korean War periods, being activated and inactivated three times as a training unit. During additional attempts to cope with and develop division organizations for possible nuclear war, the army cast aside the traditional and battle-tested triangular configuration. On September 21, 1956, the 101st became the army's first pentomic division—a five-sided organization that was heavy in command structure and light in combat power. By 1964, the army recognized the pentomic division as cumbersomely organized and lacking the combat power a division-sized unit required. That year the 101st Airborne became a ROAD (Reorganization Objective Army Division) division—a battle grouping of nine infantry battalions, a cavalry squadron, and three artillery battalions, giving the division commander better ground mobility, firepower, and command and control. Its mission changed as well to include air assault operations utilizing helicopters.

Lt. Gen. Jack V. Mackmull (U.S. Army, retired), was one of the early enthusiasts and innovators of the air assault concept. He wrote recently that "the Air Assault concept was a direct result of the Department of Defense Aerial Mobility Requirements Board, better known as the Howze Board. This Board, chartered directly by the Secretary of Defense, charged with recommending new and innovative ways for the Army to use helicopters, concluded its deliberations in 1964. The final report contained several new and innovative Army Aviation organizations. The Air Assault Division, Air Cavalry Combat Brigade and the Air Transport Brigade were the principal large organizations. . . .

"The Air Assault Division was designed to be more than an infantry or Airborne Division whose infantry could be transported by helicopters. Real tactical mobility was designed to be more than previously described in Airmobile Operations literature. The Division would be organized and equipped to accomplish all functions of land combat using the unique capabilities of now and future helicopters. This required completely new and untested doctrine, tactics, organizations and equipment to support Air Assault Division combat, combat support and combat service support operations. . . .

"Air Assault Division operations envisioned not only Air Assault infantry being delivered to objectives by helicopters, but prior reconnaissance and security in the objective and en route areas provided by division Air Cavalry units. Pickup Zone (PZ), en route and Landing Zone (LZ) security for helicopter transported Air Assault infantry was provided by organic helicopter gunships as part of the combined arms team. General fire support for Air Assault Division operations was provided by an Aerial Rocket Field Artillery Battalion of three firing batteries with helicopters equipped with 2.75″ Folding Fin Aerial Rockets [FFARs]. As a direct result of Howze Board recommendations, the XM-103 105mm lightweight howitzer was developed for emplacement by CH-47A/B medium lift helicopters. A battalion of CH-47s is organic to the division. . . . Contrary to popular belief by personnel not conversant with the Air Assault Division, the CH-47s are not strictly logistical aircraft but are used as multi-mission assets. CH-47s routinely engage in combat, combat support, and combat service support operations.

"The Air Assault concept is as much psychological as it is physical. Troops quickly learn to effectively use the unique organizations of the Air Assault Division. The ability to take these unique organizations, combine them together to promote synergism and employ them on the modern battlefield is at the heart of the Air Assault concept. Troops believe in the Air Assault Division in the same way as they do the Airborne Division. The traditional Airborne greeting and response of 'All the way, Sir—Airborne' has been adopted as 'All the way, Sir—Air Assault' by Air Assault troopers of the 101st. Morale, esprit-de-corps and performance are visible signs of soldiers' belief in the Air Assault concept."[9]

By 1965, the Vietnam War was heating up, and the 1st Brigade of the 101st Air Assault Division joined the battle at Cam Ranh Bay on July 29, 1965. The "Nomads of Vietnam" engaged in twenty-six separate actions in three of the four tactical zones in-country. The fighting was fierce. Two men of the 101st—1st Lt. James A. Gardner and Sgt. 1st Class (SFC) Webster Anderson—won Medals of Honor.

In December 1967, the rest of the 101st arrived in Vietnam and established a base of operations at Bien Hoa. For the next four years, the division operated from Quang Tri in the north to Saigon in the south. During the 1968 Tet Offensive in January, one platoon of the 2d Brigade battled on the rooftop of the U.S. Embassy in Saigon. Operation Nevada Eagle, whose objective was to secure the lowlands of northern Vietnam and which lasted from May 17, 1968, until February 28, 1969, was the longest single campaign ever fought by the 101st. Afterward, the division launched into the A Shau Valley, one of the most important Viet Cong and North Vietnamese staging and supply areas. During the operation, the 3d Battalion of the 187th Infantry Regiment assaulted Dong Ap Bia Mountain in a famous battle against some of the best North Vietnamese troops. After the A Shau battles, the valley was open for U.S. armored vehicles and the use of long-abandoned airstrips.

On July 1, 1968, the division underwent another name change to the 101st Air Cavalry Division. That designation lasted only until August 29, 1969, when the division became the army's second airmobile division—the 101st Division (Airmobile). In its history, the division went from parachutes and gliders to helicopters, marching forward with the technology and improvisations of the modern army.

In 1969 and 1970, the division supported the civic action programs of pacification and of the Vietnamization of the war effort. In Lam Son (military plan and operation) 719 in February 1971, the division airlifted South Vietnamese forces in an attack across the Laotian border. In Lam Son 720, it backed the 1st ARVN (Army of the Republic of Vietnam) Infantry Division in its invasion of the A Shau Valley.

In late 1971 and early 1972, the 101st Airmobile—the last U.S. division to leave the Vietnam combat area—redeployed to the States. Vice President Spiro Agnew along with a former commander of the division and then-army chief of staff, Gen. William C. Westmoreland, greeted the 101st Airmobile at its official homecoming ceremony at Fort Campbell on April 6, 1972.

For the next eighteen years, the division went through other reorganizations, trained in the airmobile concept, assisted the National Guard and the Reserves in their summer training, sent the 1st Battalion of the 502d Infantry to the Sinai Desert for a six-month tour of duty with the UN Multinational Force and Observers, and deployed troops to various training exercises throughout the United States, Egypt, Europe, and Honduras.[10]

The air mobility concept advanced in 1969 was conceived by such dedicated and imaginative "air assaulters" as Gen. Harry Kinnard, a career airborne innovator; Gen. Jack Tolson, who commanded the 1st Cavalry Division (Airmobile) in Vietnam and, later, XVIII Airborne Corps; and General Mackmull, who commanded the 1st Aviation Brigade in Vietnam, the JFK Special Warfare Center, and XVIII Airborne Corps. Their air mobility concept was about to be put to the test.[11]

One briefer in the Gulf War era described the uniqueness of the Air Assault Division as "flexibility plus lethality plus agility equals utility across the full operational continuum" and as the division being "free from the tyranny of terrain." Another way of putting it is in the oft-misquoted words of Gen. N. B. Forrest: "Getting there fustest with the mostest." (Apparently, according to *The Military Quotation Book,* what he did say was, "I can always make it a rule to get there first with the most men.")

The 101st Airborne Division (Air Assault) is a one-of-a-kind organization. A quick glance at its organization chart reveals a unit somewhat like a standard U.S. Army division. Each of its three infantry brigades has three infantry battalions; its division artillery has three 105mm howitzer battalions and a battery of 155mm howitzers; its support command has a maintenance battalion, a supply and transportation battalion, a medical battalion, and an aviation maintenance battalion; and it has a Military Police (MP) Company, a signal battalion, an engineer battalion, a chemical company, an air defense artillery battalion, a military intelligence battalion, and a light equipment company.

But what sets this division apart from the normal infantry division is its combat aviation brigade. In the brigade are three assault helicopter battalions, each with thirty UH-60 Black Hawks; two attack helicopter battalions, one with eighteen

AH-64 Apaches and the other with twenty-one AH-1 Cobras; one medium assault battalion with forty-five CH-47 Chinooks; a combat aviation battalion with thirty UH-1 Hueys; and an air reconnaissance squadron (the "Cav Squadron" to the men in that unit) with sixteen AH-1 Cobras, four per troop (or company-size unit). And not clear from a standard organization chart of the division are its paratroopers: a company-sized long-range surveillance detachment and a sixty-man Pathfinder detachment in the aviation briagade headquarters company. During the six months of its covering force role before the start of Iraqi hostilities, attached to the division was an aviation brigade from the headquarters, U.S. Army Europe (USAREUR).

The tactical strength and uniqueness of the division lie in its method of entry into a battle area—by helicopter. Helicopters can move a force rapidly into combat, fly over terrain that would block truck and vehicular movement, build up forces rapidly by shuttling men and equipment, fly at night, and give the division and unit commanders flexibility with routes, target areas, and timing. In short, they are "air mobile."

But the division does have its weaknesses, all well-recognized by its planners. The division's ground mobility is extremely limited once the helicopters unload their cargo and troops on the landing zones. The helicopters can bring in a number of light vehicles, but the infantry units are limited generally to foot mobility. Extremes of weather inhibit helicopter operations. Massive helicopter operations require heavy class III (fuel) and class V (ammunition) supplies and are subject to enemy air defenses. And the units on the ground in the battle zone are particularly vulnerable to enemy NBC warfare.

Various helicopter configurations—airlift, attack, reconnaissance, and command and control—give the air assault division commander a war-fighting capability unique in the annals of combat. The helicopters permit him to reconnoiter and "see" the enemy and gauge its strength; to tailor his forces to meet his mission; to focus his combat power against enemy strength; to seize the initiative, both offensively and defensively; to build up his forces rapidly; to shift power where needed; to achieve surprise by the speed of his attack; and to bring accurate and devastating fire on enemy command and control, depots, bridges, rail lines, and road junctions.

The 101st Airborne had worked long and hard in developing and perfecting the air mobility concept. Its officers and troops were inured to the flights with simulated battles in the training areas around Fort Campbell, to the loading and unloading of personnel and cargo helicopters, and especially to the demanding maintenance and logistics of helicopter operations.[12]

At Fort Campbell during the months before deployment, General Peay had long discussions with Brigadier Generals Shelton and Adams; his chief of staff, Col. Joe Bolt; and brigade commanders and staff to develop the key logistical concepts for the 101st's combat campaigns. General Peay said, "They tried to visualize how to do things—how to set up FOBs [forward operating bases], LABs [logistics assault bases], etc."

After the war, in a letter to the author dated January 12, 1993, Lieutenant General W. G. Pagonis, the outstanding logistician of the Gulf War, said that General Peay "was a superb commander who really understood the importance of logistics!

"He always reviewed all the log issues personally and ensured not only that the tactical operation could be supported—but that he took care of his troops—a truly great leader."

Their work, training, and know-how were about to be put to the test in a harsh environment, the likes of which the troopers of the division had never felt—not in the sands of the training area in California, not in Panama, not in Egypt, not in Germany, not in Vietnam. Saudi Arabia and Iraq would be different.

Divisional vehicles and equipment are loaded onto rail cars for the move to the port of Jacksonville, Florida. From there they will be shipped to Saudi Arabia.

5 | Reassembly and Preparations at Fort Campbell

Major General Peay, a graduate of Virginia Military Institute in 1962 the commander of the Screaming Eagles, was on leave in Virginia Beach, Virginia, the weekend of August 4, 1990. It was his first break since he had assumed command of the 101st Airborne a year earlier on August 3, 1989. He was in a cottage along the beach when he received a phone call from his assistant division commander (ADC) Brigadier General Henry H. (Hugh) Shelton.

"Montie Hess [the 101st's G-3] just got a 'heads up' call from Tom Needham at corps," Shelton told General Peay. "Needham says that there is a possibility that we might deploy a force to Saudi Arabia. He did not give us any specific numbers. He did tell us to get our DRB ready to go." General Shelton then went on to tell General Peay that it was not necessary for him to return immediately, that things were under control. Shelton did not have any air flow or ship flow data (schedules of aircraft and ship types, arrival times, and locations) yet; but he would alert the first division ready brigade (DRB-1) and start deploying the initial elements of the 101st when he got the official word.

After alerting General Peay, General Shelton remembers, "I convened the command element in the division briefing room, gave them a good rundown on what I knew to date, and started the process of getting the DRB-1, the first major force, ready to start to deploy."

On Monday, August 6, Gen. Edwin H. Burba, Jr., the commander of Forces Command (FORSCOM) at Fort McPherson, Georgia, called General Shelton and told him, "You guys are going, and we are going to find some additional attack aviation to marry up with you." General Shelton then knew that at least some part of the 101st Airborne was going to Saudi Arabia, but he still did not know who, when, or how.[1]

On August 8, advance command and control detachments from the XVIII Airborne Corps and 82d Airborne Division arrived in Saudi Arabia. The next day, General Burba's headquarters issued its Operation Desert Shield deployment order to the 101st Airborne Division. The division followed up that order with its own fragmented order (Frago) 90-1, providing guidance to its units on canceling leaves, freezing retirements and permanent change-of-station moves, and listing deployment criteria. Also, the division's assault command post (ACP) began preparing to move out.

"One of the realities of serving at Fort Campbell," wrote one of the division's historians after the war, "is that the first major mission encountered is getting the force to the battlefield. Rapid deployment doesn't just happen. Rapid deployment is part and parcel to all training at Fort Campbell. Little things like alert notification rosters must be accurate. Many times, soldiers are called to assemble late at night and in the early morning hours just to check the accuracy of current lists. The whole process of getting to the battlefield is constantly trained, checked, and modified."

In early August 1990, that attention to details paid off for the 101st Airborne's methodical but rapid change in posture from a division in diversified training at scattered sites to a reunified division about to be committed to combat thousands of miles away. The order to deploy galvanized the division and unit staffs into many long days and nights of seemingly endless and hectic action. The commanders and staffs saw little of their families during this phase of the operation. "When the word came to deploy," wrote the historian, "it seemed that every sinew and fiber at the installation began to perform their individual function with an end result of a tremendously effective and smooth deployment for the force."[2]

Many actions had to be carried out simultaneously. Most important, division units and personnel had to return from off-base training and operational missions. The experience of Colonel Hill, commander of the 1st Brigade, was somewhat typical. "When the invasion started, when Iraq invaded Kuwait, I personally, with a lot of my staff and two of my battalion commanders, was at Camp Attebury with the National Guard. . . . We had just gotten up there and as soon as the invasion started, the division began getting reports and alert notices. . . . I had a secure phone at Attebury so I started talking just about daily to the ADC [General Shelton]. My concern was, should I come back?

"My brigade was DRB-3 [third division ready brigade] so I'd be the last to go out anyway. The decision initially was to stay up there. Then on the morning of the 10th of August, only reason I remember is it was my birthday, ADC called me and said you need to get back on down here. He called me early in the morning and said that he'd already dispatched a UH-60 to get us. It's about a three-hour ride up there. I was back down by mid-afternoon.

"One of my battalion commanders who was left here had been already cut over to the 2d Brigade who was the DRB-1 unit in case they got called out and went rapidly by air. I was in a briefing with that battalion, showing me what they were up to, and a guy walked in and handed me a deployment order. Really a hell of a feeling. I mean, you train all your life for that kind of thing. . . . That started us on the track. . . ." Colonel Hill will never forget his forty-fourth birthday.[3]

Another group away from Fort Campbell was Lieutenant Colonel Berdy's 2d Battalion of the 187th Infantry Task Force, which was at the Jungle Operations Training Center in Panama. He brought his battalion back to base via U.S. Air Force C-141s and C-5s and commercial aircraft as soon as his brigade commander at the time, Col. John W. McDonald, alerted him.

Lieutenant Colonel Bridges and most of his battalion, the 3d Battalion of the 327th Infantry Regiment, part of the 1st Brigade, were training cadets at West Point when Colonel Hill called him with the news that the brigade was deploying to Saudi Arabia. About 9:00 P.M., Bridges notified his men over the barracks' public address system that they were going to deploy. According to Bridges, the attitude of the men was one of "quiet professional confidence—not bravado." Bridges canceled the rest of the cadet training and took his battalion back to Fort Campbell in several truck convoys and civilian buses.[4]

The other units of the division—the 2d Battalion of the 502d Infantry preparing to deploy to the Sinai, Company A and headquarters batteries of the 2d Battalion of the 44th Air Defense Artillery (ADA) Battalion at Fort Knox training other West Point cadets, and the task force on the Honduras training mission—returned to Fort Campbell by August 17. The last of the helicopters serving in Honduras, however, did not return until August 24.

One of General Shelton's first actions after he knew the division would be deployed was to get permission from General Peay to send an advance element with the 82d Airborne Division to Saudi Arabia. "I sent an ADVON [advance party] of five good guys over to Fort Bragg to deploy with the 82d," he said later. "The key guy was Maj. Keith Huber, the current operations officer from the G-3 section. We also sent Maj. John Sapienza, the aviation liaison officer who was fluent in Arabic. He had spent a year with the Saudi forces, part of the defense attaché office over in Saudi. Early on, about the fifth or sixth of August, and this is when we knew it was getting serious, we were also tasked to send about eighteen or twenty of our guys from the 311th MI [Military Intelligence] Battalion, our Arabic language specialists, to deploy with the 82d. The 101st is oriented in Arabic language skills, whereas the 82d has Spanish skills."[5]

At about ten in the evening, August 7, Lt. Col. David Eggle, battalion commander of the 311th MI Battalion (CEWI—communications, electronic warfare, intelligence), assembled his company commanders and a portion of his staff in his battalion conference room. He gave his men, known as "the eyes of the Eagle," the following instructions: in six hours, select twenty-three of the battalion's best Arab linguists and prepare them to deploy to Saudi Arabia with the 82d Airborne

Division out of Fort Bragg. Two hours later, Eggle's team had selected and notified the men, who were told to report to their respective companies with their TA-50, or Table of Allowances 50 (personal, government-issue), equipment.

At 2:00 A.M., all twenty-three soldiers were assembled in the battalion classroom for further processing by a team from the division's headquarters—it included the G-1 (personnel), G-4 (logistics), Judge Advocate General (JAG), Division Support Command (DISCOM), and medics as well as the staff of the 311th MI. The processing team issued the twenty-three men their DCUs (desert camouflage uniforms) and NBC suits from contingency stock, gave them the necessary shots, updated their wills and powers of attorney, briefed them as well as they could on the situation in Saudi Arabia, and checked their equipment. At four in the morning, a CH-47 Chinook landed on the division parade field and then flew the linguists to Fort Bragg. Sfc. Millard L. Moore, an Arab linguist and a platoon sergeant in A Company of the 311th MI, was the noncommissioned officer (NCO) in charge of the group that deployed to Saudi with the 82d Airborne Division. One of the Arab linguists, Sergeant George, from headquarters of the 311th MI, claims the honor of being the first Screaming Eagle to set foot in the sand of Saudi Arabia during Operation Desert Shield.

The next 101st Airborne soldiers to deploy to Saudi Arabia were the five troopers from the division's advance party. The ADVON reported to Fort Bragg on August 12 and arrived in Saudi Arabia on the fifteenth. "Major Huber and Captain Lake from the G-4 Section simultaneously stepped onto the airport tarmac at Dhahran so that they could both claim to be the first 'Screaming Eagle' in the Kingdom of Saudi Arabia," noted the division's historian. Apparently the division historian failed to note Sergeant George's arrival a couple of days earlier.

When the alert came, besides getting units of his division back from their far-flung summer commitments, General Peay also was faced with the task of filling up the division, which was at 86 percent of its TO and E strength. Two weeks after the alert, fillers began to arrive at Fort Campbell; however, they were of almost all ranks, not just privates. Therefore, morale in the units suffered until the new NCOs, replacing "veteran" but junior NCOs, learned their tasks and the idiosyncracies of their officers and men, and eventually proved their worth.

Before deploying, the unit commanders at Fort Campbell had their men spend as much time as possible in the field, training for what they thought they could expect in Saudi and Iraq. But as the deployment progressed, the units had to prepare and pack their equipment for shipment, so unit training with equipment necessarily fell off. Commanders then concentrated on individual training, physical fitness, individual weapons qualification, and NBC combat. Rifle platoons even went through exercises at the post's urban warfare training area to prepare for the possibility of street and house fighting in Kuwait City.

The commanders also briefed their troops extensively on the rules of engagement that would apply in combat and on some facts about Islamic culture—basic do's and don't's. All of the soldiers learned, for example, that alcohol in any form was strictly forbidden and that women play a distinctly different role with fewer freedoms. During this phase, almost one-third of the division also went to predeployment schools for training in such critical areas as field sanitation, M-60 machine gun and M-249 SAW techniques, and combat lifesaving skills.

One advantage the division enjoyed in Operations Desert Shield and Desert Storm is that the division has been focused on possible conflicts in that part of the world. The division had a Southwest Asia focus as one of its many war plans, as General Peay pointed out after the war. Thus, it had trained for the high-intensity Southwest Asia environment for several years.[6]

While they waited to deploy, the battalion and brigade staffs tried to war-game possible Saudi, Iraqi, and Kuwaiti situations using maps, aerial and satellite photographs, and intelligence updates. The intelligence came from numerous sources, including the G-2 (military intelligence) staff of XVIII Airborne Corps and even the media. The commanders and staffs scrutinized everything they could lay their hands on about Iraq's war machine—its morale, its weapons, its tactics in the Iran-Iraq War, its training under the Soviets, and its potential for using chemical warfare.

The division's past focus on Southwest Asia again was of great help in studying the Iraqis. "These sessions gave the staff an opportunity to familiarize themselves with the Iraq order of battle, equipment, movement rates, and the battalion tactical SOP [standard operating procedure]," said Colonel Bridges after the war. "Later these planning sessions proved to be invaluable as the staff was required to put together several plans in relatively short time and simultaneously. One of the most important lessons my staff learned from these exercises was that we would have to seize and hold areas far larger than we usually trained for. Doctrinally, my battalion could expect to defend an area with a frontage of no more than five kilometers. When we did the map exercises, we realized we'd be defending areas with a frontage of 7 to 10 kilometers . . . it scared the hell out of us. In fact, during the ground war, we ended up holding an area with a frontage of 12 kilometers."[7]

At the division level, planning went on apace. The DRB-1, the 2d Air Assault Brigade, was ready to deploy as scheduled because the division had developed and practiced a "good outload [departure] sequence over the years," according to General Shelton. "By the tenth, it was obvious that the 82d was going, and the 101st was beginning to get aircraft schedules. Word came down that they did not want us to send an infantry heavy force early on but an aviation heavy force, primarily Apaches and Cobras so that 'the aircraft could take on tanks.' We were told that the 2-229th Apache [2d Battalion of the 229th Aviation Regiment, an AH-64 Apache battalion] from [Fort] Rucker [Alabama] would be attached for this operation, and we figured them into our airflow, but they would be attached to us in-country. About the tenth or eleventh, we started to get the air flow and that was when we realized this was 'no kidding—we're going to war' once that air flow started coming in.

"There was some confusion. The 5th Special Forces Group, which is also located at Fort Campbell, was given an air flow and we were given an air flow. Then all of a sudden things started changing dramatically. 5th Group was told, 'No, you're not going to pull out early, you stay where you are.' Our air flow started to change almost by the hour. It was somewhat confusing to say the least. We were being given the air flow data by Corps. We also have an ALCE [air lift control element] at Campbell, headed by an Air Force officer, Lt. Col. Tom Vissey. He was getting information from the Air Force that did not match with the information we were getting from Corps. He was responsible for outloading the division and the 5th Group."[8]

Even though the DRB-1 was ready to go on schedule—eighteen hours from its alert—the division was required to change its outloading sequence. Allegedly, word came from General Schwarzkopf to send the Apache battalion first.

The first two aircraft to depart from Fort Campbell were C-5s, carrying six AH-64 Apache helicopters each; General Shelton; the aviation brigade commander, Col. Tom Garrett; the Apache battalion commander, Lt. Dick Cody; and 144 soldiers. The planes left at 5:00 A.M. on August 17 and landed at Dhahran International Airport at noon the next day. The temperature was 128 degrees. "When I walked off the airplane," remembered General Shelton, "I'll be very frank . . . I thought I was standing in an engine backwash. And as I walked across the ramp, . . . away from the plane, I noticed that the backwash did not go away. It was the darndest thing I had ever seen."[9]

After he landed, General Shelton went to the corps's command post to see Brig. Gen. Ed Scholes, chief of staff of the XVIII Airborne Corps.

General Scholes had led the advance elements of the corps to Saudi Arabia. According to Scholes, the lead element of the corps was the 4th Battalion of the 325th Infantry of the 82d Airborne Division, which had taken off from Pope Air Force Base adjacent to Fort Bragg at 3:00 A.M., August 8. Only fifty-seven minutes later, Scholes and seventy-seven soldiers, one communications vehicle, one pallet of equipment, and the ACP (Assault Command Post) for the XVIII Airborne Corps, took off from Pope in a C-141 Starlifter. Shortly before nine the following morning, he and his crew landed at Dhahran.

"There was one Army guy there," Ed Scholes recalled. It was Lt. Gen. John J. Yeosock, commanding general (CG) of the Third Army, the army component of Schwarzkopf's Central Command.

"Welcome to Saudi Arabia," said an obviously tired General Yeosock. He had been up late at meetings in Riyadh with the advance elements of CENTCOM. Yeosock was no stranger to Saudi Arabia, having been the army's program manager (PM) for modernizing the Saudi Arabian National Guard (SANG). Not only did he help the Saudis buy and integrate new equipment, but, as the officer who ran the program, known as the "PM SANG," he worked intimately with many Saudi VIPs, including members of the royal family. For two years, Yeosock operated with the Saudis in the fields of logistics, training, and writing doctrine, and with the man who became Saudi Arabia's crown prince. With such a relationship, Yeosock became the liaison between the staff and the king, an extremely important position in a country where the royal family is dominant.

Yeosock told Scholes, briefly and directly: "Don't screw it up with the locals." Yeosock then introduced Scholes to Maj. Gen. Mohammed bin Saleh al-Hamad, the Saudi eastern area commander, and to Lt. Col. Ed Lindbaum, who worked in the U.S. military mission. Lindbaum had arranged transportation for the corps's advance party: sedans for the officers and an "assortment of sputtering Bangladeshi buses, painted in psychedelic colors," for the troops. The base at Dhahran was 30 square miles surrounded by fences, and the convoy drivers had a hard time finding their way out of the area. Eventually they found the highway leading to an old Saudi training base west-southwest of the airport. Here General Scholes would establish his CP and what would eventually become known as "Dragon City," the new home of the XVIII Airborne Corps.[10]

The few men on the ground initially felt that they were all alone and a long way from home. They knew the Iraqis were somewhere to the north, massed with hundreds of tanks and artillery pieces, but there was so much work to be done that the troops and the staff gave little thought to how exposed and vulnerable they were. Lt. Col. Richard Rowe, a staff planner with the airborne corps, remembered that he was impressed with the "matter-of-fact manner that pervaded the assault command post." He also remembered watching a televised news conference that said "there were 5,000 of us in Saudi Arabia. But there was only one other planeload of troops in Dhahran at the time. There was nothing. And all these Iraqis were massing on the border. As we got off the plane, we were looking around to see what was going to fall on us."[11]

"In the meanwhile," said General Shelton, "our Apache battalion started downloading their Apaches off the C-5 and set up a small element right there inside a hangar at Dhahran and started rebuilding the Apaches."

The mission for General Shelton and his small advance staff was to find a place to house the division, with all of its troops and equipment, as it arrived. General Shelton's meeting with General Scholes was revealing.

"I will tell you right now that this was the damndest thing I had ever seen," Shelton said later, describing how he sought a place to house the division. "It was a land grab, like the California gold rush. 'Find something,' were the orders. 'Go look at King Fahd.' " On paper during the Exercise Internal Look at Fort Bragg, the division had been based at the King Fahd International Airport (KFIA) as its initial staging area in-country. It had seemed only logical to General Shelton that that is where the division should go, and it was about 20 miles from where Ed Scholes had set up the ACP for the corps. But what Shelton didn't know was that the Saudis had redeployed the Special Forces out of Riyadh, and they had "sucked up all the buildings."[12]

King Fahd airfield was an unfinished international airport about 35 miles north of Dhahran along the Persian Gulf and about 150 miles south of the Kuwait border. Built as a monument to the king, the troops would find out later that at least the completed section was a magnificent facility.

That evening, Major Huber went out to KFIA. There an air force lieutenant colonel told him, "I'm not the guy in charge of anything, but I've been told that I am the mayor, and if you can find something, I'll let you have it." Major Huber spent most of the night looking around and finally decided on two buildings on the far side of the airfield, away from the terminal area. He got the keys and informed General Shelton, "Boss, I've done the best I can. I've got a sewage treatment plant and a water treatment plant that I think maybe we can use as a headquarters."

Later that same evening, General Shelton accompanied Major Huber back out to KFIA. "Basically, what we had," remembers General Shelton, "was a lot of sand. The Saudis used stuff called marabel to compact and get some stability in the soil, and then, in this area, they rolled and packed the soils on which to build some structures." He also remembered the heat. It was 130 degrees at KFIA. He described it as standing in a scalding hot shower while holding a hair dryer blowing directly in his face. He wrote that in a letter back to the division and said the unit commanders used his statement in briefing their troops as to what they could expect in Saudi.

General Shelton decided that he could put the CG, a war room, and part of the division's operations section in the water treatment plant, which would also protect the division's communications. He assigned the G-1 and G-4 sections to the sewage treatment plant. One of the big problems he had was to find shade for the troops stepping off the transport aircraft after the long flight from Fort Campbell. The only buildings near the terminal had been claimed for Special Forces by Col. Jesse Johnson, General Schwarzkopf's Special Operations staffer, and he was not willing to share any of them.

General Shelton was disappointed. "This was one of the few instances," he said, "when I found Americans in Saudi not willing to share. The attitude was, 'Tough shit, I got here first. So hit the road.'

"They finally offered us a parking ramp with three levels. It was a modern, all-concrete structure just outside the terminal area itself like you might find at O'Hare [International Airport in Chicago]. They also told me that I couldn't have any of the parking ramps or any of the runways to park our aircraft. I was concerned. I was looking for some hardstand to keep the aircraft from ingesting all of the sand. So I occupied by force in that area. I said, 'I got Apaches coming in, guys, and I'm parking them right out here.' They said, 'You can't do that—that's where the 130s [C-130 Hercules] have to turn around.' I said, 'No, you've got plenty of room down here to turn the 130s around.' That's where my Pathfinder training came in handy. I told them, 'I'm parking the damned Apaches right here.' Twelve Apaches had come in on the first two C-5s and six the next day. There were eighteen Apaches on the ground within two days, ready to go."[13]

The parking ramp had twenty-five hundred parking spaces per level. Shelton figured that he could shelter seventy-five hundred troops under cover in the ramp and get them into some shade as soon as possible. But he was anxious about putting so many troops in one place: "Beirut was on my mind." He added that he and General Peay were concerned about security the whole time they occupied

46

the parking ramp. Shelton had the local engineer take a look at the structure. It was a very open area, but "we ended up putting our aviation brigade [personnel] in the parking ramp because there was no other place to put them," Shelton said. "And it afforded them an immediate place to get some shade as soon as they got off the planes. We also started flowing in with them the 2d Brigade headed by Col. Greg Gile. The first concern I had was to get some tents put up for the rest of the troops to live in. I could put 7500 in the parking ramp temporarily, but, meanwhile, I've got to have a base facility to put the division in. General Peay and I discussed this at length before I left. His intent was, 'Let's get a base camp going, something we can operate out of' to include all of massive requirements for the maintenance and supplies for the hundreds of aircraft."

In actuality, Generals Peay and Shelton continued to talk regularly as the division planned at both ends—in Saudi Arabia and at Fort Campbell, Kentucky.[14]

Later, General Scholes sent Shelton to see Gen. William G. ("Gus") Pagonis at CENTCOM's forward headquarters in Dhahran. General Schwarzkopf was still in Tampa, Florida, at this point, so General Pagonis, normally the assistant chief of staff for logistics (the J-4), served as CENTCOM's forward commander. After hearing Shelton's problem, Pagonis arranged for a Saudi contractor to come out to KFIA and erect tents. (These tent contractors enjoy a huge business renting tents to the millions of pilgrims on their hajj to Mecca.)

The first group of workers were Yemenis, but, according to Shelton, a couple of different groups helped during the tent-building process. The workers were slow and frustratingly inefficient. "The tents were going up and falling down," said General Shelton, who by then was getting deeply concerned. "The clock was running," he continued. "I've got the air flow coming, and I see a fairly rapid buildup now." And a great deal had to be done in a short time. The hajj tents could accommodate four men each, but the general had the work crews attach two together so that a squad could occupy one double tent. The tents were square, pyramidal, brightly colored, with colorful designs on the inside, and made out of a highly combustible, nonwaterproof cloth that could burn in twenty-five seconds. After General Shelton saw one worker accidentally ignite one with a lit cigarette and the tent burned to the ground, no smoking within twenty feet of the tents became the rule for the 101st Airborne.

Cots were also an immediate problem. Initially, General Peay had decided that the troops should move to Saudi with as little extra gear as possible, to rough it, and cots did not make the initial cut. When General Shelton saw that the ground area where his troops had to set up was covered with a dusty powder and that the intense heat would make sleeping on the ground miserable, he called Fort Campbell and told the troops to bring to Saudi Arabia as many cots as they could lay their hands on. In the meantime, he also asked General Pagonis for a supply of cots.

Back at Fort Campbell, the deployment of the division was in full swing.

Vehicles of 2d Brigade, 101st Airborne, are loaded onto C5-As on their way to Saudi Arabia.

6 | Deployment from Fort Campbell

After General Burba told General Shelton "you guys are going" on August 6, General Peay and his division staff were bombarded with phone calls, directives, air and ship flow data, and visits by staff officers from higher headquarters with yet more information and advice.

As the dust and papers settled in his headquarters, General Peay realized (a) he was going to deploy his entire division, and (b) he would have to send part of the division by air and the rest by ship. His first priority was sorting out how each unit would deploy. It soon became clear to him that higher headquarters was giving him enough air flow to send out his DRB-1 and part of his aviation brigade by air. The bulk of the division's personnel would fly on commercial aircraft to Saudi Arabia, and the rest of the division's equipment would go by ship. Because the DRB-1 was always ready to deploy by air, this made the task easier.

Set up in the basement of Building T95 two blocks from the division headquarters and near the center of the post, the division's Emergency Operations Center (EOC) became the hub of the deployment actions. "C Day began at 071200S (071700Z) [the seventh at noon, Fort Campbell time (5:00 P.M. Greenwich time)] Aug 90 with official manning of the EOC at 1330 hrs.," wrote the division historian, Capt. Ida M. McGrath. The EOC operated twenty-four hours a day. Representatives of the general and special staff sections plus staffers from chemical, signal, air, and other support groups manned the EOC. "For the next several weeks," wrote Captain McGrath, "these people working together would push out thousands of personnel, tons of equipment and supplies and manage to do so pretty smoothly."

The EOC scheduled briefings twice daily for the commanding general, garrison and major units' commanders, and their staffs. The briefings covered the latest information on weather, intelligence, operations, air and ship flow, logistics, administration, and personnel. "Due to vast video capabilities," Captain McGrath continued, "numerous people were exposed to the command and control decisions made from these briefings by viewing them on one remote television and one screen."[1]

Even after the EOC began operating on August 7, many of the troops thought that the manning of the EOC and all the rumors about a deployment were simply preludes to yet another "drill." But it soon became apparent that this was not a drill involving just one brigade, a task force, or selected troops. The most unconvinced observer of the post's hectic activities quickly discerned that the whole division, plus the 5th Special Forces Group and the division's Corps Support Group, would move out in a matter of days or weeks.

As the orders and directives flowed down the chain of command, units scrambled to account for their troops and equipment and to get the personal lives of all personnel in order. Everyone realized the division was going to war.

On August 11, processing for overseas replacement (POR) began. The DRB-1, or the 2d Brigade Task Force, processed its troops in the Gertsch Gymnasium in its brigade area. In addition to its own three organic infantry battalions, the task force included the 1st Battalion, 320th Field Artillery Regiment; the 1-101st, 3-101st, and 9-101st Aviation Battalions; Team B from the 311th MI Battalion; B Battery of the 2-44th Air Defense Artillery Battalion; B Company of the 326th Engineer Battalion; A Company of the 101st MP Battalion; and the 2d Forward Area Support Command/Forward Service Support Element (FASCO/FSSE). By the close of business, 2,285 troops had been put through the administrative mill.

When Colonel Gile recognized that this was no ordinary alert for the DRB-1 Task Force, he and his staff made adjustments in their plans for deployment. Ordinarily, for example, soldiers deployed with only their rucksacks, or rucks. But as the mission and transportation assets became clearer, Colonel Gile ordered his troops to take duffel bags as well.

By August 13, all DRB-1's vehicles were ready for shipment, and, by the fourteenth, all pallets were ready. The following day, thirty nondeployable soldiers left for Jacksonville to guard the division's shipments at Blount Island Terminal's port.

The rest of the division processed through the Deyer Field House. Captain McGrath described the POR process this way: "A soldier entered with medical record/shot records and an innate fear of the dreaded GG (gamma globulin) shot that all deploying soldiers would receive in the butt. The first station was battle roster number verification. Next came life insurance and death benefits, wills and powers of attorney, banking, shots, glasses, dental [services], and the chaplain's corner. I thought it very appropriate to have his presence since the entire atmosphere seemed to signify death instead of life. Perhaps the chaplain's table should have been first so that [his] literature, to include Bibles, could be read while soldiers stood in lines. They were so long, one wondered if an end was in sight.

"As coordination continued for DRB-1, other issues confronted the EOC. While G-1 worked on bringing in replacements for shortages within the Division and G-4 worked logistics, the G-3 worked aircraft priorities, ship schedules, convoy movement to the Port of Embarkation (POE) at Jacksonville, Florida, and off-post mission taskings. . . .

"All of this and more going on, and the personal knowledge of knowing you may be leaving your family and friends any day. I believe this became the hardest factor to cope with. Due to delayed transportation and other factors, a waiting game commenced. One minute, the unit would be saying good-bye to their loved ones and the next minute the airflow was suspended for the 101st due to the need to get the Marines into Saudi Arabia. . . .

"As major issues were resolved, simple coordination efforts turned into mini-nightmares. A clear example of this was the establishment of a guard post on the POE. A Frago requesting individuals for the Brigades to go down and provide security for upcoming shipments proved arduous to accomplish. Everybody seemed to complain and call the EOC to get out of the mission. Patience by the G-3 staff was exceptional. . . .

"With few exceptions, everyone on Fort Campbell worked throughout the [first] weekend. Monday morning brought the now routine staff briefing and with it the continual frustration of not getting anyone on the telephone from higher headquarters. As LTC Hess stated, 'You know why it's quiet between now and an hour from now? Every headquarters in the Army is having a staff meeting. If I were the enemy, when should I hit?'"[2]

Colonel Hill remembered the commanders' and staff meetings in the EOC. "All brigade commanders, separate battalion commanders, and division staff attended the both sets of daily meetings, one at 0830 [8:30 A.M.] and one at 1700 [5:00 P.M.]. As soon as the thing started in the operations center, the CG started having these daily meetings. There would be an intell [intelligence] update and whatever ops [operations] data was happening. We would certainly get a deployment update and we would work out all problems.

"At the time it was very frustrating but even in hindsight it was a remarkable job to get everybody over there. Truly remarkable feat. It was in fact frustrating because you wanted to get it all there faster. You wanted to be sure that your boat got there with the troops [who came by plane] so you didn't have a whole bunch of troops doing nothing with no equipment. We really had a fairly decent schedule. No herky jerky kind of thing."[3]

When the 101st Airborne received the draft operations order for Desert Shield from XVIII Airborne Corps on August 8, preparations for its move overseas intensified. By now General Peay determined how the division would deploy. Colonel Giles, his DRB-1—the 2d Air Assault Brigade Task Force—and a heavy aviation element would fly from Fort Campbell to Saudi Arabia in C-5s and C-141s. Colonels Hill and John McDonald, the commanders of the other two DRBs—the 1st Brigade Task Force and the 3d Brigade Task Force—knew that their equipment and some of their personnel would make the trip by ship. The bulk of their troops would fly. And Col. Tom Garrett, the commander of the aviation brigade, knew that a large portion of his aircraft would be in the first airlift phase of the operation. It was up to the EOC to sort out the details and coordinate the departure of the troops by air and their equipment by sea.

The units moved their vehicles to the ready line to prepare them for shipment. "Trucks, engineer equipment, weapon systems, and people were everywhere," Captain McGrath wrote. "Relatives started coming in to see their loved ones because many thought that the Division would be gone in a week. Satellite dishes from local and national networks established themselves across the street from Gate 4. At any time, people expected the units to depart for Saudi Arabia. The PX [post exchange] and Commissary were swamped as soldiers did their last minute shopping. The auto shops were busy as spouses did tune-ups and maintenance checks on their POV's [privately owned vehicles]. Local restaurants did a booming business due to the influx of people in the area. Both Clarksville and Hopkinsville saw an increase in the issuance of wedding licenses."[4]

Trying to deal with the "unknown" was one of the more frustrating aspects of this deployment. In the past, when 101st Airborne troops went on any training or operational exercises, the troops knew when the exercise began, where it would be held, and when they would return. Most important, they knew they would be coming back. With Desert Shield, the troops did not know exactly when they would leave, how intense and long the combat would be, when or if they would be back, or what conditions they would find in Saudi Arabia. They only *heard* how hot it was, how much sand there was, or just how diabolical Saddam Hussein was.

Thus, General Peay constantly reminded his commanders that "to control people . . . [and] your equipment, practice control. The type of discipline you instill now will determine how many lives are lost during conflict."

At 7:00 P.M., on August 13, the Military Traffic Management Command (MTMC) notified the EOC that on August 17 the *American Eagle* (incidentally, the same ship that carried the division's equipment to Vietnam) and the *Cape Lobos* would be available for loading at the port of Jacksonville's Blount Island Terminal. Eight other ships would be ready shortly. The first major troop movement from Fort Campbell started at 7:00 A.M. on August 15, when a large convoy of 438 vehicles from the 3d Brigade started the 787-mile trip to Jacksonville. Teams from the Corps Support Group had already left Fort Campbell on August 12 to set up refueling points for the convoys along the way.

En route, the drivers received tremendous encouragement from the American public. "The convoy was the first element to really experience the overwhelming support of the American people," remembered Colonel Bridges. "As it traveled the interstate to Atlanta, people lined the overpasses and cheered. . . . Young ladies drove alongside pledging their love and exposing their breasts. Morale was never higher!"[5]

As the vehicles passed through Chattanooga, Tennessee, and Atlanta, Georgia, the crowds on the overpasses were especially thick. Locally, a radio station in Clarksville, Tennessee, had given out flags and people had made their own banners for waving at the troops. Some banners were specific: "God bless you, we love you, and kick butt."

The drivers would see more of this enthusiasm over the next three weeks while they took equipment, vehicles, and troops from Fort Campbell to Jacksonville. Pilots flew helicopters, bound for the sea trip, to Camp Blanding, Florida, to be prepared for shipment.

Operations at Jacksonville were relatively smooth. The first ship to depart, the *American Eagle,* left Blount Island Terminal on August 19 for Ad Dammam, Saudi Arabia. This ship's load was typical of the other ten: 4 AH-1 Cobras, 26 CH-47 Chinooks, 8 UH-60/EH-60 Black Hawks, 3 M-998 Humvees (high-mobility, multipurpose wheeled vehicle) with TOWs, 10 M-167 Vulcan antiaircraft artillery, 9 105mm howitzers, 428 vehicles/trailers, 148 containers, and 5 "miscellaneous pieces." By September 10, the last ship to sail, the *Saudi Hail,* was under way. The ten ships carried a total of 5,258 pieces of equipment to Ad Dammam.

Each of these ships also carried a "handful of 101st soldiers serving as equipment supercargoes," according to one after-action report. The ships crossed the Atlantic Ocean, transited the Suez Canal into the Red Sea, and then steamed to the Persian Gulf port of Ad Dammam, just north of Dhahran. The trips averaged twenty-three days.

"The sea transport was not without problems," wrote another after-action reporter, "as a number of the cargo ships of the Navy's contingency fleet were in poor repair." Delays at sea were not uncommon. From start to finish, the sea transport took forty-six days. By the completion of the deployment, the division had moved 296 helicopters to Saudi Arabia by air and sea: 109 UH-60 Black Hawks; 43 CH-47 Chinooks; 50 OH-58 Kiowas; 36 AH-1 Cobras; 19 AH-64 Apaches; 36 UH-1 Hueys; and 3 EH-60 Quick Fix Black Hawks. Not included were the 18 Apaches of the 2d Battalion of the 229th Aviation Regiment.[6]

On August 7, Lt. Col. William H. ("Bill") Bryan, commander of the 2d Battalion, 229th Aviation Regiment, an AH-64 Apache battalion, was in his office at Fort Rucker, Alabama, the home of the U.S. Army Aviation School. The 2-229th Aviation was the only "go to war" unit at Fort Rucker. The rest were all school units. At about 8:45 P.M., Bryan received a phone call from Brig. Gen. Bob Frix, the assistant commandant of the school, who told him to report to his office. Bryan had an inkling that Frix's call was significant. Bryan had heard some "rumblings" about his battalion—its major problems, its state of maintenance, its operational rate, and its personnel.

Bryan and his executive officer, Maj. George Hodge, reported to General Frix. Frix gave them the alert and said that the 2-229th Aviation would deploy to Saudi Arabia with the 6th Cavalry Brigade (Air Combat) (CBAC). Known as the "6th

Seeback," the 6th CBAC is a unique, three-Apache battalion, self-contained, attack helicopter force. Frix also told Bryan to pack an overnight bag and get ready to fly that afternoon to Fort Hood, Texas, to meet with Col. Thomas J. Konitzer, the 6th CBAC's commander.

Bryan went back to his office, briefed his staff, and packed his bag. Then General Frix called with the news that the 6th CBAC was not going to Saudi, and the 2-229th Aviation would now be reassigned to XVIII Airborne Corps, its parent unit. Bryan's unit should be ready to fly to Bragg at 2:00 P.M. About an hour later, Bryan got another call from General Frix. This time Frix said Forces Command had not decided yet where the 2-229th Aviation would be assigned, but the unit should still get ready to deploy; it was definitely going. On August 9, FORSCOM decided that the 2-229th Aviation would deploy from Fort Rucker on August 12 and join the 101st Airborne Division in Saudi Arabia.

Because it was the only unit deploying from Fort Rucker, Maj. Gen. Rudolph Ostovich, commander of the Aviation School and Fort Rucker, could use the entire post's facilities to ensure that the 2-229th Aviation would deploy properly. Bryan said that he got "all out support." Each day at 4:00 P.M., Ostovich held a staff meeting to go over details and issue orders. The MTO and E of the 2-229th Aviation was "lean," and General Ostovich made certain that the battalion had enough of everything.

By the twelfth, the battalion was ready to fly out, but the air flow had been interrupted to take sorely needed cargo handlers into Saudi to off-load the scores of planes coming into the theater. The air flow was ready by August 15, and at 9:00 A.M., the battalion's troops lined up in front of their helicopters on the Fort Rucker runway. General Ostovich gave a speech in a ceremony that was covered by four TV stations. Afterward, the troops boarded their aircraft, took off, flew in a circle around Fort Rucker, made a run over the airfield, and then headed for Lawson Field at Fort Benning. A convoy of some fourteen vehicles, including four M-998 Humvees, six two-and-a-half-ton trucks, and four HEMTTs (heavy expanded mobility tactical trucks) left Fort Rucker at about the same time.

An hour later, the planes landed at Lawson. Civilian contractors met the planes and quickly readied them for loading onto C-5As and C-141s. The first plane left at 1:00 A.M. on August 19 and over the next five days was followed by nine C-5As and ten C-141s. The wheeled vehicles of 2-229th Aviation flew out on C-141s, also. The planes landed at Dhahran after stops at Westover Air Force Base, Massachusetts, and Rota, Spain. Lieutenant Colonel Bryan was on the third sortie. Once in Saudi Arabia, he supervised the reassembly of his planes and the brief acclimatization of his troops. By August 23, the battalion was on the ground and ready to operate from King Fahd International Airport.[7]

The first combat force to deploy from Fort Campbell—the first division ready brigade (DRB-1) made up of an aviation task force and the 2d Air Assault Brigade Task Force—flew out of Fort Campbell Army Airfield on August 17. The next day, the 3-502d Infantry flew out, followed by headquarters company of the

2d Brigade, TF slice elements (combat support and combat service support parts of division support units), and the 1-502d and 2-502d Infantry battalions. In the task force was part of the 2d Squadron of the 17th Cavalry Regiment (2-17th Cavalry), commanded by Lt. Col. John Hamlin. This package included the squadron's long-range surveillance detachment, its Pathfinders, two command and control UH-60 Black Hawks, three EH-60 Quick Fix electronic eavesdropping and jamming helicopters, and the Troop A 17th Cavalry Regiment scout platoon and headquarters. Other elements in the task force included B Company, 7th Battalion of the 101st Aviation Brigade with its CH-47 Chinooks; and Task Force (TF) 9-101st, consisting of the 9th Battalion of the 101st Aviation Brigade with additional command and control UH-60 Black Hawks, EH-60 Quick Fixes, and Pathfinders from 2-17th Cavalry. The aviation elements left first, followed by the infantry elements of the task force.

A total of 60 C-141s and 50 C-5As carried the task force's 2,742 soldiers, 117 helicopters, and 123 pallets of equipment. (A C-5 can carry six AH-64 Apaches or six UH-60 Black Hawks or three CH-47 Chinooks or thirteen OH-58 Kiowas, and a C-141 can take a smaller load of two Apaches or two Black Hawks or three Kiowas.) The first elements landed at Dhahran on August 18, and the entire task force closed, or was all together, thirteen days later.

The deployment of the air element started smoothly but soon ran into difficulties. The EOC staff was beset with myriad problems. For example, higher commanders made several last-minute adjustments to the Time-Phased Force Deployment List (TPFDL), causing the "deployment to become hectic and required constant reconfiguration from Transportation," read an after-action report.[8] Captain McGrath spelled out the complexities of the EOC's workload. "On 14 August, the 101st was fourth in priority for military air, behind the 82nd ABN [Airborne], Marines and 24th ID [Infantry Division]. By the 17th, its priority had changed to number two. Planning for the airflow centered around three echelons, A, B, and C. Initial load plans were dependent upon a specific number of C-5As and C-141s. However, we soon discovered that more C-141s were arriving instead of C-5As. As chalks [each chalk is one aircraft load of soldiers and equipment] from the Aviation Brigade moved through the inspection station at the ready line, it soon became apparent that a change in load configurations would have to occur, if A echelon were to go first. So, when LTC Hess said 'No' to redoing the chalks, Corps G-3 questioned why it was taking so long to move the first echelon. This would be a problem throughout the military airflow. As more and more people became involved in the system, the more complicated it became. . . .

"There would be many unsung heroes in this deployment, from the desk clerks who produced slide after slide for briefings to the personnel of the DRF-9 [Division Ready Force] who pushed the units onto the airplanes. The meetings/briefings never let up. So much information had to be given in such a short period of time. To some, these were known as 'rump' sessions due to the inordinate amount of time sitting. The Army Vice Chief of Staff, Gen. Gordon R.

Sullivan, came to Fort Campbell on the 12th and he was to be the first of a long list of distinguished guests. . . ."[9]

The EOC faced a formidable task. Moving a whole division from the United States across an ocean to another continent, ready to fight a war on landing, was not easy, no matter the rehearsals, the stand-downs, and the prior planning. For all involved, it was similar to uprooting a city of eighteen thousand people—complete with its transportation, its restaurants, its post offices, its car and truck garages, its airport, its grocery stores and drugstores, its hardware shops, its hospitals, its police force, its barber shops, its laundries, and its homes—and moving the whole package thousands of miles away, replanting it, and making it totally operable immediately, no excuses.

And throughout the process, General Peay cautioned his staff and commanders about such sobering details as accountability. "Buy only what you need," he would tell them at briefings in the EOC, "but be sure to account for it. Ask yourselves, if we had to go before Congress and justify, can we?" He also urged his staff and commanders to label and identify the division's military vans (milvans) and conex (container express) containers clearly with solid markings. He reminded them of the off-loading docks during the Vietnam War, when hundreds of containers sat around unopened and deteriorated because no one knew to whom they belonged.[10]

The deployment, however, continued apace. On August 17, the EOC got word that the *American Eagle* was ready for loading, the first planes carrying the lead elements of the first task force left Campbell Army Airfield, and Army Chief of Staff General Carl E. Vuono dropped in. On August 19, the military convoys of DRB-3 left for Jacksonville. And by the end of that weekend, all military convoys for the 101st Airborne Division were completed, and commercial, long-haul trucks would transport the remaining equipment and supplies to the port.

Next, the EOC deployed the bulk of the division's manpower from Campbell Army Airfield in commercial aircraft from the Commercial Aircraft Reserve Fleet (CARF). Thirty-six planes carried 13,500 soldiers from September 5 through September 25. Some of the military C-5As and C-141s landed for refueling in England and some in Spain. At the refueling stops, the soldiers would dismount for a few hours. In Spain, U.S. Air Force wives and the USO (United Service Organization) had set up a reception station that included a small PX and free cookies and shaving gear with towels, razors, and shaving cream. After reboarding, the next stop, eight hours away, was Dhahran International Airport in Saudi Arabia.

One soldier recorded the experience of landing in Saudi Arabia this way: "When the C-5A came to a halt on the airfield in Dhahran, soldiers gathered their weapons and personal gear and began the long climb down the ladders and to the front of the aircraft. As the huge nose of the aircraft slowly lifted toward the sky, soldiers began to experience the Saudi heat.

"As the forces rapidly moved from the plane and secured their rucksacks, they began to search for sunglasses to protect against the brightness of the sun. Soldiers then strapped on their rucks and began a 1/2-mile road march to some very large tents to await transportation.

"Even for well-conditioned soldiers, the march was torture and uniforms were soaked with sweat when the march had ended. Boxes of water were consumed before the buses finally arrived. The plastic bottles were everywhere and no soldier went anywhere without them.

"The ride to King Fahd Airport [35 miles north of Dhahran] was torture and a mad rush to the latrines by a newly arriving busload of soldiers was a common sight. The next 24 hours for soldiers was spent in the parking garage on a cot or an air mattress simply drinking water. The aviation brigade troops bunked in the parking ramp for the duration because the ramp was close to where their aircraft were based."[11]

For the EOC, the bottom line was that the Aviation Task Force was mission ready in Saudi Arabia by August 22; the 2d Brigade Task Force was mission ready by September 12; the 3d Brigade Task Force by September 20, and the 1st Brigade Task Force by October 1. The 101st Airborne was about to get involved in a war that was unprecedented in the annals of warfare.

November 1990: G-1/G-4 area of Camp Eagle II. Note showers in foreground.

7 | Camp Eagle II

Shortly after he landed in Saudi Arabia, General Shelton sent a number of messages back to the division at Fort Campbell alerting the commanding general and subordinate commanders to, among other things, the heat. "Hell cannot compete with the heat in Saudi Arabia," he told them. But no verbal comparisons or advance warnings could convey what it was like to step off an air-conditioned plane and wilt under the oppressive 120-degree to 140-degree heat on the tarmac. Only time and an acclimation period at the base camp for the 101st Airborne troops would prevent massive heat casualties in the desert. Thus, General Shelton and his advance staff proceeded apace with the monumental job of receiving the incoming troops and equipment and of building the base camp at King Fahd International Airport.

Maj. Al Columbus was the logistics representative in General Shelton's advance party. He set up a reception task force to process the troops landing by civilian chartered aircraft at Dhahran and the troops and equipment from the ships docking at Ad Dammam, and he helped build up the base camp at KFIA. "He knew the business backward and forward," said General Shelton. "[Major Columbus] did a great job getting the flow moving to King Fahd. He knew logistics better than any one guy I ever met in the Army."[1]

Major Columbus worked with the division's Port Reception Task Organization, a 377-man force subdivided into ten different groups. There were some twenty-one teams organized to handle all of the operations and problems involved in off-loading the ships, including medical setups, vehicle marshaling, driver selection, maintenance, line-haul escort, aircraft rebuilds, container accounting and movement, and convoys.

After a few days at KFIA, General Shelton, working with General Pagonis and his civilian crews and using his own men from the 101st Airborne, had set up the division base camp on an all-out work schedule. They finished Camp Eagle II (CE II)—Camp Eagle I had been the 101st's base camp in Vietnam—in time. As the soldiers came from the port at Ad Dammam and from the airfield at Dhahran, everyone had a place to put his or her head. And General Shelton had pushed hard on General Pagonis to put in a water system so that the base camp had showers.

Building the necessary latrines, however, was initially difficult. General Pagonis had called in one of his young quartermaster (QM) captains and told him to get a Saudi contractor and make some "Vietnam-type latrines—ASAP [as soon as possible]. We'll need lots of them," Pagonis told him. "We've got hundreds of people living in the same area." The young, post–Vietnam era captain said, "Yes, sir," and walked away, quite perplexed.

In about four hours he came back to General Pagonis and said, "General, I need to see you a second. Just what is a Vietnam-style latrine? I've never been there." After listening to General Pagonis's patient explanation, the captain hired local contractors to build hundreds of latrines. They used rectangular wooden boxes with four holes, covered with lids, above four halves of 55-gallon drums. The back was hinged so that the drums could be pulled out for cleaning and disinfecting. Unlike Vietnam, where the latrines had to be burned out daily and then smoked up a large area and stank, CE II's latrines were serviced twice a day by SSTs, or "s———sucking trucks," according to General Shelton. Using the SSTs avoided having to burn out the latrines and prevented sanitation problems.[2]

On August 22, Bravo Company, the company on ready alert, was the first element of the 326th Engineer Battalion of the 101st to leave Fort Campbell. A small advance party went along to help establish the base camp at King Fahd. Over the next three weeks, the remainder of the battalion arrived, closing in on Camp Eagle II on September 17.

When Lt. Col. Robert VanAntwerp, the battalion commanding officer (CO), arrived, he set up a facilities' engineer cell whose mission was to improve the quality of life for the division's soldiers. The engineer cell planned water lines, contracted for and distributed showers and latrines, and supervised the grading and black-topping of roads throughout the camp. Considering the unstable nature of the situation and the threat of terrorism, the engineer line companies also emplaced wire barricades, bunkers, gates, and perimeter wire at vulnerable points around the camp. The engineers also hired local laborers to lay one million square meters of asphalt for roads, helipads, and a large, battalion-sized assault pad from which an entire battalion could be lifted at one time.

The battalion also built the division's ammunition supply point, multiple guard towers, and the battalion motor pool. Colonel VanAntwerp said that the hardened ammunition storage facility was so solid that it "would really have been protected against almost a direct Scud attack."

Camp Eagle II was a 2-mile-by-3-mile camp of five thousand tents completely surrounded by sand dunes. One soldier said that "Camp Eagle II resembled nothing so much as a Civil War era's massive fields of white tents." The camp itself was erected on a Saudi-built semi-hardstand. The Saudis had solidified the area's topsoil by spreading a limestone-type substance over the desert sand, hosing it, and then packing it down with huge rollers. The resulting surface made a firm base for roads, streets, and tent floors, but it was so hard that in some areas the camp builders had to use large power drills to dig holes for the tent stakes. When a drill broke, the building crew poured water into the hole to soften the ground. Other tent builders drove in the stakes with sledgehammers.[3]

Each battalion area was a rectangle of tents, accurately lined up in rows of double tents surrounded by sand-bagged walls half as high as the sides of the tents. The troops filled millions of sandbags to make these walls. Latrines and showers bordered the ends of the streets between battalion areas. And in deference to Saddam Hussein's promise of terrorist attacks, hundreds of rolls of concertina wire encircled the camp. Anyone coming into the camp had to go through a series of guard posts and vehicle checkpoints.[4]

Surrounding the tent city's living areas were vast parking areas for helicopters that were spread out to avoid damage from incoming rockets. Near the runways at KFIA were other helicopters lined up on the parking ramps and taxiways. The parking garage near the KFIA terminal housed the troops of the division's aviation brigade. Outside the camp itself were tactical installations and communications vehicles under huge, desert-colored camouflage nets.

As the days wore on, the commanders and troops added amenities to make life in CE II more livable. Temperatures were so high during the first weeks of the deployment that the troops were kept under cover as much as possible from 10:30 in the morning until mid-afternoon. Most of the hard, "muscle" work was done in the evenings. By November, there were semi-enclosed showers, floors and carpets in most tents, and mess and recreation tents. To pass the time, *Newsweek, Time,* and the Desert Shield edition of *USA Today* were available. Nine 16mm projectors showed fifty movies weekly. The troops could also use twenty 37-inch TVs, twenty videocassette recorders (VCRs) with a choice of three hundred movies, and six camcorders. Fifty commercial 4x4 trucks from Japan made their way to CE II for nontactical chores. General Peay brought in a PX staffed, additionally, with several local vendors. During the division's 180-day stay at CE II, the soldiers drank 21.6 million bottles of water and 1 million sodas. In December, a telephone bank was set up, and, for the first time since deployment, troops could call home—but only after waiting in long lines for hours. Many units erected street signs—"Cold Steel Boulevard" for one artillery unit, for example—to help locate themselves in the massive, spread-out tent city. And outside the camp, the engineers built ranges for small-arms firing and helicopter refueling points in dry lake beds.

One of the troopers in the camp said that it eventually became a first-class installation, but "never let it be said that Camp Eagle II was a nice place to live or even to visit. Mosquitoes, sand vipers, scorpions and spiders also shared the camp. The heat was miserable and the dust got into everything. Yet, hot chow, a cot to sleep on and a tent to get under after 30 days of sleeping in a hole under a poncho on the desert floor was an improvement. The laundry service was superior to washing your own clothes in a bucket if you didn't mind getting back some other soldier's underwear."[5]

Outside the tent city, Col. Joe Bolt, the division's chief of staff, set up the division's headquarters in the water treatment building. Two concrete structures, with a connecting overhang, housed the division's Operations Center; war room, where both the classified and unclassified briefings were held; and the living and working area for General Peay and his staff. These buildings were higher than the G-1/G-4 compound and tent city. The view from the division headquarters was a montage of "miles and miles of tents" and a "spectacular sight at dusk," according to one division staffer. "Many a day would find one or more persons looking out over the sandbags to experience the beauty and quiet of this desert horizon."[6]

After the heat, the sand was the second most annoying problem in the Saudi desert. "Not only was it underfoot, it was in and on everything," wrote Captain McGrath later. "Unlike the sunken sand we first experienced after debarking the aircraft, the sand around Camp Eagle was harder and coarser. . . . The sand appeared like a mist and coated the green cots, mosquito netting, sand bags, and everything that wasn't covered with plastic. The sand extended into books, papers and food. It is no exaggeration to state that it covered everything. It covered your skin and frequent showers didn't rid you of it. Boots looked almost white, instead of the black finish. Soldiers did continue to polish their boots, but it was a real battle as the sand left its mark on them."[7]

The 1st Brigade of the 101st Airborne was the last major combat unit to leave Fort Campbell. Col. Tom Hill, the CO, flew out on September 13. The rest of the brigade was "pushed out by my operations officer within four or five days," he recalled. "I think we all closed by the 17th or 18th of September."

Colonel Hill was amazed at what had been accomplished at Camp Eagle II. "We landed at Dhahran," he remembered, "got on some buses and rode to King Fahd where the ADC, General Shelton, and a small part of the assault CP and a few DIS-COM players had done an incredible job of getting the division base camp . . . going. I was absolutely flabbergasted by what they had accomplished in less than 30 days. Overwhelmed with the tents, the shower facilities, the latrine facilities, the organization that was already set up. [It was] truly remarkable because when they landed there was absolutely nothing, zippo, I mean nothing. Really had done yeoman work. . . . That initial effort, the first 15–20 days served the division and finally the rest of the theatre throughout the entire time . . . I think the people leaving Saudi Arabia today are still going down to King Fahd and going through the King Fahd International because of the foresight of General Shelton. Because when they landed, it was he and Pagonis and a couple of other people and that was about it. Everybody creating a theatre. Really remarkable job. The division experienced zero morale problems, virtually zero discipline problems. I put a couple thousand soldiers into that base camp and into tight living conditions and to my knowledge had no thievery among the soldiers, none. I had very few altercations or fist fights.

"The division commander's decision was, let's establish this base camp from which we can then move in an orderly fashion out into the operation and training area as needs dictate. I think that was an incredibly wise decision. Soldiers appreciated it. They went over there expecting nothing and said, hey, this is terrific. And they were saying it up until the end."[8]

The 5th Battalion of the 101st Aviation Regiment—a UH-60 Black Hawk outfit—left Fort Campbell for Saudi Arabia on the evenings of September 17 and 19 aboard CARF aircraft. After arriving at CE II, Lt. Col. Russell E. Adams, the CO, wrote later, the battalion "began a 3–4 day acclimatization period while waiting for equipment to arrive. The unit was billeted on the second floor of the parking garage adjacent to the terminal building at KFIA. The battalion headquarters was established in the main terminal building near the Aviation Brigade headquarters. Living conditions were much better than expected. Soldiers were under cover of the parking garage. . . . Two soldiers shared a living space that corresponded to a parking space in the garage. The biggest problem was the lack of privacy. . . . Life in the desert included capturing many scorpions and snakes, and observing migrating herds of camels and goats on their way south. Each afternoon my soldiers listened to the 'Voice of Peace,' Radio Baghdad. The rock and roll music was welcome, although some of the propaganda was depressing. We were all surprised to hear, however, that 'Baghdad Betty' announced our wives were being unfaithful with none other than television's Bart Simpson!"[9]

The musical instruments for the Screaming Eagle Band, forever after known to the troops as the "First Band in the Sand," did not arrive until October. Initially, therefore, the band members supplied the security force for the division's Tactical Operations Center. One soldier being processed through a checkpoint said that it gave him "an unbelievable sense of security to know that as he was being processed through the gate he was being watched by a steely-eyed piccolo player manning an M-60 machine gun."[10]

When the band's instruments did arrive, it played on many occasions for the troops throughout CE II. Not only did the band play military music for ceremonies and play "Taps" every evening, it staged country-and-western and rock music shows, and its "Horny Horns" specialized in "the blues." The band even took its shows on the road for other units.

Captain McGrath flew to Saudi Arabia with the last of the troops from Fort Campbell. At Fort Campbell, she had worked in the Emergency Operations Center (EOC), getting the troops processed for the movement to Saudi Arabia. Finally, after most of the troops had left, it was her turn to deploy. "My trip to the JOA [Joint Operations Area] was smooth," she wrote later, describing her trip and her reactions to Saudi Arabia. They were typical of the thousands of troops who flew into the area.

"Along with 173 other soldiers, I departed Fort Campbell at 0900 hours on the 24th of September. There is a nine-hour difference between Saudi Arabia and our home in the U.S. Arriving at the airport in Dhahran at noon on the 25th, our trip had taken 18 hours with quick fuel stops in Gander, Newfoundland, Paris, France, and Cairo, Egypt.

"The arrival was really uneventful. We departed the plane, walked across the runway to experience our first steps in Saudi sand. It was something else, as we sunk about six inches everytime our boots went forward. We were ushered into two huge Saudi-style reception tents and felt relieved just to get out of the sun. It was over 100 degrees. A detail of soldiers, within our ranks, was dispatched to bring over two dozen cases of bottled water. None of us hesitated to grab one [a bottle] and begin drinking. A second detail unloaded the rucksacks and duffel bags that we had stored in the belly of the plane. We were sweating excessively and all we had done was walk a few minutes from the plane to the tents. I wanted to sit down so bad, but was afraid I would not be able to get up again. After the first of many in-country briefs about customs and courtesies, rules of engagement, and cautions about avoiding heat exhaustion, we piled into buses for our journey to King Fahd International Airport (KFIA). Over an hour later, we arrived at the partially completed airport. Construction materials lined both sides of the road going in. Large cement barriers forced the bus drivers to slow down and go through guard checks. These drivers were foreign nationals who were working for the Saudi Arabians. They came from various countries like Pakistan, the Philippines, India, etc. Rarely would I see an Arab.

"We formed a five-line formation with officers in the front rank. In front of us was a space of about fifty feet. Beginning with the officer rank we filed back to a large semi-trailer truck where our bags were located. The bags were thrown down for us to grab one, any one, and take it back to the space in front of the formation. After our rank came everyone else and gradually the amount of baggage grew to fill up the space. Most people had two bags, a duffel and a ruck, and some had three. There were over four hundred bags for 174 personnel. Upon completion of the layout, we walked around and found our individual bags. Mine came intact, but others were not so lucky. Aerosal shaving cream cans busted. Tied-on items had broken away. I saw boots lying alone, a broken radio that someone had stuffed between the ruck and its frame, liquid shampoo coming through the bags where the bottle had broken, and other bags that were unidentified because the name tag and baggage tag were missing.

"Now we were really loaded down. On the plane we had load bearing equipment (LBE), gas mask, weapon and helmet. Then we had our baggage. The LBE would vary with the unit, but the Division standard was a web belt consisting of two canteens, two ammo pouches, first aid kit, and suspenders. Flashlights, bayonets, chemical bags, the gas mask, and other items would also be attached, depending on the unit and individual preference.

"Many of us had written letters on the plane and wanted to get them in the mail as soon as possible. I took several to the mail room which was in reality a paper box, stating USA on the outside. It was situated in the garage. I became fascinated with this place. Several stories high, this garage had very few, if any, vehicles parked in it. Instead it was the homes for hundreds of soldiers from the Aviation Task Force. Situated on concrete, cots, boxes, mosquito netting, and all the comforts available were spread everywhere. I had expected to see a lot of tents, but instead there was this parking area for shelter. In the days and weeks to come, the command became more and more concerned about the high concentration of troops in such a highly terrorist-possible target. People remembered Beirut where over 200 Marines died from terrorist activities. Plans were already under way to vacate the garage for tents on the sand. The war broke out before this could be fully implemented.

"As I walked around, the soldiers were sleeping, eating, hand washing clothes, writing letters, playing cards, cleaning weapons, reading, talking, laughing and living. There was no war going on. The mood was gay and expectant. A positive atmosphere prevailed. The mail/supply/mess/orderly room/community recreation area was very busy. Behind the paper mailbox sat a clerk busily typing away on a laptop computer.

I would see many of these being used—some for official business such as memorandums, and some not so official as soldiers wrote their loved ones back home.

"I couldn't believe the amount of apples, oranges, and sodas being distributed to everyone. The supply seemed endless. Expecting to eat MREs [meals ready to eat] and T-rations, this fresh fruit was so much appreciated. However, most of us didn't eat. For one thing, we had three meals on the plane and a couple of snacks. For another, we were anxious to get to our units. We were impatiently waiting for transportation for the last final leg of our journey. Two double-decker buses arrived an hour after dark.

"We rode for about 20 minutes, driving through more barriers and past more guard checkpoints. It was dark and there was not a cloud in the sky. Since it was dark, it was not so hot. The talking by this time was a low murmur as soldiers exchanged unit names and sections that they belonged to. We were not replacements; we were just the last of the division to arrive. There were folks from almost every major unit on post and in particular from HHC [Headquarters and Headquarters Company], Division. So, it was natural to assume that we would be split up. The bus pulled into a fenced-in area. Again, we off loaded all of our stuff and waited. Several NCO's started shouting out units and telling people to move one way if you were in the HHC, 101st PSC [Personnel Service Company], 101st Finance or 101st MP Company and another way if you were in the rest of the division. Those in the former group, including myself, would stay at this compound. All the rest would await their unit representatives and further transportation to their homes for the next several months.

"This compound was in reality a water treatment plant and a sewage treatment plant. It had been under construction prior to our arrival, but was not in operation. One enormous cement structure stood in the middle. Several smaller buildings sat outside. Large towers dotted the site. Along one half were Saudi tents, picnic tables, and a cement pad where the Mobile Kitchen Unit (MKU) sat. Vehicles lined the fence. Guard posts were positioned on top of the structures and around the camp. An enormous area to house the 101st Abn Div (AASLT) [Air Assault] Headquarters support staff, the Army Post Office (APO) for the division, and three other companies.

"Of course, I couldn't see at all that night. I was dead tired and wanted to sleep. I would get two days to become acclimated to the climate, but many people would not even get that. After checking in, I found my way to my assigned tent and slept 12 hours. Thus ended my first 24 hours in-country."[11]

Camp Eagle II became the home away from home for the 101st. It provided almost all of the facilities available at Fort Campbell. Helicopter maintenance, complete dental and eye care, and all medical requirements were met at CE II. And as the division moved into its next role, the camp became a base to which the troops could return after thirty days "up-country" for laundry, hot chow, showers, and body and equipment maintenance. Even when the division moved into its combat role, CE II remained open and operational, manned by a small task force that could move supplies and replacements forward.

As one soldier succinctly put it, "Camp Eagle II served the division well."[12]

Troops of Company A, 1-502d Infantry, pull guard duty around FOB Bastogne.

8 | Tactical Operations

Through August, the 101st Airborne Division continued its deployment. The division's Advanced Command Post (ACP) became operational in Camp Eagle II on August 26 as more and more ACP personnel arrived in country. The medevac planes were operational and performing missions. Two EH-60 Electronic Black Hawks were attached to the 82d Airborne Division. The division historian reported that "high temperatures in the 120 to 130 [degree] range plagued the soldiers, but everyone kept busy doing one of four things: work, sleep, drink fluids (around 9–12 quarts a day), or go to the restroom a lot. There were no days off—no rest for the weary."[1]

By late September, the strategic deployment of the division was finished. The 101st Airborne Division (Air Assault) was established and operational in Camp Eagle II. Now General Peay was faced with the tactical phase of his division's reason for being in the desert.

The 101st Airborne Division (Air Assault) is the only division of its kind. Other units may use helicopters to transport some of their units, but these follow the "air mobility" concept. They essentially move troops and equipment by helicopter from one secure area to another secure area. The 101st Air Assault Division, however, totally merges and integrates its ground and aviation units and can land mission-tailored combat forces directly onto an objective or into the main battle area under hostile conditions. The division conducts combat operations at a high tempo and, in addition to its organic division artillery battalions, has firepower intensity with two attack helicopter battalions and an air cavalry squadron.

By far, the most significant and unique aspect of the 101st Air Assault Division is the habitual relationship and integration of its air assault–trained light infantry soldiers and army aviation. The resulting concerted effect allows the combat

67

infantrymen, with supporting fire from artillery and attack helicopters, to strike with speed, precision, tactical advantage, and surprise over extended distances of up to 95 miles and over terrain and obstacles that would slow a normal ground operation.

In an air assault operation, the division's attack helicopter battalions, with direct and indirect fire and their powerful antiarmor capability, provide flanking protection for the assault helicopters carrying the infantrymen. In addition, the attack helicopters suppress enemy air defenses, radars, and other weapons en route to the objective area; they prepare the landing zones with rocket and machine-gun fire; they watch over the landing zone and objective area to neutralize enemy resistance; they block enemy movements to the objective area; and they provide reconnaissance and security.

In a sense, the attack helicopters, unlikely as it may seem, may even take on and accomplish the normal infantry mission of holding a piece of terrain. If, for example, an enemy column of tanks, armored personnel carriers (APCs), and trucks was making its way through a defile, across a bridge, or along a highway, the attack helicopters could rapidly be "on station" to attack the column, knock out vehicles to the front and rear, and stop the column. Other attack helicopters could blast the convoy with rockets and machine guns. Additional helicopters could then come on station and maintain a presence over the area, thereby holding the terrain for as long as necessary. Attack helicopters give the division's commander a new, widely effective weapon and a broadened perspective in applying combat power.[2]

The division's total air assets are formidable. They include three assault battalions with UH-60 Black Hawks, two attack helicopter battalions with AH-64 Apaches and OH-58C Kiowa Scouts, a medium helicopter battalion with CH-47D Chinooks, a command aviation battalion with UH-1 Hueys, and an air reconnaissance squadron armed with AH-1F Cobras and OH-58C Kiowas. Along with the attached 2d Battalion of the 229th Aviation Regiment and its Apaches, Kiowas, and Black Hawks, General Peay initially had at his disposal 330 helicopters: 109 UH-60s, 43 CH-47s, 63 OH-58s, 36 AH-1s, 37 AH-64s, 36 UH-1s, 3 EH-60s, and 3 UH-60Ls.

When he received the alert for Desert Shield, General Peay was not a newcomer to the air assault concept. During two tours in Vietnam, he was first a field artillery battery commander in the 4th Division in the central highlands and later an operations officer of a field artillery battalion with the 1st Cavalry Division (Air Mobile). From 1987 to 1988, he was an assistant division commander of the 101st Airborne Division (Air Assault) at Fort Campbell and assumed command of the division on August 3, 1989. During his career, he was also exposed to the higher levels of the military establishment. He was a senior aide to the chairman of the Joint Chiefs of Staff; G-3 of I Corps at Fort Lewis, Washington; and executive officer to the chief of staff of the U.S. Army.[3]

Given his background, General Peay knew his division's advantages: The 101st Airborne could operate without being hampered by terrain obstacles;

deploy quickly when it got the word to go; rapidly build up forces in the objective area; be flexible and move quickly left, right, or full speed ahead; and, with the latest night vision devices, operate in the dark. He also knew its weaknesses: a ground mobility generally limited to foot movement once the infantrymen arrive on the objective and deplane; a dependence on fairly decent weather conditions; a heavy tail of logistics support for fuel and ammunition; a vulnerability to enemy nuclear, biological, and chemical warfare; and a very definite vulnerability to enemy air defenses. All of these factors, along with the established army guidelines below, influenced the way the division planners in the EOC prepared for combat.

"The air assault division is deployed as a maneuver element of a contingency corps, a forward deployed corps, or as part of a joint task force," states the *Air Assault Division and Brigade Operations Manual.* "Rarely will the division be deployed independent of a higher headquarters into a theatre of operation. The air assault division operates from a position on the battlefield that allows its superior tactical maneuverability and mobility to be used throughout the assigned area of operation. When employed in a global role, the air assault division is not intended to meet a heavy threat force in open terrain. It is employed under conditions that will provide it a calculated advantage due to surprise, terrain, threat or mobility."[4]

Col. Tom Garrett, commander of the 101st Aviation Brigade, was among the first senior officers to arrive in theater. After the war, he reminisced about the conditions he found initially and how the unique capabilities of the 101st Airborne blended into the situation.

"The capability we brought to the place was enormous," he said. "The vastness of the nothingness, I mean just wasteland went on forever and ever and ever. The trails that would show on a map wouldn't be there and most of the trails were very rugged so if you were ground-bound in a vehicle, you weren't going any place very fast. And you couldn't cover the distances or see or operate except for a very small area. Of course the helicopter, with the tactical and operational mobility that the 101st possesses, made it perfect to go in early and at least watch and respond over a great area. It allowed us to operate from the base camp and rotate units forward and bring units back to refit and do some good maintenance at some facilities that were a little bit better than being out in the middle of the desert.

"The helicopter, as we're organizing the 101st, not only did allow us to have combat maneuver units, attack helicopters and cavalry, it had the assault helicopter battalions bringing the infantry soldier into the air assault business with art. We were also able to move combined arms teams that had the same mobility. Then with our Chinooks and our Black Hawks we were able to sustain that force and resupply it over those great distances. It took the whole team."[5]

At the XVIII Airborne Corps's level during the fall, the planning for the defense of Saudi Arabia went on apace. The corps's staff, managed by its chief,

General Scholes, "settled into a daily and weekly routine intended to push the commander's intent as far down the chain of command as possible and circulate ideas," wrote Tom Donnelly in the February 24, 1992, edition of *Army Times.*

> The prime planning instrument was the Corps' battle management cell. Comprised of representatives of the Corps' major operating systems, the cell met every day at 9 A.M. This was where the hard details of the evolving defensive scheme were worked out. Intelligence officers discussed the latest information about Iraqi force dispositions and trench lines. Maneuver planners discussed possible courses of action, and staff members would try to figure out how to synchronize artillery, aviation and logistics effort in support.
> The week's work was punctuated every Wednesday afternoon, when the principal Corps operations officers met with brigade commanders and division staff principals. This meeting, which came to be called the "Council of Colonels," again reviewed possible courses of action, while giving the brigade and other commanders the opportunity to state requirements for carrying out their assignments.
> Corps commander [Gary] Luck held war councils with his major subordinate commanders every Thursday evening. The main agenda was to discuss the latest courses of action as envisioned by the Corps; Luck wanted to hear how bold thinkers like [Maj. Gen. Barry] McCaffery [CG of the 24th] and Maj. Gen. Binnie Peay, commander of the 101st Airborne Division, responded.

The confidence of the commander up and down the chain of command grew as the forces flowed into Saudi Arabia. In the last weeks of September, the commanders and their staffs were putting the finishing touches on the plans for the defense of Saudi Arabia. The plan for XVIII Airborne Corps was Desert Dragon IV.

On October 4, according to Donnelly, "CENTCOM [Central Command] held a senior leaders' map exercise at Dhahran Air Base that allowed Schwarzkopf to review the air and land defensive plans. Satisfied that all was in order, the final Desert Shield plan was published the following day. In a series of 13 war games throughout the month, planners refought Internal Look, with two lead Iraqi echelons and the Republican Guard attacking from its positions near Basra. One prong of the attack was to head west along the King Khalid Military City [KKMC]–Riyadh axis, the other down the coast toward Al Jubayl, Dhahran, Ad Dammam and the oil fields."[6]

By November 5, the XVIII Airborne Corps was fully combat ready with the 82d Airborne, the 101st Airborne, the 24th Infantry, and the 1st Cavalry divisions and the 3d Armored Cavalry Regiment. The total combat power of the corps included 763 main battle tanks, of which 123 were the potent M-1A1 Abrams; 444 howitzers and 63 MLRS (multiple-launch rocket systems); 1,494 fighting vehicles and APCs, of which 596 were M-3 Bradleys; 24 Patriot and 24 Hawk missile launchers; 227 attack helicopters including 145 AH-64 Apaches; and 18 nonmechanized infantry battalions, equipped with 368 M-998 Humvees with TOW missile launchers (Humvee TOWs).

By this time, the 101st Airborne Division was deployed well forward as the covering force and ahead of the rest of the corps. The XVIII Airborne Corps was ready for its first combat mission.

An M-102 howitzer section of 3-320th Field Artillery conducts a live-fire exercise at King Faisal Range, Saudi Arabia.

9 | Covering Force

Through late August and early September, U.S. forces began to build up in Saudi Arabia. But in those early days the force levels were thin. At Central Command, General Schwarzkopf had to cover and defend vast areas of desert with small, lightly armed airborne and air assault troops against an overwhelming enemy force equipped with thousands of heavy tanks, armored personnel carriers, and scores of artillery pieces. The Iraqis' Scud missile and chemical warfare potentials posed ever-present threats, compounding the defensive posture of the coalition forces.

The first U.S. unit on the ground was the twenty-three hundred–man 2d Brigade—the 325th Parachute Infantry Regiment—from the 82d Airborne Division. It arrived on August 8 only thirty-one hours after it was alerted and six days after the Iraqis invaded Kuwait. The brigade deployed immediately as a covering force south of the token Saudi forces that were arrayed in a thin line south of the Kuwaiti border. Even when the entire 82d Airborne was "in theater," the lightly armed division became known, although somewhat sarcastically, as a speed bump across the line of advance of Saddam's forces.

The major problem, as the U.S. forces built up in country, was that the commanders and staffs did not know what Saddam was planning. Fresh in Schwarzkopf's mind were two realities, one past and one present: first, Saddam's blitzkrieg through Kuwait with his Republican Guard divisions; and, second, Saddam's situation in Kuwait, where many of his more than one hundred thousand troops were poised in battle formation on the Kuwait–Saudi Arabia border. Schwarzkopf could neither believe that attacking Saudi Arabia was Saddam's final goal nor assume that Saddam would be content to sit where he was in Kuwait. Such an assumption was illogical, suicidal, and, at the time, seemingly idiotic. Schwarzkopf had to develop an operational plan based on an Iraqi attack into Saudi Arabia, and he had to be ready to defend against it.

The ground commanders of the coalition forces recognized that Kuwait's poorly deployed armed forces—only 50,000 men, 245 tanks, 430 APCs, 72 artillery pieces, 35 combat jets, and 18 armed helicopters—could not have posed a formidable obstacle to Iraq. Thus at 2:00 A.M. on August 2, Saddam's T-72 tanks rolled unopposed past the customs shed at Abdaly, down the undefended six-lane highway toward Kuwait City, and on to the capital. After machine guns, artillery shells, and helicopter gun ships blasted Kuwait City, Iraqi forces torched the residence of Kuwait's ruler, Sheikh al-Sabah. As Iraqi tanks closed in around the palace, the emir and his family flew to Saudi Arabia.[1]

Saddam overran the ill-prepared Kuwaiti force in three days, which was ridiculously slow according to one senior U.S. planner at Central Command. After having reviewed that operation, he criticized the Iraqi generals for going through Kuwait City: "They got all bogged down trying to get through Kuwait City. Any armored-mechanized commander will tell you that the thing you don't want to do is go into a major metropolitan area with your armored forces, regardless of the reason. You just cut it (the city) off and let your trailing reserve infantry clear the thing; the armor keeps going."[2]

But, mused the planners all along the chain of command from the White House to Riyadh, why did Saddam stop at the border when he had a wide-open, practically undefended path all the way to the oil fields of Saudi Arabia? CENTCOM planners had assumed that, after seizing Kuwait, Saddam would charge into Saudi Arabia's industrial belt, which extends from the port city of Al Jubayl south along the Persian Gulf to Ad Dammam. In those early days of the war, the only thing standing between Saddam and the Saudi oil fields was a battalion of the Saudi Arabian National Guard, or less than one thousand men.

Not knowing Saddam's plan of action made for some restiveness on the part of the in-country senior coalition planners and commanders. They knew that Saddam's total land forces consisted of nine hundred thousand men in sixty-three divisions, only eight of which were Republican Guard units. But, nonetheless, Saddam did have 5,747 tanks, 1,072 of which were Soviet T-72s, and most of these were in Kuwait. He also had ten thousand light armored vehicles, about three thousand five hundred artillery pieces, and three thousand heavy equipment transporters (HETs). Schwarzkopf had concluded early on that he could dispose of Saddam's air force after a short initial period and that Saddam's navy did not pose a problem; but Saddam's ground forces definitely were a threat. Schwarzkopf and his commanders down the line increasingly felt that an Iraqi attack into Saudi Arabia could come at any moment.[3]

Col. Tom Garrett, CO of the 101st's Aviation Brigade, had arrived in Saudi on the 101st Airborne's first plane with General Shelton and was uneasy with what they found. "We went in to find that we had very few combat forces in any position to do anything," he remembered. "The 82d Airborne had one infantry brigade on the ground, and an Apache battalion positioned close to the Saudi port of Al Jubayl. But it wasn't an entire battalion. It didn't have much of a support structure, so they were pretty lean.

"The Saudis weren't on the border in the force we thought they were, so what we found was a very tenuous situation and a very dangerous situation should Saddam have decided to continue south.

"We were obviously concerned, "Garrett continued. "It's our mission to go in first, but based on what had just happened, and the strength and the speed with which the Iraqis took Kuwait—a capability nobody thought they had—if he had made his move . . . it was going to be pretty exciting for us." Garrett felt that if his units were forced to defend against a sustained Iraqi attack down the eastern Arabian peninsula, his task force would run out of ammunition within "a couple of days."[4]

General Peay had left Fort Campbell on August 27 but was delayed at Dover and did not arrive at KFIA until August 29. He was impressed with what General Shelton, a few men from the division, and a swarm of civilian contractors had been able to accomplish in such a short time. After an initial briefing and a quick look at Camp Eagle II, General Peay went to the XVIII Airborne Corps's headquarters at Dragon City between Dhahran and KFIA and met with Generals Luck and Scholes.

As commander of XVIII Airborne Corps, General Luck already had the corps's mission: "On order, establish a defense in sector to defeat attacking Iraqi forces; defend approaches and critical oil facilities vic [vicinity] Abqaiq-Al Hufuf; defend the approaches to Ad Dammam–Dhahran enclave; ensure the integrity of MARCENT's [Marine Central Command] western flank and facilitate transition to offensive operations."[5]

General Luck was well aware of the 101st Airborne's capabilities. In 1975, he had been the commander of the division's 2-17th Cavalry and then became the division's G-3. In 1984, he was the assistant division commander. From 1986 to 1989, he was the commander of the Joint Special Operations Command and moved then to command the army's Special Operations Command. On August 28, 1990, he assumed command of XVIII Airborne Corps. He was obviously well qualified in both Special Operations and the workings of the army's only air assault division—the 101st.[6]

As early as August 30, General Luck had tasked the division to deploy well forward in a defensive posture. To comply, Colonel Garrett had his men ready the AH-64 Apaches for combat as fast as possible after they rolled off the C-5As that had brought them in-country. The helicopters were ready in a couple of days and loaded with the ammunition the units had brought with them to Saudi Arabia. In those early days, the logisticians had not yet built up large stockpiles of supplies.

On September 1, the division deployed an aviation task force with an infantry platoon and some combat service support elements in the vicinity of An Nuayriya, a small town that straddled the intersection of several major roads. "We were able to take over the screening mission from the 82d as far as being a trip wire," remembered Garrett.

General Luck gave General Peay his mission and discussed some of its inherent problems. In formal military terminology the 101st Airborne's mission was this: "101st conducts covering force operations in sector; provides attack helicopter support and fire support to eastern province area command forces to disrupt and delay Iraqi forces, and assists in passage of lines of EPAC [Eastern Province Area Command] forces; on order, guards in sector to protect the western flank of the XVIII Airborne Corps and provides a brigade to the XVIII Airborne Corps as theatre reserve for contingency operations; prepares for and conducts future operations as required."[7]

General Peay also met with General Schwarzkopf shortly after he arrived in country. "I think I saw General Schwarzkopf within a week to 10 days, as I recall, after closing in country," he remembered. "I conducted some initial briefings with him, [and] he passed on some of his early-on concepts, because our division was given the covering force mission, which I thought was one of the great missions to have early on in terms of learning, adapting to the desert, the harshness of it. . . . The ability then to refine our operating procedures and work with distances, and to work with other forces during that maturation period that, I think, was very valuable in the Desert Storm part of it."

The development of the division's initial mission flowed down the chain. "General Schwarzkopf and his staff laid out the initial mission," General Peay said. "General Luck then took that mission and developed a corps plan. Actually, the ARCENT [Army Central Command] headquarters developed the mission, passed the mission to the corps, the corps developed the mission at the corps level, laid out the general concept of how the corps commander wanted the covering force fight to take place and he assigned missions to all the divisional and nondivisional units within his command. Internal to the mission given the 101st, we developed our plan within the corps commander's intent, who developed his plan within the Central Commander's intent. We developed our plan and then we went through a series of back briefs where, in detail, we briefed that plan out. Now that plan changed over time as forces were added to the theatre."

As more and more forces from the 101st Airborne and other units arrived in theater, General Peay and his staff continued to modify the covering force's composition and disposition. "After we got pushed further north," General Peay recalled, "our aviation brigade was chopped back to us, and as our forces closed, we developed a more robust covering force plan nightly. And finally, of course, within about 60 days on approximately 15 October, our entire division and attachments were present in theatre. All those forces were under our operational control for the covering force fight. And so as they closed in country, then we adjusted our covering force plan, nightly, weekly, monthly and back-briefed it to our corps commander. So that's kind of how it took place. We developed it within the corps commander's intent, back-briefed it to him for his approval."[8]

For the Desert Shield portion of the war—the covering force and defensive phase—the division's task organization included additional units. For example, the 3d Armored Cavalry Regiment (ACR) from Fort Bliss, Texas, was also under General Peay's operational control (OPCON). It was a potent force armed with 123 M-1A1 Abrams tanks, 116 M-3 Bradley cavalry fighting vehicles, 26 AH-1 Cobras, and 24 self-propelled 155mm howitzers.

The 12th Combat Aviation Brigade (CAB), commanded by Col. Emmitt Gibson, was a V Corps unit normally based in Wiesbaden, Germany. "General [Crosbie] Saint, then the CINC [commander in chief] USAREUR, and then LTG [Lieutenant General] Joulwan, Commander of V Corps, allowed me to tailor the brigade to support my anticipated mission," wrote Col. Gibson. "The major units of the brigade consisted of two AH-64 attack helicopter battalions; Task Force

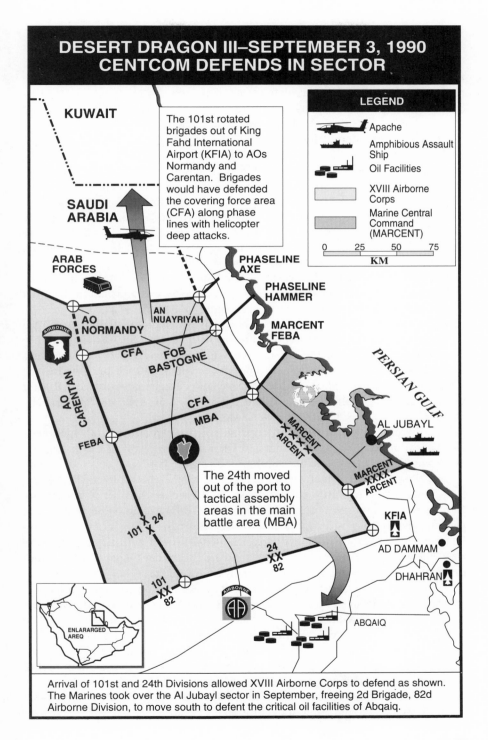

DESERT DRAGON III–SEPTEMBER 3, 1990
CENTCOM DEFENDS IN SECTOR

KUWAIT

The 101st rotated brigades out of King Fahd International Airport (KFIA) to AOs Normandy and Carentan. Brigades would have defended the covering force area (CFA) along phase lines with helicopter deep attacks.

SAUDI ARABIA

LEGEND

Apache

Amphibious Assault Ship

Oil Facilities

XVIII Airborne Corps

Marine Central Command (MARCENT)

0   25   50   75
KM

ARAB FORCES

PHASELINE AXE

PHASELINE HAMMER

AO NORMANDY

AN NUAYRIYAH

MARCENT FEBA

AIRBORNE

CFA

FOB BASTOGNE

PERSIAN GULF

AO CARENTAN

CFA

MBA

FEBA

MARCENT
X X X
ARCENT

AL JUBAYL

The 24th moved out of the port to tactical assembly areas in the main battle area (MBA)

MARCENT
XXXX
ARCENT

KFIA

X 24
101 X

AD DAMMAM

24
XX
82

DHAHRAN

101
XX
82

AIRBORNE

ENLARARGED AREQ

ABQAIQ

Arrival of 101st and 24th Divisions allowed XVIII Airborne Corps to defend as shown. The Marines took over the Al Jubayl sector in September, freeing 2d Brigade, 82d Airborne Division, to move south to defent the critical oil facilities of Abqaiq.

77

Warrior consisting of one Black Hawk company, one half of a CH-47 company, and a platoon of UH-1Hs; an OH-58D company (which I attached to one attack battalion but provided each attack battalion a platoon during operations); an aviation intermediate maintenance company; a DS [direct support] ground maintenance detachment; a chemical platoon; an air defense platoon; and a tactical air control party and weather detachment from the Air Force. All total, the brigade consisted of 101 aircraft, 377 vehicles, and 1566 soldiers. . . .

"The 12th was alerted for deployment on 14 August 90. Initially, tasked to deploy by air, the first battalion was ready in 72 hours. 5-6 Cav, an Apache battalion, was ready to deploy; however, as General Schwarzkopf adjusted his immediate, in theatre requirements, the mission eventually changed to deploy by sea. The brigade deployed ground equipment on 13 trains from four different railheads to the ports of Livorno [Italy] and Rotterdam [the Netherlands]. All aircraft were flown to Livorno and loaded on a RORO [roll-on roll-off] ship. The soldiers were flown to Saudi Arabia, arriving approximately two weeks before the equipment. The brigade closed in Saudi Arabia on 2 October 90."[9]

Once in Saudi Arabia, the brigade and its thirty-seven AH-64 Apaches, seven CH-47 Chinooks, and twenty-two UH-60 Black Hawks was attached to the 101st Airborne. It remained attached until early January 1991.

Also attached to the division were two artillery brigades—the 75th and the 212th—that were normally a part of III Corps based at Fort Sill, Oklahoma. They were in direct support of the division. They had multiple-launch rocket systems (MLRS), M-109 155mm self-propelled howitzers, and M-110 self-propelled 8-inch howitzers. The 2d Battalion of the 229th Aviation Regiment from Fort Rucker was also attached to the division. It had eighteen AH-64 Apaches, thirteen OH-58C Kiowas, and three UH-60L Black Hawks.

The division's mission was to defend an area known as Area of Operations Normandy, or AO Normandy, about 130 kilometers northwest of Camp Eagle II and approximately 85 kilometers south of the Kuwaiti border. It covered a 4,600-square-kilometer area, about 90 kilometers by 50 kilometers. To defend it, the division established a forward operation base (FOB) within the area of operations. Initially XVIII Airborne Corps had named the FOB Essex, but on September 2, it gave the division permission to rename the base Bastogne in honor of the division's historic World War II stand at that Belgian city. From Camp Eagle II to FOB Bastogne was 195 kilometers—a fifty-two-minute Black Hawk flight or a three-and-one-half-hour drive along MSR [main supply route] Audi.

To the north, between AO Normandy and the Kuwaiti border, there was a thin line of Saudi Arabian troops. To the east, U.S. Marines were deployed in a covering force and to the west were Arab and additional Saudi forces. The 24th Infantry Division was deployed in a pocket in the southeastern quadrant of the corps's sector, with the 101st Airborne to the north and west. The 82d Airborne Division and the 1st Infantry Division (Mechanized) were in the southern part of the corps's zone. In all, the corps's sector was roughly the size of New Hampshire and Vermont combined. In the event that the Iraqis attacked south from Kuwait, the 101st would take the brunt of the offensive.[10]

In FOB Bastogne, the 326th Engineer Battalion renovated several existing buildings in a deserted ARAMCO (Arabian-American Oil Company) oil compound to use as a command post and as medical and maintenance facilities. An abandoned airstrip outside of town was transformed into a massive logistics base with stores of fuel, ammo, food, and spare and repair parts. Tapline (Trans Arabia Pipeline) Road, described by General Peay as "a one-lane super highway," ran through AO Normandy from the northwest to the southeast corner and roughly paralleled the Saudi Arabian border with Iraq and Kuwait. The troops who had to drive vehicles along this road referred to it as "Suicide Alley" because of the heavy civilian traffic, with buses, trucks, and cars driven by locals who were not bound by traffic regulations. Accidents were frequent and massive.

Turning FOB Bastogne into a livable, operational support center for the troops manning AO Normandy's defenses was not a simple task. For example, when the 3d Battalion of the 502d Infantry first arrived at Bastogne, the troops found hundreds of camel and sheep carcasses in the surrounding desert. Black flies swarming everywhere were so oppressive and massive that the troops dubbed them "the national birds of Saudi Arabia." The division surgeon sent preventive medicine personnel out to investigate the dead animals. One report said that "they determined that it was Saudi custom to take an old or diseased animal into the desert, tie its front legs together and leave it to die. Soldiers built bunkers and fighting positions in the animal graveyard to the north of the city and waited for the attack that never came."[11]

The 326th Engineers worked hard on the site for the division's assault command post and the support command at FOB Bastogne, removing tons of dirt and debris. For the hundreds of helicopters that logged inside the FOB, the engineers added an oil and fuel mixture to the sand and layered it with sheets of plywood to form a helipad. After a few weeks, the engineers and troops added tents, showers, and latrines to FOB Bastogne.

The 101st Airborne officially assumed control of FOB Bastogne from the 82d Airborne Division on September 4, 1990. The mission included an aviation screen in AO Apache to the north. On the previous day, however, corps had relieved the division of providing medevac helicopter support to the corps.

An Nuayriyah was the town around which FOB Bastogne was based. It was situated at the intersection of Tapline Road and a number of other north-south roads coming from Kuwait and headed for the Saudi Arabian capital of Riyadh. By the time the 101st Airborne had arrived at FOB Bastogne, An Nuayriyah had swelled with thousands of refugees from Kuwait. The Screaming Eagles' hatred of Saddam grew with the refugees' horror stories about their treatment by the Iraqi soldiers occupying Kuwait. The division's soldiers, well indoctrinated with the need for security, still remained careful with the refugees. As one soldier put it, "With the promise of terrorist attacks by Saddam Hussein, almost everyone in the civilian communities was suspect."

General Peay divided AO Normandy into five sectors. The two aviation brigades patrolled the northeast sector; the 1st Brigade had the northwest sector; the 3d Armored Cavalry Regiment had responsibility for the southeast corner; the

2d Brigade and the 2-17th Cavalry Squadron, operating out of FOB Oasis, covered the southwest sector; and the 3d Brigade had the area between the 2d Brigade and the 3d ACR.

Colonel Hill, CO of the 1st Brigade, was well aware of his mission. "Had the whole scheme unfolded the way we thought it would," he said later, "I would have been the first American unit engaging in ground combat." He added that his brigade was spread out over a stretch of desert 70 kilometers wide by 35 kilometers deep.[12]

After the war, General Peay also talked about the division's exposure of the 101st in the covering force role. "I wouldn't say we were worried," he said. "It's the normal concern you have in any combat situation as you're going through the vulnerable time frame of closing forces, closing logistics in the country, nightly hauling ammo from the port, while you're trying to take on the security role. So, it wasn't the exposure of being so far north, which we were. We were four hours by road, an hour plus by Black Hawk helicopter, to Bastogne, situated just south of the Saudi forces, so the concern was the ability to quickly close logistics so that you had the fighting capability to go along with the structure that you had laid out on the ground. But, again, . . . there was no state of panic or anything like that. It was the kind of things that go with the projection of forces in a barebones theatre and the buildup that you expect to undergo as you close."

In the early days of Desert Shield, Saddam had forces deployed menacingly close to the division's area of coverage. In AO Normandy, General Peay said later, "We were opposed by three [Iraqi] divisions—two directly in front of us, and the third . . . we felt was going to come from the northwest, come south and then punch into our side down Tapline Road."

AO Normandy, the covering force's zone, was in front of the planned main battle position. This is the way General Peay explained the situation and the plan of battle if the Iraqis chose to attack: "The two (Iraqi) divisions would come directly south across Tapline Road. . . . Actually, we were postured to the north of Tapline Road, with the 24th Division in the main battle area to our south. . . . The concept was that we'd fight the covering force on down south and pass through the 24th . . . the main battle area. The third (Iraqi) division, though, (a mechanized division) was going to come from the northwest and then cut to the southeast, down Tapline Road on our flank. We had 180 HUMVEE TOWs, and we task-organized one company of infantry with one company of TOWs so that we had the security capability for the TOW team. We had enough infantry in there to also assist in the labor required with the ammunition. We put in those positions with great detail and we rehearsed and rehearsed and rehearsed these plans. And, in addition, it was not the HUMVEE TOW fight alone. It was a combined arms fight using the U.S. Air Force, four battalions of Apaches, and one battalion of Cobras plus our cav [cavalry] squadron Cobras. So we basically had six battalions of aviation. We also had two full heavy field artillery brigades from Fort Sill and we had the Armored Cav Regiment from Fort Bliss. So it was much more than just a HUMVEE TOW fight.[13]

OPLAN 90-3 (Operation Desert Destiny) was the 101st Airborne's "mature" theater OPLAN for the defense of Saudi Arabia. Dated October 15, OPLAN 90-3 was "extensively rehearsed and would have been executed had Iraq attacked . . .

Saudi Arabia," concluded the division's Command Report. "The division based OPLAN 90-3 on intelligence predictions that an Iraqi attack would have the objective of seizing and controlling the petroleum handling facilities at Dhahran and Abqaiq within 72 and 96 hours. Of the nine divisions that Iraq then had in forward positions in Kuwait, it was expected that Iraq would commit six to the initial assault.

"One mechanized division and two armor divisions would make the main attack while one each mechanized and armor division would make a supporting attack. A third infantry division would make a fixing attack and Republican Guard Force Corps [RGFC] forces would exploit any successes within 48 hours after the initial assault. The 101st expected to be hit head on by one division, followed twelve hours later by a flank attack by a second division."[14]

General Peay divided his OPLAN 90-3 into five phases. In Phase I, the entire division would deploy to AO Normandy. This meant that, in addition to the two infantry brigades and the 3d ACR already in position in the covering force area (CFA), he would assign air and ground movement priority to the following units: the infantry brigade task force at Camp Eagle II, division artillery, the division main command post, the remainder of two aviation brigades, and then the Division Support Command (DISCOM).

Phase II of the plan would start with Saddam's forces attacking Saudi Arabia. Once the battle in the CFA began, the 101st Airborne would fight as long as possible in its sector with TOW missiles and Apaches and Cobras before giving up its positions. The 3d ACR, operating out of FOB Bastogne in defense of An Nuayriyah, would be the main force in the covering force operations. The 3d ACR would then hand off the battle to the 24th Infantry Division (Mechanized) from Fort Stewart, Georgia; it would be deployed in defensive positions directly south of AO Normandy. Once the 24th Infantry took on the fight, the 101st Airborne would defend the 24th Infantry's western flank.

Along with the Apaches, the 180 TOWs mounted on Humvees were the division's primary antitank and anti-mechanized-vehicle counterpunch. The division's engineers dug between seven hundred and one thousand fighting positions for the HMMWVs. Each TOW company was paired with an infantry company to furnish added security and additional bodies to help move ammunition. They had three fighting positions located about 500 meters apart, according to CSM (Company Sgt. Maj.) Jonathan Smalls of 1-502d Infantry. "If the Iraqis attacked," he said, "the TOWs would hold them off as long as possible from the primary position before retreating to the secondary and tertiary positions."

During Phase II of the OPLAN, on order, the 1st Brigade Task Force would conduct a battle turnover to the 2d Brigade TF. The 1st would then move to AO Carentan, which occupied six thousand two hundred square kilometers of land along the XVIII Airborne Corps's western flank. Also on order, the 12th Combat Aviation Brigade would conduct a battle "handover" with the 3d Brigade TF and the 3d ACR. The 12th CAB would occupy Assembly Area Clarksville and become the division's reserve force. The 2-17th Cavalry would screen northwest of the division along Tapline Road. When it had completed support of the EPAC (Eastern Province Area Command) forces, the aviation brigade would assign operational control of one attack battalion to the 1st Brigade TF, move to FOB Oasis, and become the division's reserve force committed to support the west flank. Phase II would end with a battle handover to the 24th Infantry Division.

During Phase III, the 101st would withdraw from the CFA, pass through the lines of the 24th Infantry, and move to guard positions in AO Carentan. After passing the lines, the 3d ACR would become attached to the 24th Infantry and the 12th CAB would be released to the XVIII Airborne Corps. The aviation brigade would remain on reserve with its priority targets being along Tapline Road.

In Phase IV, the 101st Airborne would occupy its guard positions with 3d Brigade in the south, the 1st in the center, and the 2d to the north. The 3d Brigade would be prepared to serve as reserve for XVIII Airborne Corps, and the 2-17th Cavalry would continue to screen along Tapline Road.

Phase V was a counterattack against the Iraqis' second-echelon forces. The 101st Airborne would support the 1st Cavalry Division, which was the main effort for the counterattack.[15]

The division conducted a training exercise in October 1990 to rehearse the passage-of-lines phase of OPLAN 90-3 down to the company level. The division was ready for battle.

"This aggressive plan for the defense of Saudi Arabia required an equally aggressive logistical support plan," wrote the division's historical officer, 1st Lt. Clifford M. Lippard. "The DISCOM was task organized to provide support to all assigned and attached units. A division support area (DSA), located at Camp Eagle II, would support division forward operating bases (FOB), which in turn would support logistical assault bases (LABs) at each brigade. Each of these light, tailored bases would be resourced from DISCOM's assets.

"LABS are designed to provide the smallest capable element forward to support logistical requirements. LABs are supported through the more robust FOBs. 3d ACR, which was only under the division's operational control, would have been supported by either the 24th Division or the 1st COSCOM [Corps Support Command]."[16]

When his forces were fully deployed in the covering force defenses, General Peay was optimistic about the division's chances for success in stopping the Iraqis. "As the forces closed," he said after the war, "and as we exercised more and more with them up north and rehearsed our plan, both in map exercises and command post exercises and so forth, I felt very, very good about our ability to do a very, very solid job of covering force fight and frankly, I don't think he [Saddam] would have gotten through the covering force. . . . Our intent was to maximize the tank-killing capability of our division." Peay not only had the TOWs but the six battalions of attack helicopters, the two field artillery brigades, and the 3d ACR under his operational control.

Lt. Col. James Donald, commander of the 1st Battalion of the 502d Infantry, put it more graphically: "Had he [Saddam] attacked, we would've eaten his grits."[17]

The scenes around FOB Bastogne and out into AO Normandy contrasted sharply with anything the troops had seen at Fort Campbell or at the National

Training Centers (NTCs). In one section of Bastogne, a control tower covered with camouflage netting rose out of the desert sand. Two men in the tower constantly monitored the flight patterns of helicopters at a refueling point. In another area, an AH-64 Apache rolled into a refueling point to receive a "hot" refuel on the recently constructed helipad on the sand while another AH-64 Apache rolled in behind it. Around the FOB's perimeter, machine gunners manned their weapons in dug-in positions. A CH-47 Chinook, with its huge blades sagging impotently, sat on a pad after making a logistics run from the rear. Ouside the FOB, infantrymen run out of helicopters and hit the sand in training exercises. The M-167 Vulcans' positions are dug deeply into the desert around the FOB and covered with the ever-present camouflage nets. Air defense artillerymen, mortarmen, and infantrymen—all in camouflage uniforms—sit in deep holes and waited for the attack. A helicopter hovering over the desert created a mild sandstorm.

Aside from the military preparations, scattered weapons positions, and deployed troops, another familiar sight outside FOB Bastogne was the Bedouin tribesman. Wearing his ground-length white tunic, white turban, and black short jacket, he calmly tended his sheep in a vast expanse of sand studded with stunted, almost dried-out bushes. The contrast between the two scenes can be measured in centuries.

In the western sector of AO Normandy, the 2d Brigade needed an FOB to support its operations. The intelligence planners felt that an Iraqi division would attack from the northwest, down the Tapline Road, and directly into the 2d Brigade's sector. To the west of FOB Bastogne, the 2d Brigade found an abandoned oasis. A division report said that "for more than 300 years, this oasis was known as the 'gateway to the Kingdom.' Bedouins would travel across the border and somehow find themselves in this small village. At the direction of the King, the village was abandoned some 15 years prior to the arrival of the Screaming Eagles. . . . Critical to the oasis was the water available there. For soldiers used to drinking bottled water, it was difficult at first to get used to drinking the highly chlorinated stuff the Brigade was now serving. However, the soldiers soon learned that by adding Kool-Aid you could almost drink and enjoy it."[18]

As at FOB Bastogne, the soldiers at FOB Oasis lived in holes outside the FOB. Their mission was to protect the vital assault landing strips and tons of fuel and ammunition stored throughout the town. The deserted, three-hundred-year-old town provided a good setting for the 2d Brigade's soldiers to practice military operations in urban terrain (MOUT) daily. The old buildings were similar in structure and design to those found throughout the Persian Gulf area. Knowing how to attack and to reduce such buildings could have great advantages if the division had to fight in an Iraqi, Saudi, or Kuwaiti city. The only buildings restricted from MOUT were the old mosque and the brigade's headquarters.[19]

The scenery around FOB Oasis was different than the surrounding desert. In the town, the buildings were old and built of some sort of concrete. They resembled small forts, especially with their narrow window openings and thick, heat-resistant walls. Huge palm trees dotted the village and were in sharp contrast to the surrounding, vast, undulating sand dunes as far as the eye could see.

Farther south of FOB Oasis was a logistics assault base that the division had originally named An Chou after the valley in Vietnam through which the Screaming Eagles had fought a couple of decades ago. The 3d Brigade, made up of three battalions of the 187th Infantry, the Rakkasans of Korean War fame, changed the LAB's name to Sukchon after one of their Korean War combat jump sites.

To keep the covering force troops healthy, General Peay rotated them in and out of AO Normandy during their mission. Each brigade spent thirty days in AO Normandy, followed by fifteen days of rest and relaxation (R and R) in the more comfortable conditions at Camp Eagle II. At AO Normandy, conditions were spartan. General Peay described it as a series of "literally five-feet-by-two-feet kinds of foxholes" with MRE boxes as pillows. He wanted to get the troops back to CE II periodically to "improve their health standards, get them out of the holes, work on their desert diseases, get them back and cleaned up." The 1st Brigade's CO, Colonel Hill, acknowledged that each time his troops returned to CE II it was good for their morale. They always checked to see if something new might have been added.

General Peay maximized the time the division was deployed in the covering force role. "Every night we refined our war plan so that whatever forces we had in the country were ready to go that night," he said.[20]

Neither did the troops just hang out in their foxholes, waiting for the Iraqi attack. Although reluctant at first, the Saudis gave General Peay permission for live-fire exercises. "Despite the challenges," he said, "during the last three months of 1990, the division got in some of the best live-fire training we've ever had." And "we rehearsed the war plan with as many live-fire exercises as we could," remembered Col. Theodore ("Ted") Purdum, CO of the 2d Brigade.[21] Col. Robert ("Bob") Clark, CO of the 3d Brigade, even ran his brigade through several battalion-size live-fire exercises at night.

The constant training in FOB Oasis and in the surrounding area paid off in trooper self-confidence and skill. "I have complete confidence in my company," boasted Pfc. Frederick Warner. "We have the highest EIB [Expert Infantry Badge] rate in the brigade and our skill qualification test averages are near 100 percent. Who else would you want out here?" Spec. Sharrod Skidmore said, "Since I've been here, I've caught on to a lot of things that make me more job proficient than before."[22]

The Saudis were also hesitant to permit the division's engineers to lay minefields and obstacles along the forward line of defense. They worried that the mines would remain embedded and unmarked in the desert sands for years to come, according to Bob VanAntwerp. So the engineers stacked mines as far forward as they could and planned to put in as many as possible during the six hours' warning of an impending Iraqi attack. "We wouldn't have gotten a lot in to tell the truth," said VanAntwerp. He decided that the best approach would be to lay minefields in key locations and try "to make him [Saddam] come where we wanted [him]. . . ."[23]

During November, the 101st Airborne also went through a second field training exercise (FTX) to rehearse its plans. The division's chain of command ran through the critical phases of the defensive plan and the timing of the 3d ACR's and 12 CAB's counterattacks, which were played out on a reduced scale. During this training and rehearsing, the division staff improved and adapted many air assault techniques—a farsightedness that would prove beneficial in the actual battle yet to come.

As their tour in the covering force role grew longer and longer, however, some of the troops became restless, wanting either to fight or to go back to Fort Campbell. Army Chief of Staff General Vuono visited the division at Thanksgiving. Some of the braver troops asked him when the division might be returning home. According to Colonel Garrett, General Vuono "flat looked at them . . . and said, 'It would take me three divisions to replace the 101st because of your capability, because of the amount of terrain you can operate over, because of the distances you can cover.' We knew right then," said Garrett, "we might rotate some units, but we weren't going home."[24]

Even in a combat situation, for these forward-deployed units, the changes in command took place as scheduled by the Department of the Army. In two cases, infantry brigades of the 101st Division changed commanders in Saudi Arabia: Col. Bob Clark had assumed command of the 3d Brigade from Col. John McDonald on November 7, and Colonel Purdom relieved Colonel Gile of command of the 2d Brigade on October 22. The changes of command were routine and had been planned before the division was committed to Saudi Arabia. As Colonel Clark explained, "The change of command was preprogrammed to change after two years of command. The flags continued to pass even though we were over there." He admitted that taking over command in the field has its advantages. "I inherited the plan. All I had to do was execute it. It was an easy way to get to know the people because you're thrown together, living with each other 24 hours a day enduring the same hardships. In many respects it was a hell of a lot easier than taking command in a garrison environment in the continental United States."[25]

General Peay struggled with this problem of changing brigade commanders under the circumstances. But he had to weigh the opportunities for his colonels, and, he said later, "at that point it was not clear that we would go to war."[26]

Amnesty International found the Iraqis' conduct in Kuwait heinous and depraved. President Bush read a seventy-nine-page Amnesty International report just prior to the December 16 taping of a public television interview with David Frost at the White House. The report cited Iraqi atrocities in Kuwait, including hundreds of cases of murder and thirty-eight types of torture from administering electric shock treatment to cutting out tongues and eyes. "Good God," said Bush, "it is so powerful, you wouldn't believe it." Saddam was evil, the president was convinced, and after reading about Saddam's depravity and sadism, the president resolved to "take down" Saddam.

In the interview, aired on January 2, President Bush said that the atrocities were horrible and hard to describe. "The torturing of a handicaped child," he began. "The shooting of young boys in front of their parents. The rape of women dragged out of their homes and repeatedly raped and then brought into the hospital as kind of basket cases. The tying of those that are being tortured to ceiling fans so they turn and turn. The killing of a Kuwaiti and leaving him hanging—this is a picture of this one—leaving him hanging from a crane so that others will see him. Electric shocks to the private parts of men and women. Broken glass inserted in—jabbed into people. I mean, it is primeval. And I'm afraid I'd get very emotional if I described more of it." He did go on to describe how a fifteen-year-old boy had been beaten on the bottom of his feet and how the Iraqis pulled out the fingernails of the Kuwaitis.[27]

As the world learned of the Iraqis' raping and looting, the Iraqis were also busy building up their defenses in Kuwait from August through December. Bush's commanders heard that the Iraqis had erected a multi-belted, hardened defense in the eastern part of the Kuwaiti theater of operations (KTO). Intelligence types predicted that the Iraqis would develop strong point defenses in the vicinity of As Salman and An Nasiriyah. The Republican Guard apparently was in reserve for the entire KTO.

During the Christmas holidays, the VIPs—from President Bush to Secretary of the Army Michael W. Stone to JCS Chairman Powell—visited the troops. As in previous wartime holidays, celebrities such as the indefatigable Bob Hope, Johnny Bench, Jay Leno, Steve Martin, and Victoria Tennant entertained them. The meals during Christmas were lavish, and the division band, now reunited with their instruments, played concerts throughout the area. "The holidays passed rapidly," the division historian put it, "as the division began to prepare for the inevitable attack into Iraq."[28]

By Christmas, the months in the desert in the covering force role had hardened, trained, and united the 101st Airborne Division (Air Assault) to a new peak of combat readiness. "I think that as every week went on," reminisced General Peay after the war, "we felt better and better about the logistical replenishments, the spare parts, the ammunition, the food stuffs, the clothing, as well as the medical buildup that was coming in. We really felt good—I can speak for the 101st about the battle desert toughening that went on with our soldiers. We'd been to the NTC, we'd been to JRTC, those are tremendous facilities . . . but the facts of life are, when you live 6 months in the desert, in foxholes, the way our soldiers did, they were basically 30 days up [in their battle positions] and 15 days back [on R and R], and when you did that over the five-month period, the 101st soldiers were simply desert tough. And there's a great confidence that develops and a great bonding developed among the soldiers and to put that on top of the fact that our division, because of the way we turned over from a personnel perspective, had been together for a year before we ever went there. And then we had six months on top of that before we crossed the line of departure, so we really were a very seasoned team, and the year before we deployed, we'd been on an enormous number of joint exercises, attendance at the General Operation Training Center, National Center, Joint Readiness Training Center, had conducted some 13 battalion level ARTEPs [Army Training and Evaluation Programs], had been on two

Corps Edrees [Emergency Deployment Readiness Exercises], so the pace and operational tempo that we had been on the year before was just perfect for blending in with the six months that we were also going to have in the desert floor. So, after 18 months of that as a team, I think that we were in a superb state of readiness for the missions that were given us."[29]

After the war, Colonel Hill reflected on the defensive phase of Desert Shield and his 1st Brigade of the 101st. "The covering force mission that the 101st had, and all of the defensive missions that the units were in will probably get short shrift because of Desert Storm. The covering force operation that we ran in, the plan that we developed and rehearsed and could have executed, I'm convinced was a real highlight because I was the northern and westernmost American unit. Had the whole scheme unfolded the way we thought it would, I would have been the first American unit engaging ground combat. There would have been some attrition by the Air Force and Apaches out in front of me. My brigade frontage was 70 kilometers wide and 35 kilometers deep. The plan would have had me passing thru [sic] the 2d Brigade in an area just about as big setting up a second area.

"In my sector, I put two battalions abreast and we moved into battle positions and each scheme was to attack and move to subsequent battle position. Each line falling back until . . . you were pushed out of an area and into passage points with the 2d Brigade. And we had tried to establish . . . a major engagement area in the center which we called Engagement Area Shotgun. Our thought was we would have been attacked from the north and the west but no matter what happened once they hit Tapline Road their focus would have been turning to the east and toward Dhahran. [There was] nothing of any value to the south except more desert. If in fact that attack happened, I could conceive the Iraqi order being attack until you hit the first hard ball [paved] road and turn left. I think that essentially is what they would have done. . . .

"And we became desert tough. The final thing, on the covering force operation, the time that we had I think we used to maximum advantage without dragging down the soldier in terms of physical or mental or morale, and I think the 15 day trips back [to CE II] helped that. Each time we came back there was something nicer in the base camp. We got some TV, VCRs, cokes, hot showers, as opposed to no showers. They got out of their holes, kicked back a little bit. It was very beneficial. I think it gave us a leg up that some of the other units didn't have. We began planning for the ground offensive action in mid-November. . . . Before Thanksgiving we rehearsed it as we moved back up for our second rotation the 1st of December. We did the first actual rehearsal for the air assault into Cobra the 1st of December. We wanted to validate the fact we could fly in 10,000 gallon gasbags, put gas in 'em, that we could set up a very large RRP [rapid refuel point] and work how we would begin the command and control and the synchronization of all that. It wasn't in the final plan but it was certain that we knew what we were going to do."[30]

The 101st Airborne Division was obviously ready for its next mission.

A 60mm mortar section conducts crew drills at FOB Bastogne.

10 | Leaning Forward

In the fall of 1990, while the coalition forces built up in Saudi Arabia, another set of combatants—diplomats—waged a verbal battle to drive Saddam out of Kuwait. By a fourteen to zero vote on August 2, 1990, the UN Security Council condemned the Iraqi invasion and demanded Iraq's immediate and unconditional withdrawal from Kuwait. It supported the United States in setting up naval and air blockades and an embargo on Iraqi imports and exports. Eventually, its opposition to Saddam's use of foreign hostages to influence world powers forced Saddam, on December 6, to release the three thousand Americans and fifteen thousand other foreigners he had seized in Iraq and Kuwait after the embargo was imposed. But the UN resolutions did not tackle the problem of what should be done if Saddam continued to occupy Kuwait. During the months that followed the August resolution, the UN passed eleven more resolutions increasing the pressure on Saddam to leave Kuwait. None of the resolutions, however, specifically authorized the use of force against Saddam. None forced the stubborn Saddam to comply. To the contrary, he literally dug in.[1]

During the early deployment of U.S. forces, President Bush took a three-week vacation to Kennebunkport, Maine. The press criticized him for vacationing while the troops he commanded deployed to a combat zone, but the president's vacation was deliberately planned. He remembered that President Carter had disrupted many plans when U.S. Embassy personnel were held captive in Iran from November 1979 to January 1981. Bush thought Carter's behavior was a grievous error. Bush would not be held hostage by Saddam.

Nonetheless, while the president was on vacation, his staff kept him fully briefed on the deployment. And he kept up the diplomatic pressure. He made sixty-two phone calls to foreign leaders, continuing his efforts to build international support for his plans. Secretary of State Baker, even though he was on vacation at his Wyoming ranch, also engaged in frequent telephonic diplomacy. It became known as "working the phones." Bush and Baker pressured Japan, totally dependent on imported oil, Germany, and the wealthy Arab states to assist Turkey, Jordan, and Egypt—all hard-pressed by the embargo on Iraq. Throughout the fall, the Bush administration "worked the chain" of other foreign leaders around the globe.[2]

The United States and the UN had several options. They could wait for the sanctions, which had cut some 90 percent of Iraq's imports and exports, to force Saddam to his knees. The experts were divided on how long that would take; estimates ran from six months to never. Another option was to compromise and let Saddam keep part of Kuwait, but that choice would not deprive Saddam of his nuclear, biological, and chemical (NBC) potential.

Bush never did believe that the sanctions would work, but he wanted to avoid the stigma of being dubbed a warmonger. As the sanctions went into effect, Bush did ask Schwarzkopf to plan an offensive operation, but Schwarzkopf and his staff were already in theater and working around the clock to build up Saudi Arabia's defenses. At that point, Schwarzkopf was also not certain how much combat strength he would need to force Saddam out of Kuwait.

As the United States and other coalition forces built up their military power in Saudi Arabia, Saddam did the same in Kuwait. By the end of October, the United States had 210,000 troops in the region, giving the coalition a total of 275,000. Meanwhile, after conquering Kuwait with 100,000 troops, Saddam had pulled his three Republican Guard divisions and two mechanized divisions back near Basra. But, by mid-fall, he had increased his forces in and near Kuwait to 430,000. (Some estimated 545,000 men in twelve heavy and thirty-one light divisions.) Obviously, the United States and the coalition had to build up their strength before they could launch an offensive operation against that kind of opposition.

"After he approved the final defensive scheme," wrote Tom Donnelly in the March 2, 1992, issue of *Army Times,* "Schwarzkopf began contemplating an offensive campaign in earnest, gathering a small cell of CENTCOM planners to consider the alternatives. But no sooner had planning begun, than the White House threw a spanner [wrench] into the works.

"From the start, Schwarzkopf had told Bush and his advisers the defensive deployment would take up to four months, and any offensive campaign would require additional heavy armored forces, perhaps as much as another corps. He estimated that it would take another six to eight months to deploy the additional troops. In October, with the defensive deployment all but completed well ahead of schedule, the White House wanted to know how soon he could attack; after all, television pundits . . . concluded a single-corps attack would succeed."

One such pundit was Marine Corps Gen. George Crist. Schwarzkopf's predecessor at CENTCOM, Crist was a CBS television news analyst during the Persian Gulf War. He remembers that, in September, before Saddam built up his forces in Kuwait, he thought that a successful offensive by the coalition forces then in Saudi Arabia was a definite possibility. However, he said, during the fall, Saddam deployed at least twenty divisions of some 305,000 troops to Kuwait; pulled the Republican Guard back to Basra; and sent another five divisions of 108,000 troops to southern Iraq and eight divisions of 132,000 troops to western Iraq. General Crist realized that by the end of October, with Saddam's buildup and deployment of armored units along the southern Kuwaiti border, Schwarzkopf would need at least two or three armored and mechanized divisions to throw Saddam out of Kuwait.[3]

In the theater, some of the senior subordinate commanders felt that they should plan an offensive with the forces on hand. They had a reasonable defense force in place, and Saddam had apparently gone on the defensive in Kuwait by digging in his forces. Maj. Gen. Barry McCaffrey, commanding general of the 24th Infantry Division (Mechanized), told his staff to develop a detailed plan for an attack into Kuwait. "McCaffrey even had a clever scheme," wrote Donnelly, "involving the 101st Airborne Division (Air Assault) and the 1st Cavalry Division, designed to finish off the Republican Guard before it could get away. But it was one thing for McCaffrey to war game an attack, quite another for the White House to be hatching schemes. Schwarzkopf was not in control of the process, and he was not happy."[4]

Schwarzkopf was unable to leave the theater, of course, to argue his case in Washington. Instead, he sent Maj. Gen. Robert Johnson, his chief of staff, on October 9. In the Pentagon, Johnson made a preliminary pitch to the "brain trust"—Cheney, Powell, the four service chiefs, and the JCS operations chief, Lt. Gen. Tom Kelly. Johnson appeared "uneasy" at the meeting, according to some of those present. As he outlined the plan, he stressed that it was not final and that a successful attack to dislodge Saddam from Kuwait, given his massive buildup in Kuwait and southern and western Iraq, would require additional U.S. forces. While the United States already had two heavy divisions in Saudi Arabia plus an armored cavalry regiment and two light divisions—the 82d Airborne and the 101st Airborne—they were insufficient for a rapid, bold, all-out, and decisive attack. The current force could only attack "head on" into Kuwait and try to find the "seams" between the Iraqi divisions.[5]

Tom Donnelly reported,

The next day Johnson went to the White House to tell Bush and his advisers about the plan, which included a preparatory air campaign. National Security Adviser Brent Scowcroft, a retired Air Force lieutenant general, accepted the air plan, but was critical of the land campaign. Johnson responded that a second Army corps should be deployed to get the job done right.

Johnson reflected the collective wisdom of CENTCOM's senior land commanders. They had looked at every option, including adding heavy forces to XVIII Airborne, but concluded that it must be a two-corps operation. "Everybody concluded (a one-corps attack) was not significantly decisive," said Lt. Gen. John Yeosock, commander of Third Army, CENTCOM's Army component. "It was a marginal solution at best. To use the Clausewitzian term, we culminated before we decisively destroyed. We may have gotten ourselves to a point where we just don't have enough to get ourselves over the hill. Wouldn't lose, wouldn't have decisively destroyed it."[6]

On October 21, General Powell flew to Riyadh, Saudi Arabia, to confer with Schwarzkopf. After Schwarzkopf's briefing, he and General Powell agreed that, given the buildup of Iraqi forces, their dug-in defensive positions in Kuwait, and their armored strength, the United States had to "think big." That meant they had to add at least two hundred thousand more U.S. troops between early November and mid-January if the coalition were to become potent enough to drive Saddam out of Kuwait. Such additions would double the U.S. Air Force, Army, and Marine forces and included three more aircraft carriers. Schwarzkopf told Powell that his "wish list" included the VII Corps from Europe. Powell suggested adding the 1st Infantry Division, or "the Big Red One" (BRO), from Fort Riley, Kansas. The BRO had worked with VII Corps in Europe on various Reforger exercises. Schwarzkopf agreed and concluded that, if the president were serious about an offensive, he would have to have VII Corps.

Back in the States, Cheney and Powell presented the plan to the commander in chief on October 31, Halloween. He bought it. Bush decided to hold off from making a public announcement until after the November congressional elections.

Because weather in the Persian Gulf turns stormy, wet, and cold in the spring, Bush agreed that a massive, decisive winter campaign would be in order. An air campaign would begin January 15 with the ground offensive blasting off in February. Bush reasoned that when Saddam saw the concerted buildup of coalition forces, he would finally realize that they were not bluffing.[7]

When President Bush ordered the second buildup of forces in late October, the major army unit present in the theater was the XVIII Airborne Corps. It was composed of the 82d Airborne Division, the 24th Infantry Division, the 3d Armored Cavalry Regiment (ACR), the 12th Combat Aviation Brigade (CAB) the 101st Airborne Division, and the 1st Cavalry Division. The corps had closed on October 22.

"Commanders' confidence was high," wrote Tom Donnelly in the *Army Times*. "In the last weeks of September, they were putting the finishing touches on Desert Dragon IV, the [XVIII Abn] corps plan for defeating an Iraqi invasion of Saudi Arabia, crushing the Iraqi Army in the process and restoring the border. Behind the covering forces (the 101st), 24th Mech [Mechanized] had planned a sweeping end run tactical counterattack against the flank of the expected Iraqi advance. They then would hand off the fight to the 1st Cav, which would sweep all before it up to the border. The popular belief was the 1st Cavalry Division would never get into the fight, as the Iraqis would never get that far.[8]

On November 2, the M-1–M-1A1 Abrams tank replacement program began. "General Vuono had helped in one sense," reported Bob Woodward in *The Commanders,* "making sure that Schwarzkopf had the latest equipment. Sometimes it had to be forced on him. Vuono had insisted that more than 1,000 of the latest modernized tank, the M-1A1, be sent to Army units that had already been deployed without this state-of-the-art model. Schwarzkopf had at first resisted because he wanted to avoid the disruption of switching to new equipment that the troops would have to learn to use. But the new tanks improved combat effectiveness and the confidence of the soldiers. The effective range of the M-1A1 was about double that of the best Iraqi T-72 tank."[9]

The one thousand M-1A1 Abrams tanks were enough to equip three divisions and one armored cavalry regiment. The army also sent into the theater six hundred M-2/M-3A2 Bradley fighting vehicles, enough to equip one division and two ACRs; more than one hundred armored combat earthmovers, enough for three divisions and two ACRs; and more than one thousand HEMTTs, the latest logistical support vehicle, without which the sweeping flanking maneuver of XVIII Airborne and VII Corps would not have been possible.

After President Bush approved Schwarzkopf's request for a second corps, the army staff had to decide which one would go. Although III Corps at Fort Hood, Texas, seemed a likely candidate to fill the role, many of its units had been "picked clean" to support those Fort Hood units that had already deployed. Neither did it have the most modern armored equipment. The 4th Infantry Division at Fort Carson, Colorado, did not have Bradley fighting vehicles, either, and the 5th Infantry at Fort Polk, Louisiana, was just in the process of receiving them.

The VII Corps in Stuttgart, Germany, had been on the line since the end of World War II. With the collapse of the Soviet Union and the drawdown of U.S. forces in Germany, the VII Corps was to "case its colors," or deactivate, shortly. It had received the army's latest armor, including the M-1A1 Abrams tank. It was thus the logical choice to deploy to the Persian Gulf.

The composition of the corps was answered by General Yeosock. According to the general, "I asked for three heavies [armored and/or mech divisions] and an armored cavalry regiment and that's what we got. Everybody agreed. . . . Implicit in anything that we would be doing was not to do it halfway. The Army had a policy that you don't just beat him a little bit."[10]

Lt. Gen. Frederick Franks, commander of VII Corps, had already sent an attack helicopter battalion to Saudi Arabia in August. He also had a small staff in Stuttgart monitoring the progress of Desert Shield. In October, the alert came that he might have to send an armored division to Saudi Arabia to reinforce XVIII Airborne Corps.

On November 8, the president ordered VII Corps in Europe and the 1st Infantry Division (Mechanized) at Fort Riley, Kansas, to prepare for deployment to Saudi Arabia. General Franks met with Gen. Crosbie Saint, the USAREUR commander, to "refine the troop roster." Because the drawdown had already started in Europe, some units were so close to inactivation they could not deploy to Saudi Arabia. "General Saint and I had a number of meetings and, based on anticipated operational requirements, we had built a corps that would deploy from Europe," General Franks remembered. "We wanted the most modern equipment force that could go."

In reality, the force that Crosbie and Franks agreed on was a mix of units from all over the European theater of operations (ETO), not just from VII Corps. They settled on the VII Corps's 1st Armored Division, commanded by Maj. Gen. Ronald Griffith, and Maj. Gen. Paul Funk's 3d Armored Division from V Corps. They also assigned several battalions from the 8th Infantry Division (Mechanized) to the 3d Armored and a brigade from the 3d Infantry Division, equipped with Bradleys, to replace a brigade from the 1st Armored Division that was still equipped with the older M-113 APCs.

The corps's third division was the 1st Infantry, the Big Red One. Its 3d Brigade was too far along toward inactivation to move to the gulf, so Saint substituted the forward-deployed brigade from the 2d Armored Division to the BRO.

That night, Franks and his staff chiefs were assembled in the Stuttgart command post. It was almost midnight when they heard the president's announcement that another corps would deploy to the gulf and Secretary of Defense Cheney identified VII Corps as that new force. "According to some of the staffers who were present," wrote Tom Donnelly in the March 2, 1992, issue of *Army Times,* "it was a calm, business-as-usual session, but one laden with a strong sense that this would be a historic undertaking.

"After the announcements, the corps operations officer, Colonel Stanley Cherrie, rode home on his bicycle. Cherrie had been wounded badly in the Vietnam War and had lost a leg, as had Franks. In the quiet chill of the German night, his thoughts were of his wife, who was in north Germany visiting friends. 'Here we go again,' he thought."

On November 10, Franks and his team of staff chiefs and division commanders arrived in Dhahran and were met by General Yeosock who gave them his standard "welcome to Saudi Arabia" speech. Yeosock and Franks, together with the energetic and imaginative head logistician, General Pagonis, sat down and discussed the imminent, massive move of VII Corps and its reception in Saudi Arabia. They talked about the airfields, the ports, and the need to move as orderly and as quickly as possible out of the ports and into assembly areas.

Next Franks and his team met with the commander of XVIII Airborne Corps, General Luck. The strong message from Luck was, Bring everything you need.

Then they went on an aerial recce of the area where they would assemble their forces once in country. "We flew for four or five hours in a Black Hawk and just basically got to the Tapline Road," Cherrie recalled. "The distances were phenomenal."

The next and most important event on their schedule occurred the next day: Schwarzkopf's briefing on his campaign plan. Also present for the briefing at CENTCOM headquarters in Riyadh were the two corps commanders and the seven army division commanders: McCaffrey of the 24th Infantry, Griffith of the 1st Armored, Funk of the 3d Armored, Johnson of the 82d Airborne, Peay of the

101st Airborne, Maj. Gen. Thomas Rhame of the 1st Infantry Division, and Maj. Gen. John H. Tillei, Jr., of the 1st Cavalry Division. According to General Griffith, Schwarzkopf's presentation was a "typical G-2–G-3 briefing."

In Schwarzkopf's view, there were three centers to Saddam's capabilities: Iraq's NBC potential, Saddam himself, and the Republican Guard. Schwarzkopf then outlined his plan of attack. First, the strategic bombing campaign would target the NBC facilities. If Saddam were caught in that phase of the campaign, fine, but he was not specifically targeted. Schwarzkopf was upbeat about the air campaign. "The campaign would be driven by results, not by a rigid timetable," he pointed out. He thought the air force would need fourteen days for the strategic campaign and three weeks for the tactical phase. After the strategic phase of the air war, the coalition air forces would concentrate on cutting off the Iraqi army in the field, thus "shaping the battlefield. I want to create a given condition," he said, "and I'll base my decision to attack on the ground when that condition exists."

Schwarzkopf wanted to reduce the Republican Guard by half before beginning the ground campaign. The ground commanders were delighted with that assessment. "I don't care how good the Iraqis were," Griffith remarked, "there were 42 Iraqi divisions up there. We were attacking with seven Army divisions and two Marine divisions. The French had one division, but it had very little combat capability; we had the British division that we knew we could count on. The force ratios were out of sync with what we would normally have in an offensive campaign."

Peay asked somewhat philosophically, "If we can bomb them to 50 percent in three weeks, why don't we take another three weeks and get the other 50 percent for good measure?"

"Once the ground attack began," Peay said, "it would be a true air-land battle, with troops covered by air all the time." The plan for close air support provided six fresh sorties of air cover over each division every twenty minutes. Schwarzkopf said that there would be "lots of air."

Schwarzkopf then talked about the ground campaign. "We are not going to attack into Kuwait. We are not going to go into the teeth of this," he said. "We are going to hit him [Saddam] out here on the wing. Our objective will be to avoid the Iraqi main forces and go after his center of gravity." Schwarzkopf put his hand on the map where the Republican Guard was located. "We are going to destroy him," he declared. "We're going to push them back against the Persian Gulf and the Euphrates River, and we're going to kill them in here."

He then looked at Franks, Funk, and Griffith. "You guys are going to be the main attack," he announced. "Your mission is to kill the Republican Guard."

After the briefing, the commanders discussed what they had heard and what it meant for their troops. Griffith said, "We were anxious for all the details we could get, but I had no idea that we would get nearly as crisp a laydown as he gave us. The campaign plan had been developed."

"What was left unsaid was how this would happen," Donnelly wrote.

The logistics of moving such massive forces so far—well to the west [of] where XVIII Airborne Corps was at the time—were intimidating. The VII

Corps contingents had set off the previous day in the direction of their planned assembly areas near King Khalid Military City, and after hours of flying had gotten only partway.

Schwarzkopf left the details of supporting the attack to Pagonis, and the commanders went directly from Schwarzkopf's briefing to one with the logistics chief. Pagonis told the slack-jawed leaders how he would make it happen by moving along the Tapline Road, a two-lane blacktop road paralleling the northern Saudi border with Kuwait and Iraq. To many of the division commanders, the road looked vulnerable. "I hoped Saddam Hussein didn't get there before us," Griffith recalls.

> That evening, the two corps command groups broke up into separate groups, discussing matters with their senior staff members. VII Corps would lead the main attack, cutting through Iraqi defenses and heading for the Republican Guard. XVIII Airborne Corps would be well to the west.[11]

By November 21, units of the VII Corps began deploying to Saudi Arabia. Coincidentally, the first Army National Guard round-out brigades were called to active duty, a move that stressed the importance of the buildup and that began to make an impression on the American public.

The VII Corps deployed from Europe with the 2d Armored Cavalry Regiment, the 1st and 3d Armored Divisions, and a forward-deployed brigade from the 2d Armored Division. Moving the corps from various locations throughout Germany to the ports of embarkation required 465 trains, 312 barges, and 119 ships. The move to Saudi Arabia required 578 aircraft and 140 ships. The first ships carrying the heavy equipment and vehicles reached the seaports of Ad Dammam and Al Jubayl on December 6; and VII Corps closed in theater on February 6, when the last elements of the 3d Armored Division arrived. The VII Corps troops were initially billeted in a complex near the Dhahran International Airport.

The 1st Infantry Division, out of Fort Riley, was also assigned to VII Corps when it closed in theater. Although the division did not begin deploying until late November, its forces were in place and ready for combat by early February.

With the arrival of the VII Corps, the army, supported by its sister services, had deployed in six months a force equivalent in size to eight divisions and their supporting forces—some 250,000 soldiers—and sixty days of supplies from the United States and Europe. In theater, those soldiers, marines, and airmen from the United States totaled 365,000.

As of November, however, Bush was not able to launch an all-out air and ground campaign to oust Saddam from Kuwait. He still needed the coalition leaders' support and the backing of the U.S. Congress. He reasoned that the best approach was to return to the UN and get another resolution passed that would authorize the use of force, thus making it difficult for Congress to oppose him.

But congressional opposition was brewing as the public's antiwar sentiments began to mount. All the "war talk" began to scare the American public more than it did Saddam. Senator Sam Nunn was angered by the president's "maneuvers." He summoned his Armed Services Committee back to Washington to hold a hearing on whether the United States was rushing too precipitously to war.

Meanwhile, Bush and Secretary of State Baker kept up the international diplomatic heat and pushed for the UN resolution approving the use of military force against Iraq. Bush was anxious to get the matter to a vote while the United States still held the rotating presidency of the Security Council. One stumbling block was Mikhail Gorbachev. He was reluctant to endorse the force resolution. But after long discussions, Baker and Soviet Foreign Minister Shevardnadze agreed to use the term *all necessary means*—a broad term that might encompass diplomacy and sanctions as well as force—in the resolution. "The United States knows what 'all necessary means' is," cautioned Shevardnadze. "Don't embarrass us. Don't push us. Don't be extreme."

On November 29, 1990, by a vote of twelve to two, with only Yemen and Cuba dissenting and China abstaining, the Security Council approved Resolution 678. It authorized the nations allied with Kuwait "to use all necessary means" to drive Iraqi forces out of Kuwait if Saddam did not withdraw his forces before January 15, 1991.[12]

Before launching Operation Desert Storm, the president still wanted a resolution of support from Congress. The White House staff and Secretary of Defense Cheney helped the president lobby Congress after the UN resolution passed. The Democrats rallied against going to war. Senator Daniel Patrick Moynihan of New York chided, "It's as if the great armed force which was created to fight the Cold War is at the President's own disposal for any diversion he may wish, no matter what it costs. He will wreck our military. He will wreck his administration, and he'll spoil the chance to get a collective security system working. It breaks your heart."[13]

Finally, after three days of debate, on Saturday, January 12, Congress granted the president the authority to go to war and to use "all necessary means," the same language as the UN resolution. The congressional resolution also specifically authorized "use of military force." The Senate barely approved the resolution, 52 to 47; the House approved it 250 to 183. Even at this late date, however, the president still hoped that Saddam would pull out of Kuwait within seven days after January 15, as ordered.

Bush told reporters after the congressional vote, "This clear expression of the Congress represents the last, best chance for peace." One reporter asked him if this congressional vote made war "inevitable." The president said no. Another asked him, "Have you made the decision in your mind?" He responded, "I have not because I still hope that there will be a peaceful solution." He added that "an instant commencement of a large scale removal of troops with no condition, no concession, and just heading out could well be the best and only way to avert war, even though it would be, at this date, I would say almost impossible (for Saddam) to comply fully with the United Nations resolutions."[14]

European and Arab mediators were still trying an assortment of freelance diplomatic options. And Bush had not given up the possibility that diplomacy might yet avert combat. For example, he had tried unsuccessfully to have Iraqi Foreign Minister Tariq Aziz come to Washington and have Secretary Baker go to Baghdad to talk directly to Saddam. The message to Saddam would have been, "Pull out or else the United States will implement to a 'T' the UN resolutions." But no amount of jockeying between Washington and Baghdad resulted in an acceptable date for the meeting. Saddam suggest January 12, but Bush countered that was too late.

Bush offered Saddam one last chance. He sent Secretary of State Baker to Geneva to meet with Tariq Aziz. On January 9, the two met for six hours and twenty-seven minutes in the Salle des Nations, a spartan ground-floor meeting room in Geneva's Hotel Intercontinental. Because Bush did not trust Aziz to deliver his real message to Saddam, Bush wrote Saddam a personal letter, which Baker gave to Aziz. He refused to deliver it because it was so specific and uncompromising. Aziz complained at length during the meeting but made no commitment or promises. "If the Soviets had not collapsed, we would not be in this position," said Aziz. "They would have vetoed every one of the Security Council resolutions." After the meeting, Baker called the president and reported, "No progress."[15]

There is an interesting sidelight as to why Saddam was so adamant about not pulling out of Kuwait and why he misread the Americans' intentions, apparently thinking all along that the U.S. deployment to Saudi Arabia was a show of force and a monumental bluff. Seated on Aziz's right throughout the January 9 meeting with Secretary Baker was Barzan Tikriti, Saddam's half brother. At the end of the marathon meeting, he telephoned Saddam and said, in effect, the "Americans are weak. They have no stomach for a fight."

The next day, Secretary Baker flew to Riyadh. He briefed King Fahd and asked his permission to launch the coalition air war from Saudi Arabian territory. The king agreed.[16]

The logistics involved in deploying forces and supporting units in Saudi Arabia was nothing short of phenomenal. The United States moved forces and supplies over greater distances and in less time than ever before in its history, despite its limitations on "strategic lift," or transport for deployment. One of Saddam's major miscalculations was to discount this effort.

Beyond the reception seaports and the airfields, there was little permanent infrastructure in place in Saudi Arabia. It had to be built up from the fine, gritty sand of the desert in the searing heat of the Saudi summer. This extremely harsh environment also challenged the ingenuity of the army's equipment operators and maintenance troops consistently to maintain their gear in operating condition.

In the first eighty days of the deployment, more than 170,000 people and more than 160,000 tons of cargo were moved to Saudi Arabia by air. More than 7.5 million square feet of cargo and equipment were moved by sea. By the time the coalition forces began the offensive on January 17, 1991, the United States had shipped some 460,000 tons of ammunition, 300,000 desert camouflage uniforms, 200,000 tires, and 150 million military meals to sustain 540,000 soldiers, sailors, airmen, and marines.[17]

The logistics miracle coordinated by Lt. Gen. Gus Pagonis (Schwarzkopf awarded him a third star midway through the war to give him authority over the two-star generals commanding the divisions) and the 22d Theater Army Area Command (TAAC) can be compared to moving the entire city of Atlanta, Georgia—all of its people and anything movable—to Saudi Arabia and then providing it full support. Pagonis and the 22d TAAC managed this massive effort with the help of active and reserve units, civilian technicians, contractor teams, and Saudi contractors and civilian employees.

With the troops and equipment of Desert Shield in theater, with the backing of the United Nations and Congress, President Bush was about to launch Desert Storm. But first, Norman Schwarzkopf had to say a "Hail Mary." It may be that, even though he was not a Catholic, he ended up saying the whole Rosary.

Screaming Eagles on exercises at AO Oasis, Saudi Arabia.

11 | Shift to the Offense

The year 1990 was coming to a close. CENTCOM staffs down to squad level were working long hours and preparing the plans for an entirely new mission: the attack out of Saudi Arabia to crush Saddam's forces. The coalition forces would no longer simply defend Saudi Arabia against them.

By mid-November, Schwarzkopf had briefed his subordinate commanders on his "Hail Mary" operation for the ground war. The Hail Mary was not a miracle however; it did not come from someone's brilliant flash of intuition overnight. It had to be planned in minute detail, examined from every angle—foremost the logistical one—and briefed down the line and back-briefed up the line.

The tactics for the Hail Mary phase of the ground campaign came from the "Jedi Knights." The term came from the movie *Star Wars*. According to Bob Woodward in *The Commanders:* "Key portions of the ground campaign had been developed by half a dozen junior officers in their second year at the Army Command and Staff College at Fort Leavenworth. . . . These majors and lieutenant colonels, nicknamed the 'Jedi Knights,' had been sent to Saudi Arabia to apply the elements of advanced maneuver warfare—probing, flanking, surprise, initiative, audacity—to the war plan.

"Working in a small top-secret corner of Schwarzkopf's headquarters, they had applied the principles of the Army's unclassified 200-page operations manual [*FM 100-5*]. Chapters 6 and 7 on offensive operations were built around concepts established in General Grant's 1863 Civil War campaign at Vicksburg. Instead of attacking directly into enemy fortifications, Grant sent his troops in a wide maneuver around the Confederate front line, and then attacked from the side and rear. This indirect approach was deemed the best way to beat Saddam."[1] According to one of the Jedi Knights, Lt. Col. (major at the time) Terry Peck on the staff of the XVIII Airborne Corps, Woodward had it about right.[2]

In his book, *It Doesn't Take a Hero,* General Schwarzkopf acknowledges the contribution of the Jedi Knights. "Not satisfied that we were thinking creatively enough," he wrote, "I sent a message in early September to the Army requesting a fresh team of planners. A four-man team of graduates from the School of Advanced Military Studies (SAMS), the elite year-long program [it followed the regular course for selected students] at Command and General Staff College that concentrated on campaign planning, arrived in the middle of the month. We briefed them on our thinking to date and then I instructed: 'Assume a ground attack will follow an air campaign. I want you to study the enemy dispositions and the terrain and tell me the best way to drive Iraq out of Kuwait given the forces we have available.' I gave them two weeks to come up with an answer."[3]

During the planning phase, the corps and division commanders were also deeply involved in the tactics' planning of the operation. General Luck might receive a plan at night, meet with his division commanders, and the next day suggest different approaches through the army commander. "The maturation and reality of the planning took place at Corps and Division," remembered General Peay. "The Corps and Division planners deserve a great deal of the credit for the innovations in the plans."

Recently, the army staff revised *Field Manual 100-5, Operations,* and it was ready for publication in the spring of 1993. The changes focus more on "multiple threats, on a power-projecting Army and on the ability to deploy," says then–Army Vice Chief of Staff Gen. Dennis Reimer, West Point class of 1962. The updated version of *FM 100-5* "really will not be a revolutionary change for the Army. We think the basic doctrine that we executed in Operation Desert Storm is fairly sound."

Schwarzkopf's strategy, as he explained it to a reporter, was to "suck [Saddam] into the desert as far as I could. Then I'd pound the living heck out of him. Finally, I'd engulf him and police him up."

In a 1992 Institute of Land Warfare paper, "Operational Logistics and the Gulf War," General Pagonis, Schwarzkopf's chief logistician, and Michael Krause wrote:

Schwarzkopf's concept of operations: First blind the enemy; if the enemy could not see, he could not position his forces to counter the allied blow. Next, have the enemy think the allied forces were coming where he expected them to come: an assault from the Persian Gulf into Kuwait, along with a land assault against the main Iraqi positions in occupied Kuwait, and a flanking attack via the Wadi al Batin to try to get around these positions. Let him fool himself into thinking what he was disposed to think in the first place. Use the air campaign to blind and cripple his command, control, communications and intelligence [C³I] mediums, threaten an amphibious assault, attack the main Iraqi positions to hold them in place and then use the agility and punching power of two corps to outflank Iraqi forces. This would cut off and destroy the much vaunted Iraqi Republican Guard forces, the operational reserves of the Iraqi army. . . .

General Schwarzkopf's concept depended upon having the enemy fool himself. The logistical buildup of forward logistical bases, far to the west of the Wadi al Batin, even to the west of King Khalid Military City and to the west of any combat forces, could be seen. The solution was not to start the buildup until the air campaign had blinded the Iraqis. Hence, the westward movement of supplies for the two corps could not start until the blinding had worked. Then, while the buildup was ongoing during the aerial assault, the movement of the two corps to their forward tactical positions could take place under the air umbrella. General Schwarzkopf's concept was predicated on logistics not revealing his intent. While logistical forward bases were crucial to support the corps and the movement of the two corps was a necessity, the establishment of these bases and movement incident thereto could be detected and would signal intent.

In fact, the building of the forward logistical bases and the westward movement of the two corps—crossing them in the process—was so incredible an undertaking that allied commanders initially did not believe it could be done.[4]

Schwarzkopf was no shrinking violet; his planning concepts followed naturally from his dynamic, extroverted personality. Retired Maj. Gen. LeRoy N. Suddath, Jr., was Schwarzkopf's roommate at West Point for almost four years. "He read widely on war," remembered General Suddath. "He saw himself as a successor to Alexander the Great, and we didn't laugh when he said it. He just assumed he would be an outstanding success."

In a recent conversation, General Suddath said that no one in A1 Company of the United States Corps of Cadets, which Schwarzkopf commanded as a first classman, "was surprised at his mega-success. We always expected it. Because his father was a West Pointer before him and Norm traveled around the world with his father on various assignments, he was trained from birth to be an officer. He was just 17 when he entered West Point. It was like the British system where the sons followed their fathers into the military profession. He trained on how to lead and fight battles. He was not a modest fellow, but he was a good guy. Everybody liked him."

Another classmate, retired Brig. Gen. Ward M. LeHardy, said that "Norm is this generation's Doug MacArthur. He's got the tactical brilliance of [Gen. George S.] Patton, the strategic insight of [Gen. Dwight D.] Eisenhower and the modesty of [Gen. Omar N.] Bradley."

There are undoubtedly a number of officers in CENTCOM and other outfits that General Schwarzkopf had commanded who would take exception to comparing him to the normally even-tempered, soft-spoken General of the Army Bradley. In the book, *DESERT STORM,* by the editors of *Time,* one of the writers held that Schwarzkopf "has had epic temper tantrums. When these erupted, said a senior Joint Chiefs of Staff officer, Schwarzkopf would start 'yelling and cursing and throwing things.' What is most striking about him is a familiar characteristic often found in military leaders everywhere: an abiding certitude, a bristling self-assurance." General Suddath disputes the statement that Schwarzkopf would start "yelling and cursing and throwing things." "That would be out of character," he said.

Schwarzkopf read military history and studied past battles. One of his favorites was the battle of Cannae on August 2, 216 B.C. In that battle, Hannibal maneuvered the Romans, twice his strength, into an attack and then, using his cavalry on both flanks, double enveloped the Romans and virtually wiped them out. The Romans lost 70,000 men out of a force of 89,600; Hannibal's Carthaginians lost 5,700.

Suddath said that "Cannae was the first real war of annihilation, the kind Norm wanted to fight. We'd talk about these things in the wee hours, and Norman would predict not only that he would lead a major American army into combat, but that it would be a battle decisive to the nation."[5]

"This was absolutely an extraordinary move," said Schwarzkopf in describing all of the work in the Hail Mary operation.

> I can't recall any time in the annals of military history when this number of forces have been moved over this distance to put themselves in a position to be able to attack. But what's more important, and I think it's very, very important that I make this point, and that's the logistics bases. Not only did we move the troops out there, but we literally moved thousands and thousands of tons of fuel, of ammunition, of spare parts, of water, and of food out there, because we wanted to have enough supplies on hand so if we got into a slugfest battle, which we very easily could have, we'd have enough supplies to last for 60 days. It was an absolutely gigantic accomplishment, and I can't give enough credit to the logisticians and the transporters who were able to pull this off, for the superb support we had from the Saudi government, the literally thousands and thousands of drivers of every national origin who helped us in this move. And of course, great credit goes to the commanders of the units who were also able to maneuver their forces out here and put them in this position.[6]

"General Schwarzkopf had a general campaign plan that he briefed us on, I guess in about the October time frame," remembered General Peay. "And it was generic in nature. It had large, sweeping moves of how he thought the Corps would fight. . . . By early December, the XVIII Airborne Corps and VII Corps had general plans they were working under."[7]

The now famous Hail Mary sweeping maneuver will be recorded in future military history books and studied at war colleges around the world. But because initially the only forces in country were the marines on the coast and the XVIII Airborne Corps farther inland, the XVIII Airborne Corps planners concentrated on the offensive maneuvers of only their corps and devised a "one-corps offensive." At this point, the president had not yet even approved the movement of VII Corps from Europe to Saudi Arabia. The planners, instead, thought that perhaps III Corps from Fort Hood, Texas, would be deployed to Saudi.

Maj. Terry Peck was one of the planners from XVIII Airborne Corps. At thirty-eight, he was a graduate of Leavenworth's School of Advanced Military Studies. The SAMS program is an all-services (joint) study program to train selected officers in all aspects of military planning, including joint operations. To choose students for the additional year of study at SAMS, the faculty administers a four-hour written examination to the entire regular class and selects the best. The other services furnish outstanding middle-rank officers for the course. Major Peck's SAMS course included fifty-two officers of the U.S. Army, Navy, Air Force, and Marines.

Major Peck worked on the Hail Mary campaign. "I arrived in Saudi Arabia in mid-August as the fourth Corps planning officer in country," he wrote. "The Corps Main Command Post had not arrived yet, and we were still developing our Corps defensive planning through a series of incremental plans called 'Desert Dragon' plans. The other three planning officers in country, Majors Lane Toomey, Rich Lowe, and Jim Deloney, already had a good handle on this process, and I focused more on terrain analysis and enemy force capabilities with an orientation toward their weaknesses and vulnerabilities and how we could strike them most decisively.

"Under the direction of Colonel Frank Akers, our Corps G-3 [and incidentally, a U.S. Naval Academy graduate], I began developing counterattack options for our defensive plans, that, overtly, went as far north as to re-establish the Kuwaiti-Saudi border, but covertly addressed the option to attack Kuwait and decisively defeat Iraqi forces in that country. We knew the Iraqi forces were four times our numbers and growing daily. We also knew that massive American casualties at any time during our operations would immediately undermine the nation's commitment to our operations. Given these realities, the direct approach [a frontal attack] was never seriously considered. We knew that we would have to commit enough forces to fix the Iraqis in place but then execute the decisive blow through indirect operations. All options were open at this point . . . airborne, air assault, amphibious, mechanized turning movement, and a synchronized mixture of all of these.

"Initial offensive planning focused on the XVIII Airborne Corps executing as a single corps, massing the 24th ID (M) [Infantry Division (Mechanized)] and the 1st Cav Div along the Tapline Road, west of An Nuayriyah, and striking north up the Wadi al-Batin and then turning east to entrap the Iraqi forces committed to the southern boot of Kuwait. As time passed, and political negotiations continued, it became obvious that a one corps option would be too risky. Iraq continued to expand its fixed defenses to the west, past the Wadi al-Batin area, and moved its mechanized forces, including the Republican Guard armor, back in depth along the northern border of Kuwait with Iraq. All of this planning was done internal to XVIII Airborne Corps prior to LTC Huntoon and I going to Riyadh."[8]

Lt. Col. Dave Huntoon, thirty-nine, a West Point and a SAMS graduate, is also a brilliant young officer who had been deeply involved in the superb planning for Gen. Carl Stiner and the XVIII Airborne Corps during Operation Just Cause in Panama. On October 1, Huntoon went from the corps's headquarters to work with the Jedi Knights at ARCENT (the army's component of CENTCOM) headquarters in Riyadh. ARCENT was located in the Saudi Arabian Army headquarters building. (In normal times, ARCENT is the army's Third Army headquarters, located at Fort McPherson, Georgia.)

Brig. Gen. Steven L. Arnold was the G-3 of ARCENT and the man whom the ARCENT commander, Lieutenant General Yeosock, charged with planning for the commitment of the army forces in the theater.

Major Peck followed Lieutenant Colonel Huntoon to Riyadh on October 3 and joined a planning cell already in operation. The seven cell members were all Jedi Knights, gathered from units across the army. The chief of the planning cell was Col. Joe Purvis from Hawaii. He had been a War College Fellow at SAMS in 1990. Two of the other members were Lt. Col. Dan Roh from the 3d Infantry Division in Germany and Lt. Col. Bill Pennypacker from the 1st Infantry Division.

"We spent the initial two days," wrote Terry Peck, "wargaming the logistics of positioning forces from their current positions to attack positions north of Hafar al Batin in north central Saudi Arabia, and to assess what we believed would be the risk involved with a single corps attack into a twenty division Iraqi force. We believed we had overwhelming advantages in speed, synchronization, training, C2 [command and control], and morale commitment to the fight, but all of those were intangibles and debatable ad nauseam, so we focused on the tangibles and quickly determined that the mere mass of forces now pouring into Kuwait and southeast Iraq from the Iraq Army made a single corps attack a too high risk operation, given that we had options. (The collapse of the Soviet Union created that option, as VII Corps became available for deployment to SWA [Southwest Asia].) But I'm jumping ahead here. After the first two days, we had determined that the one corps option was a non-starter. We toyed with airborne and air assault options to block the road north out of Kuwait to Basra and link up operations using the 1st Cav Div or the 24th ID(M), but it was just too costly in lives, given the option to wait for another corps to arrive. As we looked at the two corps option over the next few days, we looked at options that went as far west as As Salman and As Samawah, and others sequentially closer in toward the Kuwaiti western border with Iraq. Of course, a hybrid of these options became the genesis for Desert Storm.

"While we were working the above mentioned plans as the primary focus, we were also asked to look at operations in western Iraq, attacking fixed Scud facilities vicinity the H-2 and H-3 airfields [numbered Iraqi airfields], to reduce Iraq's launch site options into Israel. We looked at numerous force mixes, again leaning toward an airborne seizure of both airfields with armor linkup, this time by the 3d ACR with attached Corps logistics. But it took almost as much logistical tail to execute this operation as it was going to take to support all the rest of the corps, and when it really came down to the details, we couldn't logistically support both an attack on H-2 and H-3 while simultaneously executing the attack to isolate and destroy the Iraqi forces in Kuwait.

"After about a week of wargaming all those options for sixteen or so hours a day, we had pretty much exhausted all the options and ourselves. I can't begin to express the level of detail we were trying to get to during this wargaming. If you can imagine, a theatre army level plans cell counting each truck in each convoy to support an operation, and timing attacks down to the number of hours and half hours necessary to breech minefields, pass units through, build hasty barriers for blocking positions, etc. We were breaking a 300,000 man force down to squads in breeching lanes in order to reach the level of detail that would make us feel confident that we had good figures for briefing the CINC and the Chairman."9

On October 7, the planning cell moved from ARCENT headquarters to Schwarzkopf's headquarters in the Ministry of Defense building, about two blocks away. Huntoon and Peck were the experts on the planning for the XVIII Airborne Corps. They combined their efforts with the other planners to expand the one-corps plans to two corps. "We argued over points," remembered Peck. "We challenged each other's options."

The planners reworked the plans for the campaign. According to Pagonis and Krause:

On December 27, 1990, the Secretary of Defense and the Chairman of the Joint Chiefs of Staff were briefed on the concept of operations by General Schwarzkopf in Riyadh. . . . After General Schwarzkopf explained his "end-run concept," the commanders from the two Army Corps, the Marines, the Air Force and the 22d Support Command (SUPCOM) presented their respective plans, in broad conceptual terms, to support the flanking movement. The logistical plans paid particular attention to the crossing of the two corps and the building of forward logistical bases to the west.

Toward the end of the briefing, General Schwarzkopf indicated that nothing was to move until after the January 15 expiration of the United Nations deadline for redeployment of Iraqi forces from Kuwait. When a head start on the movement to get log [logistics] bases in place was requested, General Schwarzkopf spoke bluntly. "That's not possible. The entire plan hinges on surprise and deception. If you start relocating your log bases tomorrow, we'd run a great risk of being detected. Hussein would shift his defenses westward. Or worse, he'd order his forces to attack before the deadline and preempt our strategy."

He concluded, "What we need to know is exactly how long it will take to get those log bases out there, in position to support the flanking maneuver, assuming you started moving out on 16 January. . . . We'll meet again on Saturday (December 29) to discuss a revised plan to accommodate these new goals."

*　　*　　*

The logisticians resumed their around-the-clock planning. Pagonis and Krause noted that after two days

> [of] frantic efforts a revised plan was taken to Riyadh, and, on December 29, the requested briefing took place. . . . The briefing followed the format of the earlier briefing, with General Schwarzkopf's introduction including the comment that the President had been briefed on the end-run plan. The commander's staff representatives presented their plans. Most of these included more logistical support than could be provided. The revised 21-day logistical plan needed to build the log bases and move the corps was then presented.
>   This briefing of the logistics plan was a turning point. The other commanders rallied to the 22d SUPCOM's support, sensing that, if all worked together, the logistical effort would succeed. Almost as a sidebar, General Schwarzkopf reflected that if his commanders were skeptical about the plausibility of the logistical effort in supporting the . . . operations, the enemy would be skeptical as well. In short, the magnitude of effort required to support the westward flank attack—"the end run"—served the deception needs.[10]

General Peay and members of his staff made three trips to King Khalid Military City and reported in to the ARCENT headquarters. The first time, he made the trip with General Shelton and Colonel Joe Bolt, his chief of staff. The second time he brought all of his brigade commanders to reconnoiter the area the division might ultimately occupy before the jump off into Iraq. General Peay remembers well the luxury of the offices and quarters in which ARCENT was billeted. "It would put a Holiday Inn to shame," he remembers. "The hot showers, great meals and meeting with old friends was a welcome change from life at CE II."[11]

Thus, the mission of XVIII Airborne Corps in the offense, one of the flanking sweeps, was to penetrate Iraq's forward defenses and to interdict their lines of communications along the Euphrates River in order to prevent them from being reinforced or from escaping from the KTO. On order, the corps would then attack east to assist in the RGFC's destruction.

As General Peay explained after the war, the 101st Airborne Division's plan for the ground war went through several modifications. Peay, his staff, and his commanders recognized that the division was going to have a large role in Desert Storm—a role that would be unique in military history.

Its mission in Desert Storm, in military phraseology, was this: "When directed, the 101st Airborne Division (Air Assault) moves by air and ground to Tactical Assembly Area Campbell, and prepares for offensive operations; commencing G-Day, conducts air assault to establish FOB Cobra and attacks to interdict, block and defeat enemy forces operating in and through AO Eagle; on order, conducts attacks to the east to assist in the defeat of the RGFC forces."[12]

To carry out this mission, General Peay had his staff develop two offensive plans: OPLAN 90-4 and 90-5. OPLAN 90-4—code-named Desert Rendezvous

One after the division's motto, Rendezvous With Destiny—was conceived during November 1990. It called for the division to conduct a wide envelopment from the west and to block Iraqi escape routes in the Euphrates River Valley in the vicinity of As Samawah.

Under Desert Rendezvous One, the 101st Airborne would launch an assault deep into Iraq northwest of Rafha, Saudi Arabia, and 420 miles northwest of Camp Eagle II. The plan had Colonel Purdom's 2d Brigade assaulting the town of As Samawah and establishing a forward operating base there. Colonel Clark's 3d Brigade would follow the 2d Brigade into As Samawah and then assault An Nasiriyah with Colonel Hill's 1st Brigade. The objective of the two-brigade assault was to interdict Highway 8, a main highway that runs through central Iraq and generally parallels the Euphrates River. After cutting off the highway, Purdom would move southeast and attack the Iraqi air force base at Tallil.

OPLAN 90-4 had four maneuver phases. Phase I was a logistics buildup, with Logsite Romeo built near King Khalid Military City. In Phase II, the division would be pre-positioned in a tactical assembly area far to the northwest of KKMC. In Phase III, the division would cross into Iraq and seize FOB Viper and Objectives Green and Silver (about 110 kilometers to the northeast of TAA Campbell). At the end of Phase III, the division would consolidate on Objective Silver and prepare for Phase IV's air assaults either to the southeast or the northwest of Silver to destroy enemy forces in the area.

Although General Peay and General Luck thought OPLAN 90-4 was feasible, they took a harder look at it and decided to shelve it. Rendezvous One had the division going too far west. "Desert Rendezvous One, the division plan, corresponded to the Corps plan," explained General Peay. "It had us much further west [than the actual attack]. That became logistically unsupportable because it required too much haul from a theater perspective to move the Corps that far west. Secondly, it became logistically untenable because it was going to take too much time and we wanted to kick off in concert with the air campaign a month later. . . . In fact . . . General Schwarzkopf wanted to bring the entire corps further to the east and not go that far west, and so we did. We brought the corps in further east. Tallil was just one of several options that we were working in the division."[13]

In one of General Powell's visits to CENTCOM, Schwarzkopf briefed him on the details of Rendezvous One. General Peay remembers that General Powell was concerned that the division might get involved in house-to-house fighting. Some of the division commanders shared his worry. "I'm glad we never executed Rendezvous One," said Lieutenant Colonel VanAntwerp later. "Rendezvous One had us going into built-up areas and destroying bridges and stuff in some of the larger towns. . . . That would have been a very risky mission for us." The 101st Airborne regularly trained for urban warfare, but the idea of street fighting and house-to-house fighting in As Samawah and An Nasiriyah didn't elate VanAntwerp. "We've practiced that enough to know that you're going to take some casualties when you're going building to building and door to door," he said.[14]

Generals Luck and Peay finally decided on Desert Rendezvous Two, or OPLAN 90-5. Like OPLAN 90-4, it had four maneuver phases. Phase I involved the logistics buildup designed, correctly as it turned out, to support a short-duration, high-tempo, high-consumption ground offensive. In Phase II the division would move from Camp Eagle II and the covering force area into Tactical Assembly Area Campbell southeast of Rafha, Saudi Arabia.

Phase III of OPLAN 90-5 was divided into four subphases. In subphase A, Colonel Hill's 1st Brigade would seize FOB Cobra, deep in Iraq. In subphase B, Col. Stuart W. Gerald and his Division Support Command would build up FOB Cobra to a "robust" level in order to support security operations in the FOB and to prepare for air assaults into AO Eagle along the Euphrates. In subphase C, a flight of AH-1 Cobras would make an armed aerial reconnaissance of AO Eagle. In subphase D, Colonel Clark and his 3d Brigade would attack AO Eagle on the ground war's second day and cut Saddam's line of communications along the Euphrates River. And on the fourth day of the ground war, the 2d Brigade would attack Objective Strike, or the Tallil airfield, and prepare for the additional attacks outlined in Phase IV.[15]

Peay eventually dropped the assault into Tallil from the plan because of the high risks in attacking such a well-defended objective. "We were concerned about the enormous air defense arrayed around Tallil," said Peay, "and the fact that it would unquestionably be a hot LZ." He decided to make it a secondary objective for Purdom's 2d Brigade and substituted Objective Gold, an Iraqi ammunition supply point about 19 miles southeast of Tallil along Highway 8, as Purdom's primary target.

"Some of the airfield targets we looked at definitely caused a lump in your throat," remembered Lt. Col. Bob Johnson, commander of the 4th Battalion of the 101st Aviation Brigade. "In addition to upwards of 50 anti-aircraft systems, most airfield targets had chemical weapons stored in bunkers, and all were defended by tanks and armored vehicles. Some of them looked like pretty tough targets, especially on paper. We looked at some of the targets and thought we were looking at some fairly heavy casualties. . . . The division's plan evolved more into: 'Let's go where they ain't'—which I thought was a smart move."[16]

During December, throughout the division the mood of the troops changed from defense to offense. And the training in the desert took on a new look that was far more than "leaning forward in the foxholes."

"I briefed my supportive commanders, I would say in the December time frame, on the general concept," General Peay remembered. "And then in January I briefed them in detail on our plan and had them start their series of back briefs, their series of rehearsals, the sand box exercises, and all the things we did at the National Training Center and at our home station. We just put them into effect over there."[17]

During the planning phase of Desert Rendezvous II when General Peay was working closely with the staff of XVIII Airborne Corps, General Shelton was forward at FOB Bastogne most of the time. "I was ready to provide forward command presence initially if we had to fight the covering force battle," he wrote. "The plan being worked at Corps was usually presented to the Division Commander and when I was back in the rear (about two days per week), I would provide my recommendations. As such, General Peay would be in a much better position to comment on the work by the individuals in the development of the Corps plan.

"In terms of the division plan, Maj. (P) Randy Mixon was the Division plans officer, and he was a real stalwart who played a very key role in the development of the plan. His knowledge of the AirLand Battle, current doctrine, operational terms and confidence in operational planning made him a highly respected individual and allowed him to have far more influence on the plan than an ordinary major would have been able to do. Major Mixon is a 'Jedi Knight.' "[18]

When handing out praise, General Peay remembered after the war, not to be overlooked was the outstanding work of Colonel William J. (Joe) Bolt, his chief of staff; his operations officer, Lt. Col. Montie Hess; and the planning perceptions of the brigade commanders.

Colonel Clark ran his 3d Brigade through scenarios that concentrated on air assaults behind Iraqi lines and then on linking up with another 101st unit. Clark conducted the training in the covering force area in the abandoned village of Ayn Quasan, dubbed "Q-Town" by the troops.

After Christmas . . . we did some pretty innovative training that you just don't have the opportunity to do here [at Campbell] because of range restrictions. . . . We did some very aggressive live fire training with all echelons from squad up through the battalion level . . . live fire manuever day and night . . . and the confidence that the soldiers got going through that really paid great dividends when we launched into the Euphrates. One battalion made an attack of an Iraqi bunker trench line complex that we built with our engineers on the desert floor patterned after photographs that had been taken of the trench line the Iraqis had built in Kuwait, taken from aerial photos, satellite imagery. We did a very credible job of replicating their actual defenses.

The 2d Battalion under Lt. Colonel Andy Berdy and our first batt [battalion] did an attack on a village and a bridge over a river. That was well done. They built makeshift buildings and a bridge and created a makeshift river that we did a live fire attack on day and night.

So when we went into the Euphrates, that particular battalion ended up attacking a built up area, an oil pumping station that had a lot of buildings and an airstrip adjacent to it. That had direct applicability. The soldiers got confidence being able to move and shoot and know where their buddy is on the right and use their night vision equipment and direct their fire against targets and avoid fratricide, which was one of my major concerns.

At the end of December, we deployed back to Camp Eagle II where we underwent two weeks of rest and marksmanship. . . . The purpose of Camp Eagle [II] was to give the soldiers a break from the rigors of desert life. Plus we had installation guard [duty] to provide security for all of CE II. But as the time went on during that first two weeks, it became apparent that the air war was drawing closer and it was very likely that our next move was not going to be back at the covering force but rather some sort of staging area for the ground offensive. Major unit commanders went on a reconnaissance of the assembly area.[19]

Since mid-December, Colonel Purdom and his 2d Brigade had been back at Camp Eagle II. "In late December, the decision was made that we would remain in Camp Eagle II rather than go back up in the covering force as the overall offensive plan was being developed.

"The brigade received a warning order on the 8th of January that a brigade task force was needed by VII Corps. . . . VII Corps had been alerted in November . . . and was closing in the theatre." VII Corps needed reinforcements because it was having difficulty moving its heavy tanks and Bradleys up to an area south of the Tapline Road.

"On the 8th," continued Colonel Purdom, "I personally was on a recon with the CG and the other major unit commanders within the 101st. Up at KKMC on the 8th, [we] got the warning order. On the morning of the 9th, the division Chief of Staff, Colonel Bolt, and I flew back to King Fahd International Airport, CE II, as my brigade task force prepared to go to work for VII Corps. AT 2300 hours on the night of the 9th, I got the execute order to move my brigade, my three infantry battalions, my artillery battalion, an Apache battalion, [and] the 9th of the 101st lift battalion. And so we executed that movement starting the next morning at 0600. We moved 500 kilometers up to Hafar al-Batin, where I was placed under tactical control of the 1st Cavalry who was working for VII Corps as one of the contingency plans. I moved basically 3800 people, 700 vehicles, [and] 79 aircraft 500 kilometers in about 43 hours. [The move was made with 39 C-130 sorties and 58 S and P tractor trailers]. As we moved up, the initial mission from VII Corps was to retain the Al Qaysumah airfield at Hafar al-Batin. I was tactically controlled by the 1st Cav under VII Corps."[20]

As the January 15 deadline for Saddam's withdrawal from Kuwait drew closer, the coalition planners were concerned that Iraq would strike preemptively down the Wadi al Batin, a 12-mile-wide, dried-up river valley that forms the western Kuwaiti-Iraqi border and continues southwest into Saudi Arabia, ending at Hafar al Batin. The planners also were troubled about the defenses of Hafar al Batin and the large military complex about 40 miles southwest of it, King Khalid Military City.

On January 13, Purdom received an intelligence message about a possible Iraqi attack down the wadi. Purdom showed a copy of the message to Lt. Col. James Donald, CO of the 1st Battalion of the 502d Infantry. Donald remembered that the message "suggested that reliable information had it that [the Iraqis] would attack down the Hafar al-Batin wadi complex, starting on the 13th, so we didn't sleep very well that night."

Colonel Purdom was surprised that his brigade was taken out of XVIII Airborne Corps and attached to VII Corps, but the 2d played an integral role in defending KKMC. "The 1st Cavalry division was located at Hafar al-Batin . . . basically 60 miles to the south and west of KKMC," he remembered. "I moved into the mission of retaining the airfield and the closest combat unit to us was 60 miles away. So we moved into the area and started preparing to defend. . . . Northwest of my position we had the Syrian division. Immediately to the north we had the Saudi forces. . . . To the north and east we had the Egyptians and then the Kuwaitis. I was in a retaining mission around the airfield and then we had intelligence . . . that there was an impending attack coming on the 14th of January. I was visited by the VII Corps commander [Lt. Gen. Frederick Franks] who basically saw the potential attack on Hafar al-Batin as a major threat . . . to the coalition forces if the Iraqis would come down and disrupt our lines of communications such as the Tapline. . . . The afternoon of the 13th he augmented me with four heavy engineer battalions to dig in my forces as we prepared to defend. And the order of battle, I was basically to detain [the Iraqis] and then the 1st Cav Division was going to do a counterattack if the Iraqis attacked Hafar al-Batin."

The 2d Brigade and the engineers dug in. They dredged an 8.5-kilometer-long tank ditch, positioned more than four thousand antitank mines, dug in all sixty of the brigade's TOWs ("Unbelievable," said General Peay), and set up a defense of the north side of Tapline Road that tied in with the most forward elements of the 1st Cavalry. Purdom's defense of the airfield at KKMC, however, was somewhat peculiar. His brigade "was put in a defend mission north at Tap Road," he recalled. "We were dug in, we had mines positioned, we did not put them in the ground since we did not get permission from the Saudis. That's kind of touchy." He explained that his brigade and the attached engineers positioned the mines this way: "You dig the hole and then you move the mines to an engineer regulating point. The engineers are there with the infantry to place the mines in the ground. If the attack was coming, we could have the mines in the ground within four to six hours."[21]

The Iraqi attack never came. Lieutenant Colonel Donald thinks that the Iraqis failed to attack because of the lousy weather. "The weather turned extremely bad around the 13th and 14th," he recalled. "Trafficability . . . [and] visibility would have been a problem [for the Iraqis]."

Unfortunately, the cold, wet weather worked both ways. "The weather was miserable. It started raining on us on the 10th and it rained off and on for a week," Purdom said. "I had soldiers in foxholes that were knee-deep in water who were trying to dig deeper."

"On 15 January, a relaxed and confident President Bush summoned Secretary of Defense Dick Cheney to the Oval Office," recorded one of *Time*'s writers, "and, as Commander in Chief, signed the National Security directive ordering his troops to battle. He gave Saddam one full day's grace for face, so the Iraqi could explain, perhaps only to himself, that he had not caved in to a deadline. Then the skies over Baghdad erupted."[22]

AH-64 Apache patrolling near AO Normandy, Saudi Arabia.

12 | The First Shots of the War

It was ten seconds before 2:38 in the black, moonless morning of January 17, 1991. Task Force Normandy's two teams of four AH-64 Apache helicopter crews hovered at fifty feet over their targets 50 miles inside Iraq. On their forward-looking infrared screens (FLIRs), the pilots saw them—two Iraqi radar sites that were linked to four Iraqi fighter bases and the Intelligence Operations Center in Baghdad. Each radar site, separated by 69 miles, offered a complex of at least a dozen targets—three ZPU-4s; a tropo-scatter radar; generator buildings; Spoon Rest, Squateye, and Flatface dish antennas; EW (electronic warfare) vans; and a barracks.

Lt. Tom Drew was at the controls of AH-64 Apache number 976. "Party in ten," he said, breaking radio silence for the first time on the mission.[1] Ten seconds later, the Apaches launched a salvo of laser-guided Hellfire missiles. Desert Storm had begun. Four and a half minutes later, the Apache teams of the 1st Attack Helicopter Battalion of the 101st Aviation Regiment had, in the words of General Schwarzkopf later, "plucked the eyes" out of Saddam's Soviet-supplied air defense installations.

Twenty-two minutes after the "Expect No Mercy" pilots of 1-101st Aviation had blasted the Iraqi radar sites, one hundred coalition planes boomed through the deaf, dumb, and blind alley that the Apaches had carved out inside Iraq. Desert Storm was under way.

Elsewhere on January 17, the troops of the 2d Brigade of the 101st Airborne Division were shivering in their defensive desert holes under the OPCON of the 1st Cavalry Division's commanding general. The desert holes had gotten deeper and more thickly sandbagged as the weeks had worn on. The 1st Brigade of the 101st Airborne was deployed in the covering force role.

At the start of the air war, Colonel Clark was "holding down the fort" at Camp Eagle II with his 3d Brigade. "I found out [about it] just before it started . . . " he remembered. "Heard it on the radio. The mood [in Camp Eagle II] was very serious. There was no bravado, no chest thumping, no wild-eyed enthusiasm. Very serious. Everybody put their war faces on. I'll tell you, the morning after it started, every radio in tent city was tuned into Armed Forces Radio. When the initial reports started being heard by the soldiers, there was just great enthusiasm. I could hear soldiers in their tents when a major bombing run was made on a certain facility. I could hear them whooping it up. It was quite an emotional high. After the first couple of days, though, I think we came to the realization this thing had a long way to go and airpower alone wasn't going to do it. Most of us who had been around for awhile were quite aware of that, but the young folks, the troops, I think it dawned on them. The common phrase in our brigade was, 'The road home goes through Iraq.' "[2]

Sfc. Paul F. Williams was on duty as the shift NCO at the division's main command post—a maintenance building in Camp Eagle II—on the night of January 16, 1991. Just before 2:00 A.M. on the seventeenth, he received a phone call from Maj. Levi Martin, a G-3 staffer of XVIII Airborne Corps. Martin gave Williams two crucial, momentous messages: the U.S. Navy had just launched one hundred Tomahawk missiles toward Iraqi targets, and ARCENT had declared that Operation Desert Storm was in effect.

Williams quickly passed the message to the command group and staff sections, which, in turn, relayed the message to the subordinate division commanders. Five months of waiting, planning, training, wondering, sweating, freezing, praying, and hoping were over.

For the young soldiers of the 101st Airborne, facing their first combat missions, it was an exhilarating moment. Their thoughts turned inward; they thought about home, their wives, children, or girlfriends. They prayed that the war would be over quickly and hoped that they would do their jobs gallantly and successfully. They realized that they would now have live targets in their sights and, at least as important, that the enemy would have them as live targets in his sights. To quote an old soldier, "The battle was the payoff." The young troopers of the division might not have expressed their emotions so succinctly, but they knew inherently that the old soldier was right. They had no way of knowing how long the war would last, although they did know that the war in Vietnam had ground on endlessly and that the United States was in World War II for more than three and a half years. They had no way of knowing that this war was going to be violent, swift, dramatic, and classically successful—a modern-day battle worthy of analysis by future generations of soldiers.

What most of the division's soldiers also did not know was that the first shots of Desert Storm, even before the air force's and navy's aerial attacks, were fired by Apaches from one of their own units—the 1st Battalion of the 101st Aviation Brigade. "And I can guarantee you they were the first shots of the war," insisted

Lt. Col. Richard A. Cody, the commander of 1-101st Aviation and West Point graduate (class of 1972).[3]

In the early days of Desert Shield, remembered Colonel Cody, "the [CENTCOM] planners had been doing some studies on [Iraq's] early warning and ground control intercept sites that overlapped and covered the entire Kuwaiti and Iraqi border. They were studying and making analyses of where to create a corridor."

The CENTCOM planners came up with three major courses of action for knocking out the radar sites that were vital to Saddam's air defense. One option had Special Operations Forces (SOF) attacking the sites with missiles. The second alternative had SOF infiltrating the area and then, from concealed positions on the ground, using hand-held lasers to guide Apaches to the targets. The third had air force fighters destroying the targets with their precision munitions.

A disadvantage of using SOF was the possibility of detection and compromise. Using air force fighters or cruise missiles, which could certainly accomplish the mission, meant that there would not be human "eyes" on the scene to evaluate the extent of the damage and whether the targets were definitely "dead." Helicopter pilots on the scene, however, could, if their missiles hit their targets, repeat their attacks if necessary, and be certain of the results.

"This place was out in the middle of the desert, and we were working on intelligence [that was] four days old," Colonel Cody pointed out. "[The Iraqis] could have sneaked another van in there or moved things around." The CENTCOM planners finally decided that the best option was to attack the radar sites with helicopters.[4]

Cody's battalion had gained a reputation for being the best prepared and maintained Apache battalion in the theater. It had an exceptional "fully mission capable rate" of 94 percent. Some critics have suggested that Cody's outstanding readiness rates "were distorted by higher maintenance levels." "The argument just doesn't hold water," Cody said later. "If you brought your Mercedes into the Saudi desert and didn't maintain it, what would happen? The Apache is an incredible, sophisticated machine. Maintain it as required and it performs beautifully." Cody also encouraged his men to be "creative in making the aircraft fit their needs." Thus, they raised helicopter warfare to an unprecedented level of successful mission accomplishment.[5]

Among fourteen Apache battalions in the theater, the commander of SOCCENT (Special Operations Command, Central Command), Col. Jesse Johnson, in coordination with General Luck of XVIII Airborne Corps, selected Cody's battalion for the mission. "I believe we were selected for the mission based upon the respect and the proven performance of the 101st's way of fighting at night with helicopters," Cody recalled. "Almost all the techniques we used were stuff this division had been doing for years. . . . It's just the way the 101st Airborne Division fights."[6]

Colonel Cody first learned of his mission on September 25 when Colonel Johnson called him and Col. Tom Garrett, the commander of the 101st's Aviation

Brigade, into his office at KFIA. "Johnson was looking for ways to knock out the radars for the air strike," Cody wrote. "He asked us if the Apaches could fly certain distances and knock out certain targets. I assured him that 1-101 could." Then Colonel Johnson got specific. "If we get the go-ahead even to train for this," he said, "it will be based on you saying that you can take it out 100 percent."

"After that meeting," Cody said, "we waited for ARCENT and XVIII Airborne Corps to OPCON us [1-101st Aviation] for the Top Secret Direct Action Mission. We started training with the 20th SOS [MH-53J] on 3 October." He worked with Col. Rich Comer, commander of the U.S. Air Force's 20th Special Operations Squadron (SOS), which belongs to the 1st Special Operations Wing normally based at Hurlburt Field, Florida.[7]

A number of staffers and commanders asked Colonel Cody before the mission if he was absolutely certain that he could accomplish it. He was totally confident because he was well aware of the Apache's capabilities. Of his four thousand hours of flying, some five hundred were in the Apache. Cody knew that he could fly the extended ranges Colonel Johnson was proposing because, at Fort Campbell, he had experimented with increasing the Apache's range. By attaching a 230-gallon tank to the wing, his Apache had an additional 1.8 hours of fuel. Twice he led groups of Apaches with wing tanks from Fort Campbell, Kentucky, to Vidalia, Georgia—a distance of 500 miles—on low-level, night, deep-attack raids.

"For millions of people," according to *Time*'s *Desert Storm—The War in the Persian Gulf*, "the Persian Gulf War broke live just after the start of the evening TV news on 16 Jan. ABC's Gary Shepard was the first American correspondent to interrupt his broadcast from Baghdad to announce that he could hear explosions rattling Iraq's capital. The camera abruptly shifted to the night sky. It was filled with intermittent flashes, the spearing glow of tracer rounds from antiaircraft [AA] guns, sporadic flames on the distant horizon. The time in the Gulf was 2:35 A.M., eight hours ahead of the White House. Before he lost contact with ABC anchorman Peter Jennings in New York City, Shepard declared, 'An air raid is underway.' That was quite an understatement."

And it happened *after* the raid by the Apaches of the 1st Battalion of the 101st Aviation Brigade.

Cody's battalion was the first unit from the 101st Airborne Division to deploy to Saudi Arabia from Fort Campbell. It landed at Dhahran on August 17, 1990, in seven C-5Bs and seventeen C-141s. The battalion had 340 soldiers of whom 85 were pilots. The 1-101st Attack Helicopter Battalion was equipped with nineteen AH-64 Apaches at $14 million per copy, designed primarily as a tank killer.

Colonel Cody describes the Apache as "a twin-engine, tandem seat, multi-purpose attack helicopter. It was designed to fight and survive in the Nap of the Earth [NOE] environment, day or night. The Apache can carry 16 Hellfire missiles [probability of kill of 95 percent at 6 kilometers] and 1000 rounds of 30mm ammo—or 8 Hellfires, 38 rockets [70mm] and 1000 rounds of 30mm. For the Task Force Normandy mission, we configured the Apache with 8 Hellfires, 19 rockets,

1000 rounds of 30mm and a 230-gallon wing tank on the right inboard wing store [440 nautical mile range]. The heart of the Apache, as a weapons system, is its TADS [target acquisition designation system]. This system has three sighting systems [direct view optics, day TV and FLIR—forward-looking infrared]. A laser range finder/designator, and a fire control computer allows the pilot to store ten targets and pre-point the TADS to these stored targets.

"The pilot flies the Apache at night with a one-eye monocle using the PNVS FLIR [pilot night vision system] and the co-pilot uses the TADS FLIR. In the 1-101st, our co-pilots also had ANVIS 6 NVGs [aviation night vision goggles] on to give them both NVG and FLIR capability.

"The pilot in command (PIC) normally sits in the back—he handles most of the flying, firing of rockets and 30mm [cannons]. The co-pilot gunner [CPG] sits in the front seat. He runs all the NAV [navigation] systems, fires all of the weapons, primarily Hellfire, but also can fly the aircraft from the front. Both are fully rated AH-64 pilots. I flew front and back during the war. On the raid, I flew in the back as PIC, with WO1 Stewmon as my CPG."[8]

The battalion was trained to combat readiness even before it deployed from the States. "You're always doing something in this unit," said Chief Warrant Officer Brian Stewmon. "You're either getting back from somewhere or getting ready to go somewhere. . . . You don't get bored."[9]

Less than two months before the Iraqi invasion made the headlines and the evening news, for example, the 101st Attack had deployed to Fort Hunter-Liggett, California, for a test exercise in which the Apaches simulated Soviet helicopters. "From Sep 89–Dec 89 and Feb 90–Jun 90, 1-101st participated in the LOS-FH Test [line of sight–forward heavy] of the ADATS [air defense, antitank system]," wrote Colonel Cody. "We flew the Apaches as Hinds/Havocs against a combined arms company team of M-1A1s, ADATS, and AH-1s. We fought a laser-scored battle drill twice a day—really honed our pilots' ability to fight against ADA [air defense artillery] with a 'degraded AH-64' since we were limited to using only two fields of view (FOV) as Hind/Havoc surrogates. Our pilots left Fort Hunter-Liggett in June 1990 as highly trained Apache pilots. More important, our crew chiefs and maintenance personnel came back to FTCKY [Fort Campbell, Kentucky] as highly trained 'Mr. Goodwrenches' because they had learned how to *sustain* the Apache in a wartime optempo—at Hunter-Liggett we launched 6–8 Apaches 2x [two times] per day."[10]

General Peay and Lieutenant General Yeosock authorized Cody to begin planning for his top-secret mission as early as late September 1990. Only Cody and a few key members of the 101st Airborne Division's command and staff group were aware of the operation and the planning that went on to accomplish it. His mission was to knock out, simultaneously, three key early warning radar sites in southwestern Iraq at precisely 2:38 A.M. on January 17. Its code name was Operation Eager Anvil. (Cody named his task force Task Force Normandy in honor of the 101st Airborne's troops who parachuted into Normandy, France, before H-Hour on D-Day 1944.) Wiping out the radar sites immediately and completely was essential because their elimination would pave a clean, twenty-mile-wide corridor for one hundred follow-on U.S. Air Force and coalition aircraft to fly through and strike targets in Iraq, undetected, on a moonless night.

Later Cody said that his hardest decision in preparing for the mission was selecting the pilots from among the battalion's twenty-four "battle roster" Apache crews. "Any one of them could have done that mission—any one of them," Cody said later. "I selected crews. I did not select individuals. I took guys who had been flying together as combat crews the whole time. I did not select my most experienced individuals and pool them all together. I actually had some twenty-two year olds and twenty-three year olds in the front seats out there."[11]

Selecting the crews "turned out to be a tough process," wrote 2d Lt. (at the time) Tom Drew. "There were many reasons why each of us was selected or not selected. Trying to maintain a balanced force to fight two different battles was a leadership challenge to say the least. My selection was based on a few reasons. They had to select a commissioned officer from my company to be the team leader of the White Team. There were only two choices—myself or CPT Douglas Gabram, my company commander. He was the most experienced commander LTC Cody had, and to balance the force, he had to remain back with TF [Task Force] 1-101. Also, I'm an AH-64 instructor pilot with over 1,000 hours of Apache time. The crew selection caused a lot of heartburn with those not selected. Some of the Warrant Officers started calling us the 'A' Team, thus making them the 'B' Team. Even though we didn't know what the mission was, everyone wanted to be a part of it."[12]

Even though Cody's difficult mission was of great importance to the overall air campaign, he recognized that his battalion pilots who were not chosen for Eager Anvil had an equally important job: to protect the division from potential Iraqi counterattack in eastern Saudi Arabia in the hours after the TF Normandy mission. "I was more concerned quite frankly . . . [about] a counterattack coming out of Kuwait," Cody recalled. Cody stressed to his crews that the TF Normandy operation was a team effort that extended down to the Apache crew chiefs who maintained the helicopters. Cody's crew chief, Spc. Bob Gage, was one of the very best Apache maintainers around. "He and co-pilot Stewmon," said Cody, "kept the old man's Apache 977 in tip-top shape."[13]

In Saudi Arabia, in the three months leading up to the mission, the Apache crews fine-tuned their combat skills. They spent hours flying hundreds of miles in six live-fire exercises and then accurately hitting targets with their Hellfire missiles, 2.75-inch rockets, and 30mm cannons. One Hellfire missile costs about $40,000. Chief Warrant Officer Roderick, one of the pilots on the mission, joked that firing a Hellfire is like "shooting a BMW downrange."[14]

"It all began on the 26th of September, 1990, that night we flew a mission against a radio tower near FOB Bastogne," wrote Lieutenant Drew. "The flight profile was 50 ft AHO [above the highest obstacle] and 120 Ktas [knots air speed] for the engagements. At six kilometers from the target, we fired Hellfire missiles. After the missile engagements, we fired Multi-Purpose Sub Munitions rockets and continued inbound toward the target. At 3,500 meters, we opened up with 30mm HEDP [high-explosive dual purpose]. Prior to breaking off the engagement at 2,000 meters, we launched flechette rockets and headed back toward the IP [initial point]. The mission went very well that night. The FLIR image was crystal clear and enabled us to pick up the target at about 20 kilometers."[15]

The original strike plan called for knocking out three radar sites. Based on that assumption, Cody formed three teams—Red, White, and Blue—each with three Apache and two MH-53J Pave Low helicopters.

"From the 25th of Sep through early Dec 90," wrote Cody later, "I was working a plan to take out three radar/EW/GCI [early warning/ground control intercept] sites. All of the intel pointed to three. Early in Dec, it was determined that the NW [northwest] radar site was not linked to the other two. So it was dropped off our target list. Drew and the rest of my crews didn't get the real intel and real target folders until I gave them an upbrief at our 'safe house' in Al Jouf on 14 Jan. Up to that time, we kept the crew in the dark as to the actual targets, the timing of the attack, and where the targets were. In December, however, I took the crews from the 'Blue' team (target #3) and put them into the Red and White Teams, respectively. I originally was the Blue Team leader with 2 crews from Charlie [C] Company. 'Red' had CPT Shufflebarger (A Co Cmdr [commander]) plus two A Co crews and 'White' had Lt. Drew (B Co Pltn Ldr [platoon leader]) plus two B Co crews. When the 3d target dropped off we went to two teams of 4 Apaches with one Apache backup."

The two radar sites were about 69 miles apart. One was just seven miles inside Iraq; the other was across the Iraqi border about fourteen miles from the Saudi village of Ar Ar. The radar sites furnished defensive coverage of the southwestern Iraqi border and protected both Iraqi air bases and fixed launchers for Scud missiles in the area. According to Cody, hitting the two radar sites exactly in unison was essential. "We had to do it . . . simultaneously so that Baghdad was not alerted to get MiG-29s and ground-control intercept systems up."[16]

Although the selected crews had been training for more than three months, they only knew that they were practicing for a special operations raid. They were unaware of the timing, the location of their targets, and the import of their mission—that they would fire the first shots of the air war in Iraq. Cody did not isolate himself from the rest of the battalion, because he did not want to raise suspicions about the highly classified nature of the Normandy operation. "I never relinquished my division mission with the 101st or the covering forces," he said later. "1-101st participated in every 101st Airborne Division training exercise and I kept an AH-64 company on strip alert at KFIA all during Desert Shield."

All of Task Force Normandy's training was done in the covering force area, "in a sandbox," according to Cody. "We never practiced the route because of the sensitivity of the mission."[17]

Lieutenant Drew acknowledged that the training was difficult. "Once the crews were selected, we began an intense training program," wrote Drew. "We practiced the flight profile and weapons engagements to destroy an unknown target that had some antennas. That was the easy part. The hard part was the hours and hours of planning it took just to practice the flight profile. The precise timing needed to successfully complete the mission absolutely required very detailed planning. Every combination of 'what if' was brought up and a contingency plan was made for it. Due to the radio silent requirement placed on the mission, we developed light signals using a very small IR light to communicate problems within the flight. We practiced one or two emergencies during every training flight, so even emergency situations were rehearsed. The flight profile we used was the toughest I've ever encountered in my ten years of military flying. 50 ft AHO, 120 Ktas, 3 rotor disc separation, at night, 0% illum [no lights], in the desert, no commo [voice communications], and we had to hit each check point exactly on time. . . . We made sand tables of the target arrays and discussed the best avenues of approach."[18]

"All their (the Iraqi) systems were up during this time," wrote Cody. "All their intelligence gathering networks were up—and everything else. So this was all done under the umbrella of joint training, just going out and practicing things. We practiced such things as what type of formation flights we wanted to fly. How low we wanted to fly. How fast we wanted to fly. All of this was done with no voice communications. What light signals (would emanate) from the Pave Lows. What techniques to indicate we're turning, we're not going to turn."[19]

To accomplish the mission, Cody had to surmount several problems. The first had to do with the distance from the selected strike base to the targets. To reach one of the targets, Cody thought that he would have to set up a forward arming and refueling point (FARP) along the route; but that would "create signature problems and raise the risk factor of the operation," he reasoned. In early November, Lt. Tim DeVito came up with the solution—the "single tank option." He had the Apache configured with its two outboard wing stores carrying a total of eight Hellfire missiles; the left inboard store, nineteen 70mm Hydra rockets; the right inboard store, a 230-gallon fuel tank; and the ammo bay, 1,100 rounds of 30mm ammunition. This arrangement gave the Apache a range of 440-plus nautical miles while "arriving at the target area with a substantial amount of firepower," Cody noted. "We had to get a special waiver from AVSCOM [Aviation Systems Command] to configure and fly the AH-64 with one tank. We did all the testing and sent AVSCOM the data."[20]

The second problem facing Cody in the planning stage was determining the effect that the Hellfire missile would have on the "soft" targets. The Hellfire is a tank killer and, as such, performs superbly. "What we did not know," wrote Cody, "was whether the missile would give us the desired battle damage on the soft targets. This was critical since the first targets to be engaged were the communications, tropo-scatter radar, and EW/GCI vans. To evaluate the missile effects on soft targets, we conducted three night range firings following route rehearsals. The targets engaged were buses and vans that replicated the mass and relative dimensions of the actual targets. After reviewing the damage to these targets, we confirmed that the Hellfires, fired from four to six km using autonomous lasing, could easily destroy these soft targets."

Cody's third problem was tactical: how could they destroy both radar sites simultaneously? Their separate sites and their linear size created problems. Accurate intelligence showed the layout of the Iraqi EW/GCI sites, and the critical, primary targets—several different Soviet radar systems with communications vans and antiaircraft artillery (AAA)—were well dispersed.

Cody accumulated all of the latest intelligence and photos and made his plan. He decided to attack each site with four Apaches, broken down into teams of two, side by side, and separated at each target site by 500 meters. He gave each Apache crew at least two primary and two secondary targets, "with all secondary targets belonging to their respective wingman." Cody planned it this way: "These primary targets would be engaged simultaneously at both sites with Hellfire missiles. Subsequent targets would be engaged by flechette and multi-purpose 70 mm rockets at 4,000 meters and 30 mm HEI [high-explosive incendiary] from 3,000 to 1,500 meters. This would ensure that all of the primary targets were eliminated simultaneously, provide redundancy and keep the Apaches out of AAA range."

The final problem Cody had to solve for the Apache and Pave Low crews was the night-terrain flight techniques to and from the targets. "Our best guess," he wrote later, "was that if the aircraft slowed to 80 kt and hugged the terrain (75 ft AHO), we could get inside the Iraqi coverage, launch our missiles and close with the sites before the radar operators 'broke' us out of ground clutter. Knowing this, it became imperative that both attack teams of Apaches arrive at their respective release points (RP) simultaneously. All of our rehearsals with the 20th SOS Pave Lows during the November–December time-frame focused on accurate fixing of update points, and arrival at the RPs [release points] and Battle Positions (BPs) with a tolerance of ten seconds."[21]

The Pave Lows made up for the lack of accurate, fine-detailed maps of the area for pinpointing targets. The Pave Lows are equipped for precision navigation with its state-of-the-art global positioning system (GPS). With the GPS, the Pave Lows are capable of flying to a predetermined point within eight grid points—about ten meters. "The Apache systems could fix only within 100 meters."[22]

"That was the main reason we had the Pave Lows with us," said Cody, "so they could use the GPS and INS [inertial navigation system] to mark our actual spot at the release point prior to reaching the target area. They would drop chem [chemical] lights on the desert floor to mark the position. We then plugged that into our fire-control computers on each of the Apaches. We were updating over that point. That eliminated any built-up error in the Apaches' Doppler system and fire-control system.

"It gave our target acquisition designation system extreme accuracy so we could lock onto the targets at twelve to fifteen kilometers away. That was very important as we moved forward because we knew that from about twenty and fifteen klicks [kilometers] . . . they would pick us up."

In the rehearsals and practice sessions, the Pave Lows would position the Apaches and then break off. Meanwhile, Cody said, "we would go in and practice our attack tactics, how we would sequentially dismember and destroy these sites by sectoring our fire, how we would lase [spot for one's wingman] if we had to, how we would fight if one guy got shot down, all the permutations and combinations of 'what if?'

"We do it well in the Army, but the Pave Lows have a precision with which they are able to hit their checkpoints right on the money. Their terrain-following radar helped us quite a bit in anticipating when we had to come up and still maintain our airspeed. The desert-flying experience they had with their systems, telling us how they were doing it and then our trying to duplicate that with our system, was the biggest challenge in those early days of TF Normandy training."[23]

During the battalions training, those commanders familiar with the mission checked on Cody's progress.

"Colonel Jesse Johnson, CINC SOCCENT, reviewed our tapes," wrote Tom Drew, "and told LTC Cody he would get back with us. We, the pilots, had no idea why we flew that mission [on the 26th of September], and were told not to discuss it with anyone. About four days later, we flew Colonel Johnson in an Apache to show him firsthand what the aircraft could do. CW2 Tim Zarnowski flew him for just over an hour. Upon returning from his flight, he seemed to be very impressed with the capabilities of the aircraft, especially the optics. Using FLIR the aircraft can magnify an image 38 times."[24]

In addition to the personal flight in an Apache, Colonel Johnson kept carefully abreast of the details of Cody's training. In late October, he took one of Cody's training videotapes to CENTCOM Headquarters at Riyadh and showed it to General Schwarzkopf. He was impressed.

The final decision to use the Apaches for the war's first strike was made at a relatively high level. Just before Christmas, Secretary of Defense Cheney and Chairman of the Joint Chiefs General Powell flew into Riyadh to review plans for the war that all thought was inevitable. The ranking officers and Cheney met in Schwarzkopf's underground "war room," located in the modern, concrete and steel Saudi Arabian Ministry of Defense building.

When the Task Force Normandy mission came up for briefing and discussion, Schwarzkopf cleared the room of those without the "need to know" and called on Colonel Johnson and Col. George Gray, CO of the 1st Special Operations Wing, to brief everyone on the mission. After hearing about the mission's details and the Apache's ability to fly at night, its low infrared and radar signatures, and the accuracy of its standoff weapons, General Schwarzkopf asked, "Can you guarantee 100 percent success?" Both the colonels said, "Yes, sir." The mission was a "go."

On January 12, General Peay and Colonel Garrett got their first complete, detailed Task Force Normandy brief. On that same date, wrote Drew, "COL Johnson took us to a secure room and briefed us on the mission. He explained the importance of what we were about to do, and that he had guaranteed GEN

Schwarzkopf 100% target destruction. At the conclusion of his briefing he asked if anyone was not willing to give up his life to complete the mission. Nobody raised his hand. During the briefing, COL Johnson told us we were to be in place at our staging base NLT [no later than] 14 January 1991." Privately, Colonel Johnson told Cody that he believed H-Hour would be January 17 at 3:00 A.M.[25]

On January 14, the two teams—each with four Apaches and one Pave Low helicopter—made their way to their isolated staging area at Al Jouf, some 100 nautical miles south of the Iraqi border. The weather was cold and rainy. The nap-of-the-earth flight was in two stages: the first leg, 220 nautical miles (nm), was from CE II to King Khalid Military City, where they refueled; and the second leg, 360 nautical miles, was from KKMC to Al Jouf. The first hour of the flight was flown through heavy rainshowers with less than a mile of visibility.

Even this flight to Al Jouf was under strict secrecy. "We even had to do that stealthily, without creating a signature," Cody said. "We rolled into King Khalid Military City—no radio calls or anything—refueled there and took right off. 3/160 SOAR [Special Operation Air Regiment] had set up a FARP for us and got our flights in and out quickly. There were already a large number of other helicopters operating out of KKMC so we would have looked just like any training exercise. No units or activities were allowed west of KKMC prior to the air war."

They flew low over the flat terrain, heading west. "We got down where nobody would be able to pick us up along the border, even if they were looking for us," Cody said. "I think we got into Al Jouf pretty much undetected. Once we were 100 miles west of KKMC, I had each Apache come up 'hot' on all weapons, testing the lasers and actually firing 10–20 rounds of 30 mm."

Al Jouf was a one-runway forward staging base that doubled as a civilian airport. "It was small, with limited facilities," wrote Cody later. It did have a control tower, taxiways, and ramps and was surrounded by a perimeter road. After the Apaches landed at Al Jouf, Cody parked them on the perimeter road to the south of the runway.[26]

"We arrived at Al Jouf at 1700 [5:00 P.M.]," wrote Drew. "Once we shut our aircraft down and collected our baggage, we were taken to our luxury condominiums. At least, that's what the Air Force told us prior to leaving King Fahd. They turned out to be shacks with little or no hot water. We had approximately 10 personnel in each hut. There was one bed, and only a few chairs. The Air Force had also told us we would have excellent contract mess facilities. By the end of the first day, we were starting to understand Air Force lingo. Condominiums meant shacks and good food meant MREs. We all joked about it, but we really didn't care. We were there to complete a mission. About an hour after we got settled in our huts, some Hajis (local workers) came in and took the only table and all the chairs. As our furniture was being taken, an Air Force MAJ came in and told us there was no security around our compound and that we would have to post our own guards. So there I was at 0100 [1:00 A.M.] on 15 January 91, pulling guard duty with my stick buddy [co-pilot]. I remember thinking, 'Do they really think we can pull our own guard duty and be rested enough to perform this mission?' The night of the 15th, the Air Force SPs [Security Policemen] pulled security for our compound and we all had a good laugh about pulling guard duty."[27]

On January 15, Colonel Cody briefed his pilots on the exact details of their missions and passed out maps and photos. He gave them their exact targets, their locations, the flight routes, the joint execution checklist, an intelligence update, and a joint operations air mission brief. "I put Newman Shufflebarger in charge of Red Team and Tom Drew as the team leader of White," wrote Cody. "I flew [with Stewmon] as Drew's wingman and had the tropo[-scatter] as a target as well as flying the final BDA [bomb damage assessment] run." On Team White, Drew's backseat pilot was CW2 Tim Zarnowski. The other members of the White Team were CW2 Thomas ("Tip") O'Neal with CW3 David Jones in the back seat, and CW3 Ronald Rodrigues with CW2 Davey Miller in the back. The Red Team consisted of Cpt. Newman Shufflebarger and CW3 Tim Roderick, WO1 Joe Bridgeforth and CW3 Dave Miller, WO1 Tim Vincent and CW2 Shaun Hoban, and WO1 Jerry Osburn and CW4 Lewis Hall.

"Up until this time," Cody wrote later, "only myself and Lt. Russ Stinger (S-2) [battalion intelligence officer] knew the actual mission. Russ had been my primary link to all of the SOCCENT and USAF intell assets."[28]

That day, the crews preflighted their aircraft and loaded all the navigation points in their computers. Drew said, "It was a relaxing day for the most part. I wasn't scared really. I was more nervous about whether or not we would do well on the mission. The night of the 15th we looked at the satellite photos of our target. We went through at least 10 dry runs while sitting in our little hut. We went over everything from the code words to down pilot procedures. The Air Force flight surgeon gave everyone a sleeping pill to ensure we stayed asleep late on the 16th. We played cards until around 0300 [3:00 A.M.] 16 JAN 91 and went to sleep."[29]

They were in the staging area, of course, when the January 15 deadline for Saddam's withdrawal from Kuwait came and went. To the TF Normandy teams, this all meant that Schwarzkopf had given Saddam's troops a brief respite in which to "cool their heels," and the president was giving Saddam another day to change his mind and avert war.

The men preparing to make the first strike discussed the impact of the inactivity. Chief Warrant Officer Roderick said that he did not know the reason for the pause, but Stewmon thought that Schwarzkopf gave Saddam enough time for the Iraqi troops "to drop their guard." Saddam did not back down. The 101st Airborne and the pilots for the 1st of the 101st Aviation were ready. Some of the troopers wanted to "fight it out"; we get paid to kill and break things, they reasoned. Others were willing to let the high-level power brokers in both governments and the UN negotiate a peace without battle. "We get paid to preserve the peace," Roderick pointed out.

The next day, Cody brought the teams out of "crew rest" at noon. The crews spent the next three to four hours checking the aircraft and weapon systems.

126

And up to the last minute, after they had been briefed in detail and were standing by their aircraft, they were not sure that they would be ordered to execute the Task Force Normandy mission. "We sat down by the aircraft and waited for the President to call down and say 'go,' and that's when we went," remembered CW2 Bridgeforth, an Apache gunner/navigator on the mission.[30]

Colonel Cody received the official go-ahead at about 2:00 P.M. on January 16. Cody was sitting in his helicopter, talking to his gunner, when a rental car sped across the tarmac to his Apache. Colonel Gray's deputy, Col. Ben Orrell, USAF, hopped out and said, "I need to talk to you." Cody climbed out, and Orrell told him, "We have just received H-Hour from the CINC. It's 170300 [January 17, 3:00 A.M.]. Your mission is a 'go.'"

"This translated into a 0238 [2:38 A.M.] strike for Task Force Normandy," Cody wrote later. "The mission was to attack and destroy two EW/GCI sites at H minus :22 [twenty-two minutes]." Once H-Hour was set, Cody gave the teams a last-minute briefing on routes, weather, and the status of defenses along the Iraqi-Saudi border.

"They scheduled a final brief at 2100 [9:00 P.M.] in the Air Force building," Drew wrote. "We finished the final preparation of our aircraft and went back to our huts. We all tried to get some sleep but were unable to. At about 2045 [8:45 P.M.] we walked to the Air Force building. When we arrived, the Air Force PJs [para-rescue jumpers] were in their combat uniforms. They had grenades, knives, and guns strapped all over them. There was none of the normal joking around. Everybody was all business. The importance of what we were about to do really hit me. I knew we were well trained and well equipped so I had a feeling of confidence. They briefed the entire mission which took almost an hour. During the intell portion, they briefed an Iraqi OP [observation post] directly on our flight route. Following the brief, we had to change our flight route to bypass the OP. Once we had everything set, we all shook hands and went our separate ways."

At about 10:30 P.M., the crews loaded up in trucks and headed for the airfield. The guards at the airfield gate made everyone show ID cards. "This was causing quite a stackup of trucks trying to get in the gate," said Drew. "[It was] kind of strange for the guard, I guess. 2230 hrs [10:30 P.M.] and all this traffic wanting to go to the airfield. When we got to the gate, we all showed him our ID cards. He asked us what was going on. We, of course, said nothing. I was thinking, 'If you only knew.'"[31]

When the word came down that the operation was on, the crews felt the usual pre-combat butterflies. "I myself stood out by the aircraft and screamed for ten minutes to get a bit of the tension off," Bridgeforth said.[32]

"Once I arrived at my aircraft," recalled Drew, "I put my maps and kneeboard in the aircraft, and made some other preparations. I still had about a half hour before APU [auxiliary power unit] crank. I laid [sic] down beside my aircraft and looked up at the stars. A lot of things went through my mind. I wondered if I would live long enough to see the sun come up in the morning, what my wife and daughter were doing at home, and how would Iraq retaliate. It was time to strap in. I said a prayer and got in. The run-up was normal, all systems go. At 0056 [12:56 A.M.] 17 JAN 91, we lifted off into a cold moonless night headed for targets in Iraq."[33]

At 1:00 A.M. January 17, Cody led the White Team of two MH-53 Pave Lows and four AH-64 Apaches out of Al Jouf into the pitch-black night for the ninety-minute flight. Twelve minutes later, the Red Team, led by Captain Shufflebarger and his copilot, Tim Roderick, departed. There were a total of nine AH-64s, one UH-60 Black Hawk, and two Pave Lows in the task force. The two extra helicopters—one AH-64 and one UH-60—were for backup command and control and SAR (search and rescue) for the teams after the strike. According to Cody, "We had some 900 nm to travel to get back to the 101st Airborne Division immediately after we fired the first shots of the Gulf War."

During the flight to the target area, the Apache pilots exercised total radio silence and turned off all navigational lights. "The illumination that night was zero percent," wrote Cody, "but both the MH-53s and the AH-64 crews were flying with both FLIR and ANVIS-6 NVGs. This combination of Apache pilots flying with the Pilot Night Vision System [PNVS] FLIR and the co-pilot/gunner using both the ANVIS NVGs and the TADS FLIR greatly enhanced the crews' night fighting capability and gave the Apache a true all/any night capability."

On the way into the target area, flying at 120 knots and 50 feet off the ground, Colonel Cody and his copilot saw, about a mile away directly across their path, what they guessed was the flash of a shoulder-fired missile. It did not endanger the flight, but Colonel Cody said to himself, "Shit. People know we're coming." Fortunately, they did not.

The main reason the Iraqis did not pick up the Apache teams was a combination of the teams' high speed, low altitude, total blackout of navigation lights, and complete radio silence. The last legs of the mission were flown at less than 80 knots to stay below the speed gates of enemy radars.

"The Pave Lows flew as our primary NAV," said Cody. "We were backed up with the Doppler Navigational System. . . . The Pave Lows had terrain-following radar, which helped them out quite a bit. We didn't have that, but our FLIR, coupled with our night-vision goggles, was just working great. So you had two different systems backing each other up. We were backing them up, and they were primary. The lead Apache in each one of those teams had a primary mission of navigation. We didn't leave anything to chance.

"The MH-53 crews dropped 'chem light' bundles at their respective RPs some 20 km south of the targets, and each Apache updated its HARS and Doppler off the GPS-spotted chem light bundles. The MH-53s peeled off and went to their respective linkup points and the Apache teams slowed to 60 kt and pressed forward to the targets."[34]

"After take-off," wrote Drew, "I initialized my weapons system and made sure everything was set. It was extremely dark. That portion of Saudi Arabia and Iraq is very sparsely populated, so we didn't have the normal lights to illuminate the area.

128

We couldn't make any radio calls so it was very quiet. We had flown in the darkness for about 45 minutes. I was concentrating on precise navigation when we began to take fire from a Bedouin camp. It appeared to be a machine gun. I was trying to get a clear shot but was unable to due to the aircraft in front of me. Then I saw a missile fired at the flight. No one was hit but the little camp was saturated with bullets. About 15 minutes later, we took fire from another camp. Basically the same events took place. When we got farther into Iraq, I couldn't see any camps, animals, or any other life forms. As we drew closer to the target, I could finally see some lights. I told the onboard computer to point the TADS (Target Acquisition Designation System) at the target. Lo and behold, all those lights out there were our targets. . . . We hit the IP, the Air Force broke off and went to their preplanned orbit, and we continued in toward the target. At a little over six kilometers we came to a hover. We were about 20 seconds early. At ten seconds I made the call, 'Party in ten.' Ten seconds later, *'Get some!'* "[35]

The Apache crews were totally radio silent until about ten seconds from their targets. "Can you imagine driving a car at night—blacked out—down the freeway for 90 minutes and not talking to the person next to you?" Colonel Cody reminisced after the raid. "Now put yourself in four Apaches, flying at 50 feet off the ground and 120 miles an hour down on the desert floor, knowing you're going to launch the first strike and you don't say a word on the radio to your front or back man. Lead [helicopter with Jones and O'Neal] never knew—I was the cleanup hitter on my team—until I fired my first missile that I was still with him."[36]

Nearing the targets, the lead Apaches squeezed their coded lasers to the center of their assigned targets and, using their laser spot trackers, locked onto the target array. At precisely 2:37 A.M., both the Red and the White teams were in position. Each crew lased and stored their primary and alternate targets and awaited the "10 seconds" radio call from each team leader.

When they were near the target area, CW2 O'Neal said to his pilot, CW3 Jones, "OK, I've got the target area."

Jones asked for the range and said, "Slowing back."

"I'm showing 12.2 (kilometers)," replied O'Neal.

"I'll keep moving," said Jones.

"I've got one of the big ones all the way on the right," O'Neal announced.

Jones zeroed in on the first target, a building. "There's the generator right there," he said. "OK."

"Aha," said O'Neal.

"Party in ten," exclaimed Drew from the lead Apache.

The FLIR screen flashed *Launch.* "O'Neal and Jones hit seven for seven with their missiles," Cody said later, praising their accuracy.

All the pilots pulled their triggers at the same time. In Drew's team, all four aircraft fired two Hellfires at their primary targets. "Time of flight was more than ten seconds, and it seemed like an eternity," wrote Drew. His first target was a trailer, and his wingman's first target was a radar antenna. The other two Apaches would fire at different antennas, control buildings, and the communications vans.

"There were people running around the site," wrote Drew. "They all seemed to pick the wrong places to go. As my missiles neared impact, two people ran inside. The missiles impacted. Direct hit! My next target was an anti-aircraft position. I checked it only to find a guy running from it. He never made it back to the site. As the team leader, I was responsible for ensuring that all the targets were destroyed. I surveyed the site. All primary targets were destroyed and burning. I had two more missiles that I could fire. I noticed that all the people were running in and out of the barracks. So, I squeezed the trigger twice. It ripped through the building and just about knocked it completely down. The next one hit farther to the right and wiped out the barracks. At this point, there was no structure left untouched. I fired about 300 rounds of 30mm at the personnel running around the site. Our last engagement was with flechette rockets. We fired six rockets, which put 13,200 flechettes going the speed of sound raining in on the target. If anybody lived through that, I don't know how. At 1500 meters we broke off the engagement."[37]

Shufflebarger's Red Team attacked its radar site with the same intensity and accuracy. The team members locked onto their targets with their Image Auto Gate Trackers, or electronic rectangles on the scopes that are designed to find and hold onto targets by identifying their heat sources.

On target, the Apache crews fired up to thirty-two Hellfire missiles and destroyed sixteen to eighteen targets at each site. Their goal was to cripple each site so that it could not be used during the next seventy-two hours. "We made sure it was not usable," said Roderick, Shufflebarger's back-seater. "It never came back up during the rest of the war." The raid itself took four and a half minutes—"a very busy four and a half minutes," Roderick recalled later.[38]

"Just incessant fire," said Cody. "Missile after missile, rocket after rocket, 30-mm after 30-mm coming from four aircraft that they [the Iraqis] couldn't even see. From the first shot, they were just running for cover. When we closed in to 4,000 meters, we engaged their ZPUs and antiaircraft artillery and put them out."[39]

During the actual attack, the crews did experience some disorientation. "When the wingman puts out two or three rockets, everything lights up," Cody remembered. "You're sitting there looking at your FLIR and then your naked eye picks up these flashes. You had to be very, very careful not to mistake that for ground fire coming at you.

"We took those things down in three and a half to four and a half minutes, four aircraft flying in pretty close proximity to each other.

"Some of us got closer than 800 meters when we finished. We used 2,000 meters as a breakpoint, but, depending on what our targets looked like, as we were breaking and as we were being engaged, some of us moved in a little closer, fired our flechette rockets, and then broke. Drew and Zarnowski covered my final run-in with their rockets and 30 mm."[40]

The teams knew every minute detail about the operation and that, "no matter what," it had to be completed. They were prepared for any contingency. If their

FLIR systems had failed, they would have used their electronic navigation equipment, and if that had failed, "we would have used our maps," Roderick said.

Cody's plan was to have one Apache per site destroy the large generator/power pits while the other Apaches obliterated the communications and tropo-scatter vans. When they had accomplished these primary missions, each crew first checked his wingman's target and then took the secondary targets under fire.

Most of the missiles were fired from 6 to 3 kilometers, the rockets from 3 to 0.8 kilometers, and the 30mm cannon from 2 to 0.8 kilometers. They were fired as the Apaches broke away from the target area.

The primary targets were destroyed within the first minute. "Neither team took fire from the AAA sites defending the targets," said Cody, "nor did we receive any small arms fire. Our APR-39s radar warning receivers did pick up search modes from the radars as we closed from the RPs, but our FLIR videos verified that the Iraqis did not realize they were under attack until seconds before the missiles were launched."[41] That they did not take any antiaircraft fire on their way in surprised Bridgeforth. "Wouldn't you expect to get shot at if you were 80 miles over the border shooting at them? We really didn't expect it to go off as easily as it did."

The search-and-rescue Black Hawk hovered at the border but was not needed. The task force did not lose any aircraft or suffer any casualties.[42]

Cody reflected that the Apache crews fully understood the significance of Operation Eager Anvil, which many believe set the tone for the overwhelming air victory in the war. They felt the pressure, Cody admitted, but the pilots kept their minds on the job at hand. "What we did was to open up a 20-mile wide corridor to Baghdad so Saddam couldn't see what was coming at him. Suffice it to say, we knew that if we didn't knock the things out, that some guys were going to get shot down." He was aware at the time of the raid that some operational types had projected double-digit pilot losses for the first day of the air war.

With their mission accomplished, the Apache teams raced south to their linkup point and the Iraqi border at up to 140 knots and 100 feet AHO. En route out of Iraq, the Apache crews knew that the coalition fighters were overhead en route to Baghdad through the now radar-black corridor. The waves of incoming tactical jets were just 400 feet overhead. "We had to link up all these attacking forces [the Apaches] at night at a new rendezvous point," Cody recalled, "and then charge back across the Saudi border—coming the wrong way. We were a little nervous."[43]

"The link-up was a very dangerous procedure," remembered Drew. "All aircraft were of course blacked out, and we were flying at around 140 ktas. The difficulty was identifying the proper aircraft. Finding the number two Apache was critical. If you fly up on number one thinking it's number two, you have a serious problem. It took me almost ten minutes to completely join up with the flight. By this time, my aircraft was shaking pretty violently. There was a two-inch hole in my number two rotor blade, which was getting bigger. I didn't know what was causing the vibrations at that time, but [it] became very apparent after I shut down the aircraft. As the flight continued, the vibrations got worse. As we neared the Saudi

Arabian border, the U.S. Air Force first wave was coming in the corridor we had just made in the Iraqi early warning system. We were flying at around 75 feet. They weren't much over that, and they were coming fast. Little dots on my FLIR picture would rapidly get bigger and bigger and come right over the top of us. It was an awesome sight. After seeing that, LTC Comer coined the phrase, 'Aluminum Overcast.' They began coming in larger groups, F-111s [Aardvarks], F-15Es [Strike Eagles], etc. . . . Through my NVGs I could see them all lining up way to the south. When they got within 20 miles of the border, they turned their lights out. It truly was like aluminum overcast."[44]

The U.S. and British bombers were on their way to the fixed Scud missile sites at an airfield in western Iraq, or H-2 on coalition military maps, and at desert outposts near the wadis of Amij, al Jaber, ar Ratqa, and Muh Hammadi. As one *U.S. News & World Report* writer observed in *Triumph Without Victory*, "All of the targets were in westernmost Iraq near Jordan; in fact, they were the Scud bases nearest Israel. The bombers were seeking to fulfill the pledge of the Bush administration to Israeli Prime Minister Yitzak Shamir."

The Apaches' flight back to Al Jouf took about an hour and a half. They arrived at 4:30 A.M., refueled, shut down, and conducted a mission debrief. At first light, with the exception of Lieutenant Drew, they launched for the return trip to King Fahd International Airport. Drew had inspected his aircraft and found that the rotor blade was peeling apart at the top. Cody left Drew at Al Jouf to wait for a new blade. "We could have put a temp patch on Tom's blade," Cody recalled later, "but I didn't want to take the risk. Everything was going well and I had the means to get a blade up to Al Jouf that day." Drew flew back to KFIA two days later.

The rest of Task Force Normandy flew the 360 nautical miles to KKMC, where Cody had stashed Hellfire missiles before the raid. He wanted the Apaches armed when they returned to CE II in case Saddam decided to retaliate and attack the covering force area. AT KKMC, the Apaches reloaded the Hellfires, refueled, and then flew the 220 nautical miles to CE II. They landed at CE II at 4:00 P.M., only fifteen hours after the launch of the attack. For the Normandy mission, the crews had flown more than thirteen hours and fired more than thirty Hellfire missiles, fourteen hundred rounds of 30mm and one hundred 70mm rockets.[45]

According to Cody, when the Apache crews returned to Camp Eagle II after the mission, they found out that there had been no pilot losses along the corridor that they had just opened. "The guys that we paved the way for never got touched," he said. "We felt pretty good, and we knew we had accomplished our mission then."[46]

The Apache crews had taken videotapes of their target runs. They have been edited together for a nine-minute tape showing the actions of all eight Apache attacks. Colonel Cody has reviewed the film countless times. The tape in one section shows an Iraqi soldier running out of a building but then dashing back inside just before the missile strikes and blows the building into the air. "When stuff starts hitting around, you naturally look for shelter, but shelter was what we were shooting at, so it was his bad day," Stewmon reflected.[47]

Drew claimed that the success of the mission was based on four factors: *training*—"We had trained so well that the mission could not fail"; *teamwork*—"A group of Americans working toward a common goal cannot be stopped"; *leadership*—"The leadership in the Task Force was truly outstanding . . . LTC Cody and LTC Comer were always positive and more important, were always on the same sheet of music"; and the *Cody Factor*—"He is extremely intelligent, and he has a strength within that drives him to be the best he can be in everything. . . . He displays confidence in everything he does. . . . In watching LTC Cody for the past eight years, I've noticed that everything he touches turns to gold." In the 1st Battalion, he was known as "Commander" Cody.

Cody insisted that the operation was a team effort. Its success was shared by all, from the pilots to the Apache crew chiefs. "It was not a perfectly executed mission," Cody admitted later. "None of them are. The fog of war is always there. But I will tell you that it was as close to perfect as you can get."

To put it mildly, Cody is a firm believer in the Apache's capabilities. "The Apache is the finest combat helicopter ever produced—bar none," he said.

Task Force Normandy proved it.

An artillery section prepares an M-102 howitzer for internal load operations into a CH-47.

13 | The Move Northwest

After January 17, when the air war phase of Desert Storm began, the coalition air forces flew thousands of air sorties every day against pre-planned targets in Iraq. Their strikes hit targets of military importance: missiles sites, command and control centers, communications centers, power generating plants, airfields and runways, aircraft storage hangars, NBC weapon development and production facilities, and bridges. The coalition's sorties involved aircraft from the air forces of Bahrain, Canada, France, Great Britain, Italy, Kuwait, Qatar, Saudia Arabia, and the United States.

For thirty-four days, from January 17 to February 24, the coalition air forces pounded Iraqi targets relentlessly. Toward the end of the third week of the air campaign—more rapidly than even the most optimistic planners had predicted—General Schwarzkopf declared air superiority, if not supremacy, after the initial targets had been virtually destroyed and Saddam's air force rendered impotent. Most of the Iraqi air force went to ground in civilian communities or in protective bunkers that were later destroyed by precision-guided missiles. The few Iraqi aircraft that took to the skies were either quickly shot down or flown across the border into Iran, where the 140 Iraqi aircraft were impounded. The term *bug out,* coined during the undisciplined, haphazard, first battles of the Korean War, might have been used to describe the precipitous cross-border flight of part of Saddam's air fleet.

Then, Schwarzkopf shifted the around-the-clock air strikes against Iraqi ground troops and their lines of communications, command and control centers, logistics centers, and armored vehicles, especially of those Iraqi units across the Kuwaiti-Saudi Arabian border. He concentrated particularly on the Republican Guard divisions.

A classic AirLand Battle, according to the dictates of the U.S. Army's *Field Manual 100-5,* was about to begin. According to one of the writers of *Time*'s *Desert Storm,*

The plan that the U.S. would follow had been worked out in immense detail by General Norman H. Schwarzkopf. "Make no mistake," one top Pentagon official said later, "this was Norman's plan from A to Z." In a sense, however, the general was simply going by the book. A relatively obscure (and unclassified) U.S. Army publication, *Field Manual 100-5,* lays out the principles of "AirLand Battle," a post-Vietnam military doctrine that has been gospel for every war college student since the early 1980s. "Don't give me a meat-grinder," Schwarzkopf repeatedly warned his planners. Instead of the World War I frontal assault that Saddam was preparing to defend against, the AirLand doctrine calls for air attacks on the enemy's rear areas to cut off supply lines, destroy command-and-control centers and strike at reinforcing units, in order to isolate the battlefield.

"The strategy is aimed as much at the enemy's mind and morale as his weapons and troops. . . . AirLand strategy requires commanders to concentrate their efforts on attacking the right thing in the right place at the right time. The enemy's crucial "center of gravity"—a term borrowed from Prussian strategist Karl von Clausewitz—is the target whose destruction will have the greatest ripple effect on the enemy's overall military operations.[1]

The Republican Guard was certainly that "center of gravity."

As late as December 1990, the lower levels in the 101st command still had not been briefed on Schwarzkopf's Hail Mary plan—to outflank and destroy the Iraqi forces.

Lt. Col. Thomas J. Costello was the commander of the 3d Battalion of the 320th Field Artillery Regiment in the 101st Airborne Division. "We knew, of course, that planning for the move against the Iraqis had been ongoing for months," he wrote. "While the plans were Top Secret, and very closely held, few of us had been given some insights into what was in store. . . . We had been assuming that the offensive would focus on Kuwait, and might possibly range as far west as the Wadi al Batin. 1-187th Infantry, under the command of LTC Hank Kinnison, had been tasked with developing and rehearsing tactics for an air assault mission into Kuwait while the other two battalions of the brigade were focusing on the covering force mission in October and November, and Hank and his guys had developed many useful lessons learned. The underlying assumption, nonetheless, was that the air assault would be as 'deep' as forty or fifty kilometers, and would be against one of the softer, but highly lucrative Iraqi targets in Kuwait itself. In fact, until the hostages were released in December, the possibility of a hostage rescue was on the menu of potential missions.

"When we returned to Camp Eagle II at the end of December, COL Clark assembled his task force commanders and staff, and revealed our planned mission to us, within the framework of the division, corps and theater plans. To say that we were dumbstruck would be something of an understatement! Up until that time, no one that I knew of had envisioned anything as bold as the move

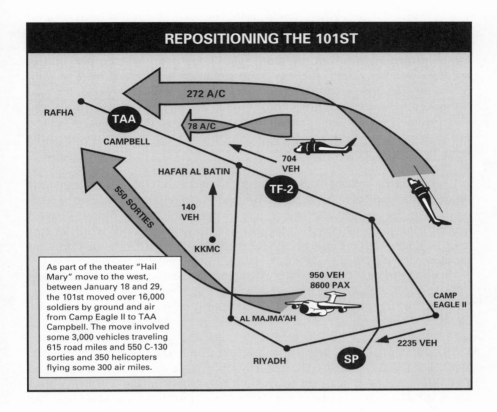

REPOSITIONING THE 101ST

272 A/C

78 A/C

RAFHA

TAA
CAMPBELL

704
VEH

TF-2

HAFAR AL BATIN

550 SORTIES

140
VEH

KKMC

As part of the theater "Hail Mary" move to the west, between January 18 and 29, the 101st moved over 16,000 soldiers by ground and air from Camp Eagle II to TAA Campbell. The move involved some 3,000 vehicles traveling 615 road miles and 550 C-130 sorties and 350 helicopters flying some 300 air miles.

950 VEH
8600 PAX

CAMP
EAGLE II

AL MAJMA'AH

2235 VEH

RIYADH

SP

well to the west and the planned air assault into the Euphrates Valley. The scope of the operation was breathtaking, and the depth of the assault was intimidating. From the inception of the division's planning, the Rakkasans of the 3d Brigade were given the Euphrates Valley mission, but the exact objectives and parameters of the mission underwent a series of changes and modifications. Initially, we were to seize bridges over the Euphrates in the city of As Samawah, hand the area off to a follow-on brigade, and then air assault to the east and seize the bridges in the city of An Nasiriyah. (Jim Mathis told me, after hearing this, that he wrote home to have his wife, Nadine, mail him his copy of 'A Bridge Too Far.')

"As time went on, that particular plan underwent revision after revision, finally being scrapped for several reasons: the bridges were targeted by the Air Force enough times that there was a high degree of confidence that they would be dropped by the time the ground campaign commenced; the NCA [National Command Authority] was uneasy about the prospects of U.S. troops getting sucked into one or more urban fights; the probability of collateral damage and unacceptable civilian casualties was too high; and so forth. The plan eventually focused on interdicting Highway 8, the main road paralleling the Euphrates, linking Basra and Baghdad on the south side of the river. Whether the bridges remained standing or not, Highway 8 was certain to be a critical route of withdrawal for Iraqi forces, particularly the Republican Guard (in this case, the road became even more critical if the bridges to the east were down, since this would then become the best route of withdrawal), and it offered the potential of being a major supply and reinforcement route into the KTO, if the battle offered the Iraqis that opportunity.[2]

The day after Colonel Cody and his highly successful Task Force Normandy returned to Camp Eagle II, the 101st Airborne began its move to the northwest in preparation for its militarily unique role in Operation Desert Storm. It was a major challenge for the division's logisticians and commanders. The staff worked long, hard hours to perfect the plan, which came from XVIII Airborne Corps, for the move. The staff then broke it down into schedules and unit assignments.

General Shelton, the division's assistant commander, outlined their work. "We were given an air and ground movement plan by Corps," wrote General Shelton, "which assigned ground routes and gave us 'block' times that we could be on our assigned routes. Likewise, they gave us the number of C-130 sorties that we would be allocated by day/time. Within those parameters, the Division staff provided a proposed movement plan to the Division Commander. While DISCOM had a part, the majority of the work was done by the G-4 and G-3. We, of course, planned to maximize the loads in the 350 helicopters which we also had to move to the Rafha TAA. DISCOM was tasked, as you would expect, to provide the recovery/beddown site enroute since, as I recall, it was a 2 1/2–3-day trip. The Division Assault CP, which I was charged to train and lead, was designated to go to Rafha and provide the forward command and control as we moved into the new area (AA Campbell). We were anxious to get started and departed the second we were cleared by Corps to move north (o/a [on or about] 17 Jan—the day the air war commenced.) We (ASSLT CP) launched in two ESSS [external stores subsystem] equipped UH-60s heavily loaded with command and control equipment early that morning for the 400 or so mile trip. I remember as we headed north that morning thinking as we skimmed across the desert floor at 120 knots, 'Here we come, you bastard; I hope you know that you've asked for.' About an hour into the flight, the missile warning light/audio activated and we went into evasive maneuvers. Still don't know what made it activate but the pilot's immediate response reinforced a key point that was to be repeated many times in the next 45 days—the way you train is the way you fight—the pilot's reaction was at this point instinctive!"[3]

At Camp Eagle II, the troops were well aware that January 15—the deadline for Saddam's withdrawal from Kuwait—was a significant date. Lieutenant Colonel

Costello wrote that "as the date grew closer, tensions continued to rise. . . . The evening of the 16th, I think, we went to THREATCON DELTA [highest threat condition], expecting an imminent terrorist attack. We carried our MOPP [mission-oriented protective posture] gear with us everywhere we went, and kevlar helmets and flak jackets became the uniform. The instructions were for everyone to sleep below the level of the sandbag barrier that we had long before built around the tent rows.

"A few minutes before 0300 [3:00 A.M.] on the 17th, MSG John Daigle, my operations sergeant, came into my tent and told me, 'Sir, I think it's started. AFN [Armed Forces Network] reports flak over Baghdad.' Shortly afterward, we were shaken by the thunder of high performance jets leaving King Fahd on afterburner. That was a real surprise; an A-10 [Warthog] wing was the occupant (and what a lovely sight they, and our neighborhood Patriot battery, were each and every day), but we had never heard fastmovers operating out of there before. I still have no idea where they came from, nor how long they had been there. They might have stopped there for fuel, for all I know.

"The entire day of the 17th was spent with knots of soldiers huddling around radios, hanging on every report out of AFN. By noon the war had been won, and the Republican Guard completely destroyed. Not a bad morning's work—there may even have been a few guys who believed it. The casualty reports, at least, were reassuring, and I tended to believe them more. I, for one, carefully watched the A-10 operations, looking for signs of battle damage as they passed overhead in the pattern, and didn't see any. The one event we were all waiting for didn't come to pass that day—there were no SCUD attacks.

"I awoke on the morning of the 18th to the air raid—which was also automatically the NBC—alarm. What an experience! To say that it was one that I will never forget is a plain statement of fact. I masked, ensured that the troops were undercover—there was really no place to go, so the best course of action was to remain inside, on the floor, and hope for bad gunnery—and tuned in AFN. The news broadcast was reporting '. . . large numbers of Israeli civilians being transported to local hospitals for treatment of nerve agent symptoms . . . from the SCUD attacks.' What a way to start the day! My long years of military experience and schooling allowed me to conclude that the war had taken a turn during the night. And this was only the second day—who said this was tough? The nerve agent casualties, of course, turned out to be victims of hysteria, but we didn't know that at the time. And the SCUDs were for real. Saddam had made good on one of his threats, so there was no reason for this kid to doubt his willingness to make good on the others. We also knew that Israeli reprisal, no matter how justified it may have been, would turn the coalition into a real mess, and nobody was betting on Israeli restraint that morning. From a prior tour in Israel as a UN observer, I had met a number of Israelis, in and out of the military, and while no expert, I personally figured the odds of Israel sitting this one out as far better than a massive Iraqi surrender and a Saudi conversion to . . . beer and *Playboy*. I'm glad I was wrong."[4]

*   *   *

Nonetheless, throughout the division, preparations for the move to the northwest went on apace. Soldiers crammed their gear into their duffel bags and rucksacks, and sergeants supervised the loading of allocated vehicles. Unit commanders made plans—when, where, how many, loading restraints—for the transportation they were going to use: C-130s, helicopters, trucks, and organic vehicles.

"In between false [air raid] alarms, we finished our preparations to move to Rafha," wrote Lieutenant Colonel Costello. "As you might guess, this was an operation of no small proportions, with little room for the unit that wasn't prepared on time and in the right place. We had loaded the howitzers and prime movers [the truck that pulls the howitzers] with everything they could hold, and still wished for more. Every vehicle was carrying a load of barrier material, and each gun truck had about ten rounds of 105 ammunition. Add it all up—ammo, section equipment, plywood, small arms basic load, rations, water, mission-essential unit equipment, and so forth—and there wasn't a HMMWV that wasn't at least 1000 pounds overweight. That did not include rucksacks, which we were handcarrying, nor duffel bags, which were being trucked up. Having ridden with the Air Force a time or two, I had horrible visions of half the loads [getting] dumped on the tarmac at King Fahd. This, however, was war, and for some reason, somebody told the Air Force. As long as the total loads didn't exceed the capacity of the C-130 to stagger off the ground, anything went. The niceties of axle weights and so forth seemed to pale in comparison with mission requirements. Was this our Air Force?

"We finished breaking down the tents and issuing the small arms basic load. Up until this time, we had been carrying only the self-protection load we had been issued back in September, about 15 rounds per pistol and rifle, and maybe 200 rounds per M-60. Now it was the big time, and another image that I'll carry with me for a long time to come is that of MSG [John D.] Daigle, SFC [Steven L.] Howard, the assistant ops NCO, SFC [Thomas U.] Sasko, the FDC [Fire Direction Center] chief, and their troops sitting around the floor of our TOC [tactical operations center] in tent city, loading magazines. The old pros, like Daigle, coached the youngsters on the fine points (three tracers go in first; that way, you'll know when you get to the end of the mag). The weather was very undesert like [it was raining] at that particular time, which added to the general sense of well-being. The hajj tents were made of some sort of cotton or burlap type material, and were never intended to be waterproof, or even water resistant. They were designed to provide shelter from the sun, and nothing else, and that's what they did. . . . On what I expected to be my last night in tent city, I went to use the facility (the luxury of sitting down, don't you know), and there I sat, about 2200 [10:00 P.M.] in the rain, thinking about home, whether I'd ever see it again, how the family was doing, what we might be doing together on that Sunday night, wondering if I'd get a SCUD between my knees before I finished, and getting some insight into how some people might fail to appreciate the charm of my way of life."[5]

The secret movement of two corps to the northwest was a huge, spectacular military operation, the like of which is rare in the annals of military history. According to General Pagonis and Michael Krause,

> For 18 critical days, 18-wheelers were transporting combat equipment and materiel, passing one point on the westward road every minute, every hour, 24 hours a day. The movement was staggering. By February 24, each of the corps was in position and the logistical forward bases stocked to the necessary levels.
> The central concept of maneuver was to sweep the western flank. As we have seen, this was intimately tied to achieving operational surprise. Hence the enemy had to fool himself into thinking that a western flanking sweep was all but impossible.
> The malpositioned corps—XVIII Airborne in the east and VII Corps in the west—had to be repositioned. . . . Mobility was the key. This meant high combat systems readiness. Complete factory-to-foxhole integrated maintenance and distribution were practiced. The Army Materiel Command and other commands and agencies were directly involved in helping to achieve the highest readiness to date.[6]

The massive movement of General Patton's Third Army in World War II offers a comparison to the even more massive movement of XVIII Airborne Corps at the beginning of Desert Storm. On December 16, 1944, Patton was preparing to drive east as the Germans launched their drive west into the Ardennes. On December 18, General Eisenhower ordered the Third Army to attack north and to relieve the pressure on the trapped and surrounded 101st Airborne Division at Bastogne. Between December 19 and 21, Patton moved his III Corps, consisting of three divisions and supporting troop units, along four separate routes that ranged from 98 kilometers to 181 kilometers in length. Altogether, Patton moved 9,404 vehicles—1,713 tracked and 7,691 wheeled—and 42 light observation aircraft.

Between January 18 and February 7, 1991, XVIII Airborne Corps moved from the vicinity of Dhahran to the northwest, near the Iraqi border and well past the VII Corps. The corps's staff paper read:

> Only two routes were available to the 100,000 plus soldiers of the XVIII Airborne Corps and those had to be shared with the normal heavy traffic of Saudi Arabian commerce and with the daily ARCENT logistics traffic required of Desert Shield forces. The typical Corps unit had to travel 665 kilometers; other elements moved up to 1,100 kilometers. . . . XVIII Airborne Corps moved three full U.S. combat divisions, an armored cavalry regiment, and nearly all of its supporting specialized groups and brigades. That translates into flying approximately 980 helicopters; driving 25,310 vehicles (20,165 wheeled and

5,145 tracked) by road; and using nearly 1,400 Air Force transport sorties to deploy an additional 2,719 wheeled vehicles, 15,876 personnel and thousands of tons of supplies, food, and ammunition into both fixed airfields and XVIII Airborne Corps–constructed assault landing strips.[7]

In its move to the northwest, the division's destination was Tactical Assembly Area Campbell, which was about 900 kilometers from Camp Eagle II, approximately 75 kilometers southeast of Rafha, and 10 kilometers southwest of the Iraqi border. TAA Campbell was immense—approximately 3,200 square kilometers.

On D-Day, January 17, the 101st Airborne began moving its pre-positioned forces from Logsite Romeo, near King Kahlid Military City, into TAA Campbell. A and C companies of the 326th Engineer Battalion closed into Campbell by 9:30 P.M. The division assault CP—General Shelton and a small staff—and quartering parties joined them in TAA Campbell the same day. The quartering parties set up the camp and assigned areas to various units.

Also on D-Day, the DISCOM commander, Col. Stuart Gerald, ordered the Task Force Assembly Area's advance party to occupy and to set up the new DISCOM site and to prepare to receive supplies. "The advanced party moved to occupy the TAA on 17 January," he wrote after the war.

> The area occupied was less than five miles from the disputed border between Iraq and Saudi Arabia. The threat was believed to be Iraqi artillery and terrorists from Tapline Road. The battalions made their way up the 700-mile convoy route to the TAA. The convoy [route] included nearly 200 miles of the dreaded Tapline Road which could be the most dangerous road in the world. At any given time, four white Toyota or Nissan pickup trucks loaded with sheep, camels or children could be approaching you four abreast on the narrow two-lane highway. . . . Corps transportation assets were not available so the task of moving the prepositioned supplies at [Logsite] Romeo to the TAA fell solely on Delta Company 426. The company had 40 five-ton cargo trucks and 9 30-foot stake and platform trailers, many of which were committed to moving supplies and personnel from FOB Bastogne to the TAA.[8]

The division's main body began to move out for TAA Campbell, per Phase II of OPLAN 90-5, on January 18. The first ground convoy of twenty-four vehicles left Camp Eagle II at 8:46 A.M. Per one of the division's briefers, the total route was 615 miles in length.

As Lieutenant Colonel Costello noted, the division also experienced its first Scud alert of the war at CE II while troops were preparing to move. As practiced endlessly, the troopers of the 101st Airborne quickly masked and prepared for the worst until the "all clear" signal reverberated through the air. Later that day, another Scud was launched—this time toward Dhahran—and was destroyed by a Patriot missile. Over the next few days, CE II had frequent Scud alerts, but after the first alert, the troops masked only for attacks aimed at Dhahran and Riyadh. From CE II, the troops could easily observe the Scuds' contrails as the missiles sped toward Dhahran and witness the Patriots streaking up in the sky to engage and destroy them in tremendous, brilliant explosions.

Over the next several days, the division continued to move from its covering force positions and Camp Eagle II to TAA Campbell. The 3d Brigade closed on January 23. Two days later, 2d Brigade was released from the 1st Cavalry Division's tactical control and began moving by ground convoy and air from Al Qaysumah to TAA Campbell.[9]

Costello and part of his battalion staff and TOC flew into Rafha on the night of January 18. "If the weather was bad where we were, it was god-awful where we were going," he wrote. "The bad weather up in Iraq was the subject of the daily weather briefing at the brigade TOC, and the weather at Rafha was evidently no better. . . . We finally got our turn at about 1800 [6:00 P.M.], loaded a C-130, and headed off into the evening skies. . . .

"I talked my way into the cockpit of the C-130 and watched, but couldn't participate, in the activity on the flight deck (no headset). The flight took about two hours and 45 minutes, and for the last few minutes of it the navigator had his radar operating. I couldn't tell squat from it, but I guess he could, because runway lights presently appeared as we broke through the overcast, and we landed, killed the lights, and followed a ground guide over to a gloomy corner of the airfield, where we were encouraged to unload with all due speed. I don't think they even set the brakes on the plane. As I was leaving, I thanked one of the cockpit crew for the ride and the courtesy, and he wished us luck. In fact, he told me that we were lucky to get in, since the weather was really dogshit. Why didn't I feel lucky?

"Anyway, we emerged from the back of the C-130, which quickly departed for its next load, and there we were, at Rafha airfield, in the dark, in the mist, in the cold, with no idea of which way was what. In the near distance I saw the revolving blue lights of a Saudi police car, and traffic passing on the road. Dennis Murphy was there, a friendly familiar face to greet us, and he welcomed me to Rafha. Smart-ass. Oh, by the way, he said, the blue lights are for us. A Saudi driver, watching a departing plane as he drove by the airport, drove into one of the howitzers as it was exiting the airport. Great. As we began organizing the aircraft loads into a convoy for the rest of the trip, word passed along the line that we were under a SCUD alert, and everyone masked. The night was getting better by the minute. The SCUD alert ended, we unmasked, and we unassed—that is to say, we expeditiously continued our movement—from the area into the desert. . . . Tapline Road after dark was something we avoided like the plague. So here we were, on Tapline Road, and it was definitely after dark. Up here, however, there was much less traffic than we encountered farther south. As a matter of fact, there was none. Not a truck, not a car, not a military vehicle, not a camel, not a thing except our little convoy and bunches of desert. If you ever want to experience spooky. . . ."

CSM Lawrence C. Douglas had met Costello at the airfield and, with his vehicle and a PADS [position azimuth determining system] vehicle, escorted Costello and his convoy to their spot in the tactical assembly area. Costello knew that after he left the Tapline Road he still had about 12 kilometers of desert to traverse and that his battalion position was about 10 kilometers from the Iraqi border. Out in the desert, moving near the head of his convoy, Costello began to doubt the ability of the PADS vehicle to lead him to his assigned position. "After covering what had to have been at least 100 kilometers due north from Tapline Road, I began to contemplate the prospects of leading the invasion of Iraq with my TOC, and began composing appropriate Stars and Stripes headlines ('Battalion Commander and TOC Captured by Iraq; 101st Artillerymen First Ground POWs; Theatre Plan Compromised by Blundering Artillery Unit of 101st; Schwarzkopf Assessing Continued Viability of Deception Campaign'). After several hours of this (maybe several minutes), still oblivious to the fact that I had a vehicle ahead of me that could tell me to a tenth of a meter where I was at, I decided to call a halt for a position check. As I suspected, there we were—two hundred meters from the blue chemlite marking CSM Douglas's bunker. . . .

"By this time, it was about 0230 [2:30 A.M.] or so, and we began to try to dig. I knew for an absolute fact that we were either on the far side of the moon or in a shopping mall parking lot, for the ground defied any hole deeper than six inches. As daylight seeped in, we were able to survey our new home, and my assessment of the night before was not far from the mark. It was the flattest, rockiest, most desolate, barren, godforsaken piece of ground that I have ever seen. The gray, hundred (maybe) foot ceiling [cloud cover] did little to add to the charm of the scene, and I could only guess what the place must be like in the middle of summer. It had nothing going for it in the winter, that was for damn sure. After careful searching, we were able to find a few spots soft enough to dig in, and had absolutely no problems motivating the troops to dig quality fighting and survivability positions—they knew where we were as well as I did. . . . As I was digging, I could only imagine how CSM Douglas, SSG Montgomery, and Specialist [Donald R.] Pirtle, who along with the PADS team, constituted our quartering party, must have felt out there by themselves while they were waiting for us to arrive (keeping in mind that we were days late by this time). None of them ever mentioned a word about it."[10]

The rest of the division continued to move northwest by aircraft and trucks over the next several days to TAA Campbell. As the division was closing in and getting organized on the ground, on January 25 General Luck gave General Peay's 101st responsibility for screening along Phase Line Razor—a northwest–southeast line that ran north of and roughly parallel to the Tapline Road. General Peay assigned Colonel Hill's 1st Brigade positions on the line's left and Colonel Clark's 3d Brigade positions on the right. About 10 kilometers north, the line of departure for the XVIII Airborne Corps ran along the disputed and largely unmarked Iraqi–Saudi Arabian border with its actual Saudi and Iraqi guard posts.

Elements of Colonel Purdom's 2d Brigade provided security for the 101st's assets in the rear half of TAA Campbell.

The 1st Brigade closed in TAA Campbell on January 26. As the brigade was moving in, General Peay conducted the first in a series of brigade and separate battalion commanders' backbriefs to get an idea of what his commanders' concepts were of the upcoming battles based on OPLAN 90-5.

On January 29, the 2d Brigade closed in TAA Campbell. Its men and equipment had moved from the area around Hafir al Batin in 656 vehicles, 60 stake and platform trucks, 15 forklifts (materiel handling equipment, or MHEs), and 78 C-130 sorties. The remainder of the division required 358 C-130 chalks (some 900 sorties) and convoys of 1,910 vehicles and 833 flatbed trucks.

En toto, the division moved a total of 350 aircraft, 4,000-plus vehicles, three battalions of 105mm howitzers, and 17,132 soldiers by both air and ground. In short, the division's entire Humvee fleet and the majority of its soldiers moved by C-130s from King Fahd International Airport to the Rafha airfield. Two-and-a-half-ton trucks and larger vehicles moved from KFIA to the TAA by ground convoy via the southern route through the Saudi capital of Riyadh. All of the division's helicopters self-deployed to the TAA.

The division's move was hampered by a transportation management system that "violated unit command and control," said one of the division's briefers after the war. "External transportation assets were piecemealed to the division from a pool of assets belonging to a variety of units. The movement would have gone more efficiently had entire units, with their own leadership, been provided to complete missions per established movement priorities."[11]

General Shelton, however, was a little more upbeat. "The move, to my recollection," he wrote, "went amazingly smoothly without substantial problems. This is particularly astonishing considering the length of the route (700 miles) and the fact that the transportation units came from all over the world (and within the theater). The sight I'll never forget after arriving at the Rafha airfield is that the first five C-130s that landed came from different units and many were reserve units, their State names proudly displayed on the side of the aircraft. The first bird to land was a Pope AFB [Air Force Base] (317th) C-130, followed by an Air National Guard plane, etc. Easy to see why standardization is so important in our business. I remember thinking as I watched those planes landing that morning, this is truly the power of the United States vividly demonstrated and we've just begun to tap our resources. . . .

"The 3d Brigade and the 1st Brigade arrived at the airfield, and we had 2 1/2 tons to carry them up to the Saudi/Iraqi border where they went into defensive positions. I do remember that when we arrived at Rafha airfield we were met by the mayor, airfield manager and several of the people (leaders) from town. They were delighted to see us—couldn't do enough for us. It was considerably colder there in the NW [northwest]. Rain was falling and the temperatures were bitter. Nevertheless we were all glad to be there. At last the wait was over. The troops understood—the road home was through Iraq and we were now one step closer. We also understood the next step was the BIG one with a lot at stake. We also knew we were well trained and ready!"[12]

With this intratheater deployment completed, General Peay had under his command a massive combat force positioned just south of the Iraqi border. His superbly trained and desert-hardened troops were in three air assault infantry brigades; the division artillery of three battalions of 105mm howitzers and an M-198, 155mm towed artillery battalion; and an aviation brigade of three attack helicopter battalions (including the attached 2-229th Attack Helicopter Regiment from Fort Rucker), one air cavalry squadron, and one utility, three assault, and one medium-lift helicopter battalions. The division also had the usual support of its air defense, engineer, signal, and military intelligence battalions, and the Division Support Command (DISCOM) with its maintenance, supply, transportation, and medical battalions and military police, chemical, and light equipment companies.

TAA Campbell was 3,200 square kilometers of flat, open, desolate, barren desert. Viewed from the air, the positions of the division's units appeared as little clusters of pale tents, tan vehicles, and camouflage nets covering weapons, vehicles, and communications centers. Plain desert separated one cluster from another. The units' positions were easy to spot from the air despite the extensive use of camouflage nets, but the nets did mask the type of unit in each location. Fortunately, no Iraqi aircraft were flying over the area to spot them.

The main terrain features in TAA Campbell were Tapline Road and the oil pipeline from which the road took its name. One of the division's briefers wrote that, during the move, Saudi "drivers weaved violently through slow moving convoys. The 101st MP Company took up positions along Tapline Road to enforce safe speed limits. The incidence of accidents involving 101st Airborne soldiers and equipment was in fact remarkably low throughout both Desert Shield and Desert Storm, given the tremendous amount of movement and maneuver by vast numbers of forces."[13]

Once the division had closed in TAA Campbell, the emphasis was on digging in, securing the area, and refining the plans for the offensive into Iraq.

"We settled into a routine after the first few days," wrote Lieutenant Colonel Costello, "in which we accomplished the bulk of our digging in. We were very tense, of course, with the Iraqi border in plain view a few kilometers away. Each element was spread out, of course, with at least a kilometer or two between them, but we knew that we must surely be visible to the Iraqi Border Guards. The brigade mounted an aggressive patrol program between our FLOT [forward line of own troops] and the actual border, and there were several sightings, each of which subsequently proved to be a false alarm of one sort or another (Saudi border guards, friendly forces from adjacent units, or other patrols from the brigade). At one point we were alerted to displace to an offset position and conduct a ground artillery raid against a border post and air defense site. That was pretty exciting as we did the reconnaissance and planning, but it was cancelled before we could execute it. The whole thing had a surreal quality about it; the weather was improving, and the days were generally sunny and pleasantly warm. We were at war, but the days were very peaceful. We could see coalition air activity overhead from time to time, but little happened in our immediate vicinity that one could associate with battle."[14]

That would soon change.

Iraqi prisoners of war in TAA Campbell's EPW camp, February 1991.

14 | TAA Campbell to FOB Cobra

Schwarzkopf's Hail Mary plan was working. His prayer was being answered. He had moved two corps, one through and over the other, hundreds of miles to the northwest apparently without being detected by Saddam's forces. General Pagonis's logistics "miracle" was a fait accompli. Now Schwarzkopf was about to exercise one of the prime principles of war: He was going to surprise Saddam.

"The need for surprise—the need to fool the opponent—had a definitive logistical component," wrote General Pagonis and Michael Krause.

> Again, General Schwarzkopf reasoned that if his commanders thought the logistical task daunting, then the enemy would think so as well. Therefore, logistical tracks in the sand could not be allowed until the opponent was blinded.
>
> The extent of this deception was not known back in the United States. Even highly classified briefings in the Army's Pentagon warroom [sic]—the operations center—kept the force position and their logistical bases in the eastern province until after the beginning of the ground campaign.
>
> The other question related to intelligence and deception was the logistical supportability of the western flanking move. Could it be done? Could two malpositioned corps be crossed and repositioned at the same time the logistical bases were being constructed? . . . It took longer than originally planned; two weeks became three. One reason, therefore, for the stretching of the air campaign from two to three weeks was the time needed to position the corps and build up the logistical bases.[1]

Once most of the 101st Airborne Division was in place, the screens positioned out front, the troops dug in, and command posts, communications vans, howitzers, Humvees, and supply points camouflaged, General Peay focused on preparing for

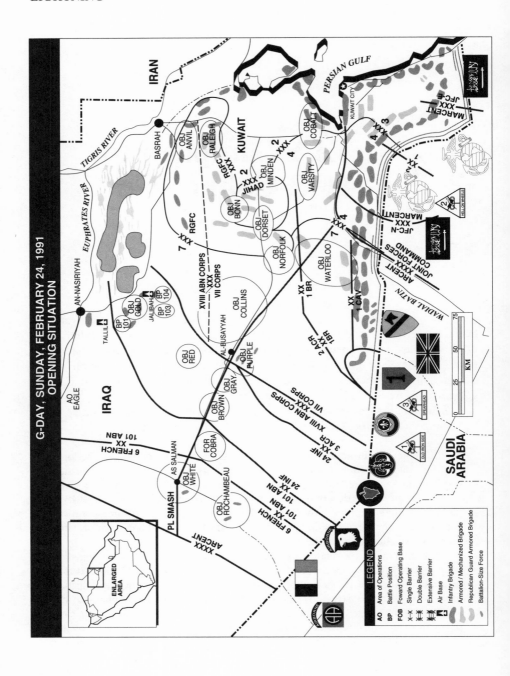

G-DAY, SUNDAY, FEBRUARY 24, 1991
OPENING SITUATION

his airborne assault force's attack into Iraq and for making military history. First, he had to conduct an intelligence preparation of the battlefield, or an "IPB" in the latest military shorthand. The first stages of the IPB involved procuring and extensively studying maps and aerial photography—a science honed to highest skills in this war and that surpassed the techniques and quality of previous battles and wars. The IPB also included interpreting intelligence gathered by the division's 311th Military Intelligence Battalion, monitoring Iraqi radar use, and studying intelligence passed down from the corps and higher headquarters. "More thorough information would be gained by the aerial reconnaissance of the 'G minus 7' operations, but in late January, that was still several days off," said one of the division's briefers.

OPLAN 90-5 was fine-tuned to reflect the information gained during the IPB, though no major changes developed. First Brigade TF [Task Force] would still lead into Iraq to establish a forward operation base, followed by Third Brigade TF blocking along the Euphrates. Second Brigade TF would then either attack into Objective Strike (the Tallil airfield) or into a critical choke point at Objective Gold. The strikes into Iraq would be preceded by several days of aerial reconnaissance [recon].

The staff developed a reconnaissance plan that called for aerial recons beginning on the seventh day prior to G-Day, the start of the ground war. This plan was labeled the "G minus 7" plan. It would prove to be very influential in the preparation of the battlefield for the coming ground war.

In preparation for combat, continuous training always complemented planning. The division used the precious few days of late January and early February to polish its air assault and command task skills.

The brigade task forces practiced sling load techniques, conducted air assault rehearsals, discussed rules of engagement and used sand tables to talk through their planned air assaults. Their direct support field artillery battalions emphasized crater analysis and fire direction control procedures while the engineers practiced breaching minefields and rigging demolitions.

The division's air defenders perfected CH-47D Chinook internal delivery methods for the Vulcan air defense cannon. DISCOM fine-tuned resupply procedures while the 7-101st Aviation [7th Battalion, 101st Aviation Regiment] tested flow rate for a rapid refuel point to be used in upcoming aviation operations. While conducting plenty of flying training missions, Aviation Brigade was careful not to fly much to the north, to avoid disclosing the division's location and power.2

Lieutenant Colonel Costello and his staff reflected the work being done by all the battalion commanders and their staffs. They refined the plans they would implement on G-Day, calculated vehicle and howitzer load configurations, and war-gamed the exact equipment they would need in the forthcoming battle. Costello slimmed down his TOC so that he had a lean team riding in on the first choppers.

"The target kept moving," he wrote, "as the Chinook pilots updated their estimates on fuel requirements and load capacity. The plan eventually evolved to the point that we knew that Task Force Rakkasan, the heavy element of the brigade that would include my two firing batteries and jump TOC, would not be able to fly the entire distance into AO Eagle. A landing site, called LZ Sand, was selected at the point the aviators felt they could reach, some 40 kilometers or so short of AO Eagle. The plan was for us to fly in the day of G+1 [the day after G-Day], land, reorganize, and move by ground to a point just short of AO Eagle, there to await the arrival of the infantry assault. Travelling by Black Hawk, they would be able to fly directly into Eagle, and would make their assault after dark on the evening of G+1. We continued to plan, rehearse, backbrief, and wait, as the Powers That Be deliberated on when G-Day would be."[3]

As unit training was being conducted, the unit commanders continued to work on common task skills. They emphasized in particular perfecting NBC defense and decontamination skills, never forgetting the threat of Iraqi chemical warfare. Unit supply teams issued to each soldier PB (pyridostigmine bromide) pills to help build up a tolerance against nerve agents and valium injectors to mitigate potentially harmful effects of atropine, which was used as a nerve agent antidote. Soldiers also continually practiced basic marksmanship skills. The 326th Engineer Battalion built small-arms ranges in the brigade sectors of TAA Campbell.

General Peay tied all of the plans and training together through daily staff meetings and biweekly updates for brigade and separate battalion commanders. The second in the series of unit backbriefs to the commanding general was conducted in early February.

Preparations for the ground operations were also under way. The division G-4, Lt. Col. Tom Shrodzki, worked closely with the corps's staff on throughput of supplies and the use of main supply routes. The division also changed its commercial utility and cargo vehicle (CUCV) fleet for five hundred new, more capable Humvees. Task Force King, named after its commander, made several round-trips between CE II and TAA Campbell to ferry new trucks to the units. The DISCOM supply units stockpiled ammunition, water, and food on unit-configured pallets for sling loading under the lift helicopters.

"As preparations for the coming ground war continued," wrote the division's briefer, "day to day life in TAA Campbell was full of contrasts between old and new. Soldiers continued to perform such age old tasks as digging fighting positions and filling sandbags. We continued to live and work in tents, bunkers, vehicles and homemade shelters (hooches). At the same time, there was a decidedly modern air to our operations. Every command post, down to at least battalion level, had at least one computer. Electronic messages were passed from laptop computer to laptop computer via multichannel telephone lines. There were also a large number of fascimile (fax) machines and photocopiers in use."[4]

Digging for the defensive positions was not easy. Lt. Col. Richard F. Riccardelli, CO of the 311th MI Battalion, described the terrain in his sector as "almost lunar-like environment. The terrain was vast and flat with small volcanic-like rock."

The troops dug as deep as they could—a few feet—before reaching hard rock. Then they built up their bunkers and positions with walls of sandbags that grew higher the longer they were in position. The division engineers used earth-moving gear to dig trenches for bunkers and to pile large berms of dirt around tents and positions. Some units gained extra protection by moving into deep wadis.

TAA Campbell was not another CE II. At TAA Campbell, the troops were dug in, ready to repel an attack from the Iraqis. On the perimeter of TAA Campbell, the troops lived in holes in the ground, covered with tarps or behind sandbagged revetments. Gone were the precisely aligned rows of tents at CE II.

Fortunately, the weather was relatively pleasant during the latter part of January and early February. Temperatures were in the upper sixties during the day, but, at night, they dropped into the thirties. Sleeping bags proved essential. The blowing sand caused the commanders to place great emphasis on preventive maintenance of equipment, especially the division's trademark and primary means of movement—the helicopters. And the blowing sand could drop visibility quickly from seven miles to less than a half mile.

In the TAA, the troops were also becoming well aware of the air war's intensity. During the day, they could see the contrails of the coalition's jets as they flew toward Iraq, and, at night, they could see the flashes of the bombs' explosions. Combat was getting closer.

Maj. Steve Chester was S-5—the staff officer concerned with civil-military operations—of the 3d Brigade of the 101st. He described life in the TAA: "Planning complete, it was a matter of waiting for the word to go. We did some patrolling of the border, but, other than that, it was rehearse, complete preparations and sleep. Life revolved around a shallow hole that alternately trapped blown sand or flooded after the fairly frequent rainstorms. The air war made itself known as the contrails of various aircraft and rumble of distant air strikes served as reminders of what the Iraqis were catching. Some other fireworks were provided by the French and 82d Airborne Division, who persisted in firing hundreds of 105mm rounds. In the middle of the night, an RAF Tornado blasted over my hole at warp speed and low enough I could feel a hot wind and the chemical alarms gave their usual false alarm. Coming out of a dead sleep, that set my heart to beating harder than anything else for several years. We found out later that the Tornado was damaged and had two MiGs on his tail. These were intercepted just inside the border by two F-15s and shot down, I was told."[5]

Scud attacks also kept the troops on the alert. Incoming Scuds were tracked by the early warning system of the division's 2-44th Air Defense Artillery Battalion, commanded by Lt. Col. Charles DeWitt. No Scud hit TAA Campbell directly, although one did land as close as Hafar al-Batin.

General Luck had not authorized any movement beyond the FLOT (forward line of own troops). But, on February 14, even though there was still no official date for G-Day, Luck authorized General Peay to send troops across the FLOT. Peay could initiate his "G-7" (the start date for the ground war minus seven days) plans. That night, division aircraft crossed into Iraq for the second time.

Lt. Col. John Hamlin (West Point class of 1972), was the commander of the division's air recon squadron, the 2d Squadron of the 17th Cavalry. Equipped with twenty-four OH-58C Kiowa Scouts, sixteen AH-1F Cobras, and thirteen UH-60 Black Hawks, five of which were command and control helicopters, it had more helicopters than any other aviation unit in the division. During the covering force defensive phase of Desert Shield, Hamlin had the mission of screening the division's northwest flank.

Hamlin and his squadron flew from CE II to TAA Campbell between January 23 and 25. During the latter part of January and the first few weeks of February, the squadron spent most of its time on aircraft maintenance. Hamlin said that "we slowed down the tempo in which we refined the aircraft and trained the aviators. . . . We found that we couldn't train or maintain the tempo the way we wanted and, they say, hone our aviators to a razor's edge because we couldn't keep up with the maintenance on the aircraft in the desert environment. And the influx of parts was a detriment as well. So we opted to optimize our maintenance efforts. . . . I don't think the aircraft would have survived as well as they did for the two weeks of the war had we reversed it, because we were able to deploy 52 out of 53 aircraft. . . ."

While the division was at TAA Campbell, the 2d-17th Cavalry flew combat patrols. "We flew principally three times during the day, first light, midday, and last light," Hamlin recalled.

> One was to pick up any troop movements along the border, between us and the Iraqi border; the second was also picking up trends of the local population's moves, for instance, the Bedouin camps, civilian vehicles, tractors, anything that would give us an indication that something was changing as well as the basic combat patrol to pick up any infiltrators and so forth that came in across the border.
>
> So I volunteered for that mission because I thought it was important for us to enhance the security of the entire region area, plus that gave me the opportunity to train my squadron while using the minimum of our outfit. It kept our skills honed as well as providing security for the division area. . . . We were engaged one time by small arms fire in the division rear and it appeared to be two or three people . . . and we were not able to capture them . . . we increased our combat patrol, but it was not a major incident. . . . Our assumption was that they were probably Bedouins that were favorable to the Iraqi side that bothered a number of civilians in that area.6

Also, during the time the 101st Airborne spent in TAA Campbell, the division's aviation elements were deeply involved in the pre-offensive operations that became known as the "G-7 Operations." Before the ground assault, the U.S. Air Force's efforts were largely concentrated on the KTO and the Wadi al Batin.

Intelligence on enemy dispositions in the division and XVIII Airborne Corps's sector was, therefore, "often out-dated or exaggerated," according to Col. Tom Garrett, the 101st Aviation Brigade's commander. "The success of the 101st Airborne Division depended on its ability to air assault deep into Iraq on the first day of the ground offensive (G-Day) and establish a 'super FARP' to support follow-on operations to the Euphrates River. With the lack of real-time intelligence in sector, inaccuracy of maps on hand, and unknown terrain suitability for FARP operations, the Aviation Brigade developed and executed a reconnaissance plan to gain the information needed."

The initial plan called for night aerial reconnaissance beginning at G-7. "Seven days would provide enough time to use stealth the first few nights to determine the actual threat, then attack to destroy forces in sector as necessary or change the plan to adjust to METT-T," wrote Colonel Garrett.

The G-Minus Plan's only flaw was that it assumed that we would know the exact date of G-Day seven days out, which was ultimately not the case. G-Day was initially assumed to be 21 February 91, and 1-101st AATK [1st Battalion, 101st Aviation Regiment] conducted the first cross border reconnaissance in 101st Division sector under the cover of darkness on 14 February 1991. Their mission was to breach the FLOT, determine enemy dispositions near the Iraqi border, and conduct reconnaissance in zone out to PL [Phase Line] GIANT (approximately 15 nm past the FLOT [forward line of own troops]). The following night, AH-64s from 1-101st again penetrated Iraqi airspace and conducted a zone reconnaissance in Division Sector out to PL Charger. During these recons, personnel and livestock were spotted in the vicinity of MSR NEWMARKET, but no hostile action was initiated by the Iraqis and the Apaches bypassed to continue their recon.[7]

In the early morning hours of February 16, a team of Apaches from Col. Dick Cody's 1st Battalion, 101st Aviation (AATK, or Advanced Attack Helicopter) Regiment flew up to the area that General Peay had tentatively selected for FOB Cobra. This was also the first flight past PL Charger, which was some 15 miles into Iraq. In this reconnaissance role, the aircrafts' advanced optics assisted the navigators by filming terrain for tactical study back at the division command post. The pilots found a built-up area near the Thaab al Hajj oasis consisting of several buildings, some vehicles, and a number of bunkers. The pilots also spotted some personnel but no weapons. Because there was no hostile action from the Iraqis on the ground, the AH-64 Apaches continued their primary mission of reconnoitering the area near the proposed FOB Cobra site.

"This recon was a critical turning point in the decision-making process," said Colonel Garrett, "as it identified a potential target along the route of flight to Cobra, but confirmed that the Cobra area itself was virtually undefended."[8]

Until noon on January 25, Lt. Col. Bill Bryan and his 2-229th Aviation Regiment had served with the 2d Brigade, under operational control of VII

Corps, to defend the airfield at Al Qaysumah (east of Hafar al-Batin). Schwarzkopf was apparently worried about a possible preemptive Iraqi offensive down the Wadi al Batin as a "spoiling attack" before the VII Corps could deploy into a firm defensive position. Some of the junior commanders, Bryan among them, thought that Iraq might attack as a political stroke before the UN deadline went into effect. Thus, the 2-229th Aviation had closed into a TAA northwest of KKMC on January 11. Egyptian, Kuwaiti, Saudi, and Syrian armored forces were already in front of TF 2-101st when Bryan's battalion came into the TAA. The VII Corps had OPCON of the 1st Cavalry Division, which had OPCON of TF 2-101st for conducting the defense north of Hafar al-Batin on January 13. Intelligence available to Colonel Bryan indicated that an Iraqi offensive was slated for that night. Bryan had an infantry platoon from 1-502d Infantry attached for perimeter defense. On January 13, Bryan moved his battalion closer to the TF 2-101st Aviation to improve communications in anticipation of a battle over the next few days. The 1st Cavalry and TF 2-101st had seven field artillery (FA) battalions available to support defensive operations around Al Qaysumah airfield.

When the air campaign began on January 17, the Multinational Coalition Forces (MCF) began to reposition. The Egyptian and Syrian forces in front of the 1st Cavalry moved out to offensive positions south of Kuwait. The 1st Cavalry and the 2d Armored Cavalry Regiment moved into the departed Arab sectors. Engineers dug fighting positions for the platoon around the 2-229th Aviation's defensive position and hardened the overall perimeter defense of the battalion TAA. At noon on January 25, the 2-229th Aviation was released from TF 2-101st to move farther west to TAA Campbell, where it rejoined the 101st Airborne Division to prepare for the attack into Iraq. Bryan also returned the infantry platoon to B Company of the 1-502d Infantry.

Once in TAA Campbell, the battalion established itself in the western sector, just south of Tapline Road. As with the other battalions in the TAA, Bryan used the engineers to harden positions in his area to protect his men against terrorist attacks. His Apaches flew night recons of the FLOT—the Iraqi-Saudi border—every other night on a random schedule to check for infiltrators in the division area and verify enemy spottings reported by other sources.

On January 29, Bryan had all five of his companies' Apaches configured with auxiliary fuel tanks. "You've got to remember," he said, "with that tank on there we could fly for almost four hours. We sat down and figured it out one time. We could have flown about 200 kilometers. That would have given us about 20 minutes station time and been able to return. That was a normal mission profile, and that was from the last point you had fuel on the ground."[9]

On February 2, the Saudis had left all of their border posts forward of the division sector. The forward elements of the 101st Airborne, therefore, were the first line of defense, or "the line in the sand," if any Iraqi force attacked across the border into TAA Campbell.

On February 17, Colonel Garrett and a company of Apaches from 2-229th Aviation flew north across the border to determine the location and suitability of the area that would become FOB Cobra. Colonel Garrett knew that the site selection was "critical to the success of the Division's plan to conduct an air assault to the Euphrates River."[10] FOB Cobra had to be extensive enough to hold an infantry brigade, a DISCOM logistics cell, up to five separate FARPs, larger sites for up to five aviation battalions, and a heavy PZ for landing external loads from heavy-lift helicopters. Before the flight, Colonel Garrett had studied all available photo imagery and maps. The staff had meticulously analyzed the photos, maps, and even soil samples to locate a suitable FOB and had narrowed the possibilities to three large "goose eggs" in the sector that corps had assigned the division. Colonel Garrett brought back videotapes along with his own personal assessment of the areas. He concluded that, in spite of a "dust problem," the staff's first choice was a suitable area for the FOB.

Encouraged by the enemy's apparent absence from the area, on February 17, Colonel Garrett designated Bryan's 2-229th Aviation as the "day" Apache battalion. Colonel Cody's 1-101st Aviation would run recon missions at night to locate targets that the 2-229th Aviation could attack during the day. Bryan also made one of his companies available to Cody for nighttime operations, if needed.

Also on February 17, Hamlin's 2-17th Cavalry conducted a route reconnaissance up MSR Newmarket, which would serve as the 101st Airborne's primary ground line of communications after the ground war started. In so doing, Hamlin's D Troop and five of his Pathfinders captured the first Iraqi prisoners.

On their route reconnaissance, the D Troop's recce helicopters found a sophisticated network of expertly camouflaged enemy bunkers in the rolling desert. From that location, the D troopers found that the Iraqis could dominate the route with firepower.

"We were doing a route reconnaissance of MSR Newmarket which was to be the division's convoy route from TAA Campbell, across the Iraqi border, to FOB Cobra," Hamlin explained after the war. "And we did that in conjunction with the Apaches from the 2-229th who were doing a zone reconnaissance forward of the Cav in the meantime. On the 17th, the Alpha Troop discovered some Iraqi bunkers, reported it, bypassed them, and the Apaches from the 2-229th were called in to destroy the bunkers."[11]

When the Apaches from 2-229th Aviation went into the area, they took some fire from the bunkers. Immediately the Apaches attacked the bunker with 30mm cannon fire. They also fired on what they suspected was a BM-21 multiple-rocket launcher.

The Apache attack was enough for ten Iraqi soldiers. They threw down their weapons and surrendered. "We went in behind the Apaches with the Black Hawks and captured 10 Iraqi soldiers," Hamlin remembered. "So the Pathfinders were on board the aircraft and Delta Troop captured the first Iraqi soldiers on the 17th and brought those people back."

Hamlin went on to explain that "one of the reasons that the Apaches were included into the zone reconnaissance was because their target acquisition system was much better than the Cobra's. They had a stand-off capability so that the brigade commander made the decision to enhance the Cav's reliability on the battlefield by putting Apaches ahead of them . . . against the threat. In this case, we found the bunkers and we called the Apaches to engage them. . . . Therefore our aviators weren't subject to taking fire."

Colonel Garrett described the capture of the first Iraqi enemy prisoners of war (EPWs). "After the Cav troops found the bunker system and reported it, the 2-229th engaged one of the first bunker systems, destroying several vehicles and armament caches. In an unforeseen development, ten Iraqi soldiers emerged from the bunkers with their hands up and waving white flags."

Garrett called forward the Pathfinder detachment from 2-17th Cavalry. The Pathfinders arrived in UH-60 Black Hawks, quickly rounded up and secured the EPWs, searched the complex, and destroyed all the enemy equipment they could find in a hurry. They were, after all, by themselves, far ahead of the FLOT, and deep in relatively uncharted enemy territory. The Pathfinders also found an eleventh Iraqi soldier—an enlisted man who had been injured, apparently by the Apache 30mm cannons. The Pathfinders also discovered that the suspected BM-21 rocket launcher turned out to be a truck loaded with mortar rounds.

The Pathfinders loaded the EPWs—one captain, one NCO, and nine enlisted men—into the Black Hawks and flew them back to the division's rear command post. They landed outside the CP's perimeter, where brightly painted civilian buses waited for them. The EPWs, with their hands behind their heads and the "Pathfinders' rifles at their backs," walked a short distance from the helicopters to the buses. Their next stop was the division EPW "cage."

Shortly afterward, a group of forty Iraqi soldiers came out of a second bunker system and attempted to surrender to the company of Apaches—certainly an unusual arrangement that was unique to the Gulf War. The aviation brigade quickly scrambled a company of UH-60 Black Hawks from the 9th Battalion, 101st Aviation Regiment, commanded by Lt. Col. Bill Brophy, and an infantry platoon from C Company, 3d Battalion, 502d Infantry Regiment. The brigade also secured approval to extract the EPWs and sweep the site for documents and equipment. Once the EPWs were flown back and deposited in the EPW cage, they were interrogated by Arabic-speaking men of the 311th MI Battalion. The EPWs provided critical intelligence about enemy dispositions in the sector as well as their apparent lack of necessary equipment to conduct chemical warfare.

The prisoners were from B Company, 2d Battalion, 17th Border Guard Brigade of the 45th Infantry Division. It was a composite unit of border guards and regular infantry. "From its previous duty against Kurdish dissidents," reported a division spokesman, "the 45th had gained a reputation as an effective counter-guerrilla force.

"The prisoners were in good shape. They wore serviceable uniforms and claimed to have had an adequate supply of food and water. They were cooperative with the Arabic speaking interrogators from the 311th MI Battalion. The captain captured in the group of eleven prisoners stated that his men had not been paid in two months and that the only communications he had with his higher unit was via vehicle courier. The Iraqi company was irregularly resupplied by vehicle. The captain readily gave information on Iraqi troop, command and air defense artillery locations."[12]

Several other outfits supported the reconnaissance in the area forward of TAA Campbell. The 311th MI Battalion provided early warning communications and radar intelligence with one of the EH-60 Quick Fix helicopters under its OPCON. The Quick Fixes took up stations south of Phase Line Razor. A U.S. Air Force EF-111 also provided early warning for the mission. C Battery of the 2-320th Field Artillery Battalion displaced forward of Phase Line Razor after early evening nautical twilight (EENT) on February 14 to provide fire support for the aerial recon.

The unexpected surrender of Iraqi soldiers to the attack helicopters on recce prompted General Peay to set up a new SOP. In Frago 20 to Operations Order 91-1, each infantry brigade commander had to put a battalion reaction force on a two-hour standby. The battalion, in turn, would have one company on a one-hour standby, and the company would have a platoon ready to move out in fifteen minutes. The reaction force, in General Peay's mind, could be used to secure downed aircraft, to collect EPWs, and to clear enemy positions. His SOP enabled the division to react swiftly to any situation that developed from the numerous helicopter recon flights over the FLOT. Only a few days later, one of the reaction forces was called into action.

During the afternoon on February 18, pilots from the 2-17th Cavalry and 2-229th Aviation flew reconnaissance missions along MSR Newmarket and in the division's zone between Phase Line Charger and Phase Line Smash. In that area, an Apache from the 2-229th Aviation fired its 30mm cannon on two unarmored vehicles carrying six to ten Iraqi soldiers. Results were uncertain.[13]

"Further daylight reconnaissance of the zone near PL Charger on 18 February by the 2-17th CAV and 2-229 AATK confirmed the presence of at least a battalion-sized element at Thaab al Hajj, astride of MSR Newmarket and under the intended flight route to Cobra," said Colonel Garrett.

"The area was named OBJ TOAD [Objective Toad], because," said Colonel Hamlin, "it was a toad in the road," threatening to obstruct convoys and movement up MSR Newmarket.

"The Division and Brigade staffs began to formulate plans for an air assault artillery raid to clear the division route of advance prior to G-Day. While the lack of Iraqi armor/mech forces and associated ADA systems encouraged this aggressive raid technique, ultimately the chain of command was reluctant to commit infantrymen prior to the official start of the ground war. As a result, the attack on OBJ TOAD proceeded as an attack helicopter reconnaissance-by-fire with a detailed contingency plan to insert an air assault infantry company or battalion in case of an Iraqi surrender."

The intelligence to date suggested that the enemy position contained about fifteen bunkers, thirty to one hundred Iraqis, mortar positions, several trucks, and two or three antiaircraft guns.

At 8:10 A.M. on February 20, AH-1 Cobras from Lt. Col. Mark Curran's 3d Battalion, 101st Aviation Regiment began a phased attack on Objective Toad. Curran cycled all three of his companies through the attack, strafing the bunkers with TOWs and 20mm rockets. Curran then turned the battle over to the 2-229th Aviation. The AH-64 Apaches from the 2-229th Aviation continued the assault, firing TOWs at dozens of bunker entrances that resulted in secondary explosions inside many of the bunkers.

"Enemy resistance was virtually non-existent," wrote Colonel Garrett later, "yet neither did any Iraqi infantrymen show any signs of surrender. By noon, the Aviation Brigade Air Liaison Officer had succeeded in getting CAS [Close Air Support] on station in the form of two teams of two A-10s loaded with cluster bombs, 500 pound MK82s, and Maverick missiles. The CAS linked up with the Air Battle Captain in the attack helicopter company, for a classic JAAT [joint air attack team] mission. The A-10s successfully scored direct hits on several bunkers with the MK82s, and cluster-bombed the area. They were prevented from unleashing Mavericks only by the lack of a compatible (armor) target in the area."[14]

After the attack by the AH-64 Apaches and the A-10 Warthogs, Colonel Garrett saw that he could continue to expend huge quantities of ordnance on the position indefinitely—without immediate results. He convinced General Peay to send up a loudspeaker team on a UH-60 Black Hawk to talk the Iraqis into surrendering. The UH-60 flew directly to the objective. The 311th MI Battalion psychological operations (psyop) team aboard dropped leaflets in Arabic and, in Arabic via the loudspeakers, told the Iraqis how to surrender. As a result, a small number of enemy soldiers left their fighting positions and surrendered, but most of the Iraqis stayed in their bunkers.

General Peay then committed Capt. Thomas Jardine's B Company of the 1-187th Infantry—the standby battalion commanded by Lt. Col. Henry ("Hank") Kinnison—and put the company under the operational control of Colonel Garrett. Its mission was to secure the area, help round up the Iraqis, and sweep the area for maps and other intelligence data. Jardine and his company landed and swept from bunker to bunker, prying out the Iraqis. Most of the enemy soldiers surrendered immediately, but there were about forty, according to Colonel Kinnison, who clearly did not want to give up without a fight. Some of them fired at the 1-187th Infantry troops, but the fire was ineffective. No casualties were incurred. "Those hard core guys . . . clearly did not want to surrender, and it could have easily swung the other way," remembered Colonel Kinnison.

Because the bunker complex was far larger than the aviators had suspected and because of the Iraqis' resistance, General Peay sent in Capt. Joseph Buche's A Company of 1-187th Infantry to help sweep the area. Colonel Garrett committed Lt. Col. Bob Johnson's 4-101st Assault Battalion to support the infantry as it entered the enemy complex and to extract the EPWs as they were rounded up. Colonel Garrett also provided four CH-47 Chinooks for the back-haul, or movement to the rear, of the Iraqis.

General Peay instructed Colonel Garrett to bring back samples of enemy equipment and weapons as well as "exploitable intelligence" and to destroy all other captured equipment in place. General Peay also sent in the division's explosive ordnance detachment and a detachment of engineers to assist this part of the mission. In addition, he authorized the operations to extend into the evening. With both companies on the ground and with the support of 2-229th Aviation and the 101st Aviation Brigade's assets, Lieutenant Colonel Kinnison's men cleared Objective Toad by the evening of February 20. Some 406 Iraqis surrendered, including the battalion commander, eight other officers, and one warrant officer.

"It was an unexpected windfall," said Colonel Garrett, "yielding an entire infantry battalion. . . . The Iraqi commander was captured along with all of his maps, orders, and classified documents. Additionally, 101st soldiers captured or destroyed a hugh cache of Iraqi weapons and ammunition, to include ZPU-4 ADA guns that were never fired at the attacking U.S. aircraft. Most important, it was discovered that this battalion consisted mainly of border troops and new conscripts, and was part of the 49th Infantry Division. Morale, foodstuffs, and well-trained troops were in short supply. The make-up of the battalion and its division confirmed U.S. suspicions that the western flank of the KTO was lightly defended and would not pose a major obstacle to the advance of XVIII Airborne Corps."[15]

At one of the nightly, made-for-TV CENTCOM briefings in Riyadh, Brig. Gen. Richard Neal presented an overview of the 101st Airborne's mass capture of an Iraqi battalion. Radio Baghdad replied that "that sort of thing only happens in American movies."[16]

Lt. Col. Rick Riccardelli, CO of the 311th MI Battalion, and his intelligence specialists had a field day with the captured Iraqis. After the war, Riccardelli said,

Within hours, we knew a lot about the Iraqis in our sector. . . . That first evening [the 20th], I briefed the Commanding General about the tactical Iraqi situation in our sector and what we had found out . . . specifically, that they did not know that American forces were there and that our assault would be a surprise, that there were no chemicals or mines in our sector, and that the Iraqi command and control system in our sector was broken. I remember that first group of prisoners well. I was with a NEWSWEEK photographer as over 600 Iraqi soldiers were lined up and tons of equipment and documents were transported from their bunkers to our location. I was struck by how healthy these soldiers looked . . . and how passively they reacted. During this evacuation, their safe from the command complex was brought to us. After piling up hundreds of classified documents, we thought the safe would have great treasures or perhaps the master war plan of Saddam Hussein's government. When we blew the door off the safe and looked inside, all that I could think of was how Geraldo Rivera felt when he opened Al Capone's secret vault in Chicago on national TV. All that was inside [the Iraqi safe] was envelopes, tea and sugar. The Iraqi commander and his staff knew what was important. . . .

From 0200 to 0400 [2:00 A.M. to 4:00 A.M.], I personally debriefed the battalion commander, a veteran of the Iran-Iraq War. I was amazed by his openness and of the openness of other Iraqi soldiers to our questions. They told us anything we wanted to know. In fact, this commander and his officers provided such detailed information about our sector that we were able to pinpoint every headquarters and tank formation. We found time and again throughout the war that the Iraqi soldiers, to incude some captured Republican Guard soldiers, didn't want to fight.[17]

On February 21, Hamlin sent air cavalry teams along MSR Newmarket and into Objective Toad. "Our Bravo Troop expanded the reconnaissance around Objective Toad to see if there were any stragglers," said Hamlin, "to see if the complex was bigger than we thought or anything else, and we did pick up three prisoners that day. One of our teams [an AH-1 Cobra and an OH-58C Kiowa] was engaged by what we think were two SA-8 missiles which in fact were close [50 meters] to the aircraft but there were no casualties."

During this reconnaissance, one of Hamlin's OH-58D Kiowas, because of contaminated fuel, was forced to land. "We had to go back in with a Chinook," remembered Hamlin, "with Apaches providing cover, and the recovery team to sling load the 58 back, heading out. The Kiowa was recovered by 2300 [11:00 P.M.] that night."[18]

The reduction of Objective Toad was a bonanza for the division in two distinct ways. First, it provided superb intelligence of the Iraqi dispositions in the division's sector and confirmed that the division would encounter few obstacles as it moved by air and ground convoy into southern Iraq. Second, capturing an Iraqi battalion boosted the morale and confidence of the Screaming Eagles as they prepared to fly into combat.

"We felt more comfortable with things after that happened," said Lieutenant Colonel Johnson. "We knew there'd be pockets of resistance and we didn't think the Republican Guards would be pushovers, but it's nice to see the rank-and-file Iraqi soldier and know that he's anxious to get home in one piece."[19]

"When we captured those prisoners, some very telling things came out," said General Peay in an interview after the war. "We found those prisoners well-groomed, we found that they had brand new weaponry, they were hungry but they were not starving. To a man, they despised Saddam. We learned through the interrogation process where his air defense was, where some of his other ground infantry was. All that told me to take more risks, to go quicker; it allowed us to solidify our plan."[20]

A few days before the ground war began, General Schwarzkopf flew into General Peay's CP for a quick briefing and a few words of advice. He left no doubt in General Peay's mind about what he expected of the 101st Airborne. "He wanted to be very sure that the leaders were competent," recalled General Peay, "that they were aggressive, understood their mission, and would want to move."[21]

With Objective Toad out of the way, General Peay decided to reduce the division's presence in the area between TAA Campbell and FOB Cobra. He wanted "to lower exposure and prevent 'telegraphing' the true target area," said Colonel Garrett.

"The day of 24 February was confirmed as G-Day, and the Aviation Brigade conducted light reconnaissance and final air mission briefs in the days prior to the G-Day air assault. Further reconnaissance found little enemy activity in sector, and plans and contingencies were solidified for the largest air assault in history."

The plan was set; the troops were briefed and had rehearsed over and over again; and the last man in the last squad knew exactly what he was supposed to do, when he was supposed to do it, and how his action fit into his unit's plan. The Screaming Eagles of 1991 were about to carry out the history-making tradition of the 1944 Screaming Eagles. But this time, instead of a gallant, heroic defense against overwhelming odds, the 101st Airborne would attack.

A 101st MP takes count of captured Iraqis in FOB Cobra, February 24, 1991.

15 | The Launch into FOB Cobra

23 FEB 91 D+37
1500 [3:00 P.M.] Phoncon with Major General Peay, 101st Air Assault Division. The CINC [General Schwarzkopf] wished him Godspeed in the upcoming attack. (From CENTCOM Log.)

In wars long gone by it was the horse cavalry—with its mobility and range far surpassing the 3-miles-an-hour foot infantry—that secured the flanks, screened the front, reconnoitered the enemy's positions, pursued a demoralized enemy, exploited penetrations and breakthroughs, and struck suddenly at weak points in the enemy's lines. In Desert Storm, again the cavalry led the attack into Iraq, mounted this time in UH-60 Black Hawk and AH-64 Apache helicopters. On the night of February 23, G-Day minus 1 (G-1), four long-range surveillance detachments (LRSD) attached to the 2-17th Cavalry were the first 101st soldiers to set foot on FOB Cobra. In two shuttles, UH-60 Black Hawks of Delta Troop of the 2-17th Cavalry, escorted by two AH-64 Apaches of 2-229th Aviation, flew the six-man teams in under cover of darkness.

"Their mission," Lt. Col. John Hamlin said, "was to report back any enemy activity entering Cobra or any reinforcements coming along the other side. They were reporting directly back into the division assault CP. They were at that point working for the division, maintaining communications on the high frequency radios. And the LRSDs, of course, are highly trained soldiers. They are adept at going in deep in enemy territory and their principal mission is to see and report and not get caught. So during the day they hide, and at night they observe. . . . They are a detachment which is organic to the 311th Military Intelligence Battalion but they are attached to the cavalry squadron." They are, in short, the "eyes and ears" of the division.

Three of the teams were inserted into FOB Cobra, and one went farther north to reconnoiter a two-lane highway, named MSR Texas, leading from Rafha north to Highway 8. The teams that went into FOB Cobra were picked up later by Colonel Hill's 1st Brigade Air Assault Task Force when it landed in FOB Cobra the next morning.

The team that went in to scout MSR Texas had an unanticipated close call. Around 3:00 P.M. on February 25, the team was spotted by Iraqi civilians, compromising its position. The team leader immediately radioed back to the assault CP and reported his predicament.

Hamlin had two Black Hawks and two Apaches on strip alert to support the LRSD reconnaisssance. "If the LRSDs were compromised," he said, "you didn't have time to react and try to form a relief effort. So the Black Hawks and Apaches were put on strict alert with total dedication to those teams out there. Our goal was to get those kids back alive." The team leader also reported that he had spotted Iraqi soldiers in vehicles, about a half mile away, traveling toward his position.

Hamlin immediately launched the Black Hawks and Apaches. He felt that if he had not extracted the team, there could easily have been a firefight, and the odds were in favor of the Iraqis, who outnumbered the team by a wide margin. "I guess the question would be," he said later, "would the LRSD have been captured or would the Iraqis surrender to the LRSD? It got exciting because the plan was always to put them in and recover them at night, using the darkness as our method of preventing them from being engaged. And because they were compromised, we had to go in in broad daylight."

Hamlin's rescue effort was successful and with only a couple of minutes to spare. When the Black Hawks arrived, the LRSD team members climbed out of their holes and scrambled aboard. The "Blackbirds" took off immediately and headed south. The crews aboard could see the Iraqi vehicles closing in on their abandoned position.[1]

Before the LRSD was picked up from MSR Texas, the division units in TAA Campbell were making last-minute preparations for the massive helicopter assault into Iraq. Troopers were cleaning weapons, packing rucksacks, checking ammunition and radios, and getting ready for what would be for most of them their first exposure to combat. All the planning, training, and rehearsals were now on the line. In the cold, dark morning of G-Day, the troops shivered in their full combat gear and awaited the signal to mount up in their helicopters. They were going to war, but for how long they had no idea. Many of the younger troops wondered, Is this going to be another Vietnam?

To the 1st Brigade fell the honor of launching the division's assault into Iraq on G-Day, February 24. According to the brigade's CO, Colonel Hill, it had the mission of "attacking across the Saudi-Iraqi border at H-Hour [the time of the main body's landing in FOB Cobra] G-Day by air assault and ground to seize and secure a Forward Operating Base [FOB], code-named Cobra, in order to facilitate

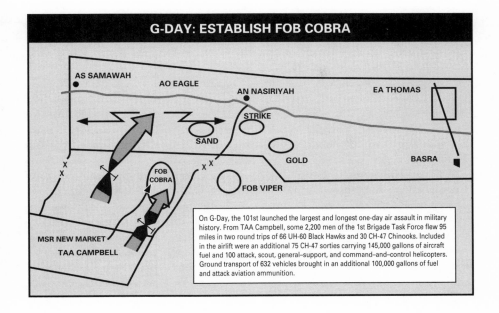

G-DAY: ESTABLISH FOB COBRA

AS SAMAWAH
AO EAGLE
AN NASIRIYAH
EA THOMAS
STRIKE
SAND
GOLD
BASRA
FOB COBRA
FOB VIPER
MSR NEW MARKET
TAA CAMPBELL

On G-Day, the 101st launched the largest and longest one-day air assault in military history. From TAA Campbell, some 2,200 men of the 1st Brigade Task Force flew 95 miles in two round trips of 66 UH-60 Black Hawks and 30 CH-47 Chinooks. Included in the airlift were an additional 75 CH-47 sorties carrying 145,000 gallons of aircraft fuel and 100 attack, scout, general–support, and command–and–control helicopters. Ground transport of 632 vehicles brought in an additional 100,000 gallons of fuel and attack aviation ammunition.

future division operations in the Euphrates River Valley. FOB Cobra was a piece of desert, located approximately 80 miles within Iraq and about 35 km [56 miles] southeast of As Salman, the main objective of the French Armored attack, also to occur on G-Day."

The 1st Brigade's plan, which had been fine-tuned and rehearsed for about three months, involved inserting four battalions (1-327th, 2-327th, and 3-327th Infantry of the 1st Brigade and 1-502d Infantry of the 2d Brigade) under cover of darkness into FOB Cobra. Once in FOB Cobra, the brigade would secure an airhead line and set up a perimeter defense of an area about 15 kilometers long and 12 kilometers wide. In addition to the infantry, the 1st Brigade would also use forty-seven CH-47 Chinooks to bring in fifty TOW Humvees with crews, necessary command and control vehicles, two 105mm artillery batteries with full loads of ammunition, and four battalion aid stations. By H+2 hours, Colonel Hill hoped to begin air landing enough equipment and fuel to set up a rapid refuel point.

Lt. Col. John Broderick's 426th Supply and Transportation Battalion, a unit from the Division Support Command, was responsible for the RRP. In effect, what the battalion was building was a giant gas station for helicopters that contained a sixteen-point refuel operation for Black Hawks and Chinooks and an eight-point setup for Apaches. Broderick planned to have the RRP operating at H+4 hours and to have on the ground 100,000 gallons of fuel by nightfall of G-Day.[2]

FOB Cobra and its RRP were of critical tactical and operational importance to the division's main combat operation—blocking, interdicting, and defeating enemy forces moving along the Euphrates River and Highway 8, the six-lane main route from Baghdad to Basra. The 101st Airborne knew that Saddam's forces in Baghdad, when either deploying reinforcements to the east or retreating from Kuwait and Basra, would have to travel over Highway 8.

The 3d Brigade, making the division's main effort on G+1, was slated to launch into AO Eagle, an area enveloping Highway 8 and the Euphrates. The helicopters, however, did not have the range to carry the 3d Brigade from its launch sites in TAA Campbell to AO Eagle and back. Therefore, FOB Cobra's gas station had to be operational to refuel the helicopters flying back from AO Eagle.

Colonel Hill also had the mission of clearing a ground supply route to FOB Cobra. Colonel Hill's executive officer (XO), Lt. Col. Jim McGarity, was in charge of that phase of the initial ground assault into Iraq. McGarity used the four infantry battalions' executive officers as his battle captains. His task force included thirty TOW Humvees; a 105mm and a 155mm artillery battery; one infantry company; two helicopter scout-attack teams to screen the front and flanks of the attacking ground column; and a combat and combat support vehicle convoy of some seven hundred vehicles, including fuel trucks carrying an additional 100,000 gallons of aviation fuel. McGarity's axis of advance was a narrow desert road named the Darb Al Haj, a perennial pilgrimage route for the Muslim hajj to Mecca.

McGarity, a Citadel graduate, called his force of some two thousand soldiers Task Force Citadel. He took some pride in the name inasmuch as three of his four battle captains were West Pointers. "In deference to General Peay, a Virginia Military Institute graduate and arch rival of the Citadel," wrote Colonel Hill, "we named the route of attack 'Newmarket,' for the Civil War battle fought by the cadets of VMI.

"In the days prior to G-Day, an extensive aerial recon of the objective area and Newmarket took place. The Achilles' heel of the RRP was the dust generated by helicopter landings. A relatively sand free area had to be found if helicopters, in large numbers, were to land and refuel safely. Additionally, we had to know if Newmarket was a decent road and free of major Iraqi troop concentrations which could slow or halt its movement or anti-aircraft weapons which could attack the air assault."

The recon elements did find about one hundred Iraqis in an area near one of the proposed landing zones in FOB Cobra. Colonel Hill and his staff decided to change the zone's location, "to our great fortune," he said.[3]

Colonel Hill had more than just the 1st Brigade to accomplish his mission. In addition to his own three infantry battalions, Colonel Hill also had attached Lt. Col. James Donald's 1-502d Infantry from the 2d Brigade. Also, Colonel Cody's 1-101st AATK Apache (Aviation) Battalion would lead the movement north as air assault security, followed by Lt. Col. Mark Curran and his 3-101st Aviation.

The helicopters that would lift the reinforced 1st Brigade were under the control of Lt. Col. Russ Adams and his 5th Battalion, 101st Aviation Regiment. His task force was made up of the majority of all three UH-60 Black Hawk assault battalions and a CH-47 Chinook battalion.

"In all," Colonel Hill wrote after the war, "the units allotted to the brigade to accomplish the mission totaled some 5,000 soldiers and 11 battalions—4 infantry, 1 arty [artillery] battalion and 1 arty battery, 2 attack helicopter battalions, the better part of 4 assault and lift helicopter battalions and numerous combat support and combat service support units, including 2 engineer companies, 1 aid defense company, 2 military police companies, 1 military intelligence company. Aircraft totaled about 200; 75 Black Hawks, 55 Chinooks, 10 UH-1 Hueys, 18 Apaches, 21 Cobras, and about 20 OH-58 Kiowa Scout helicopters." Colonel Hill commanded a formidable air assault force.[4]

On the afternoon of February 23, the day before G-Day, Colonel Hill, his staff, and commanders pre-positioned all 107 assault and heavy-lift helicopters into fifteen company-size pickup zones (PZs) and five heavy-lift PZs throughout the brigade's area in TAA Campbell. That evening, the troops moved to their assigned areas and hunkered down near their helicopters, not unlike the paratroopers of the WWII 101st Airborne Division who slept under the wings of their C-47s in England prior to their parachute assault into Normandy on D-Day.

The weather in Saudi Arabia varies widely between extremes. The summer's blazing, suffocating, enervating heat gives way to the wet winter cold. Late February 1991 turned out to be no exception. H-Hour on G-Day was numbingly cold and wet, and a dense fog blanketed the departure areas. When the 101st Airborne's pilots left early that morning to recon the route from TAA Campbell to FOB Cobra, the fog was so thick that General Peay decided to postpone H-Hour from 6:00 A.M. to 7:00 A.M. and later to 8:00 A.M.

The 1-9th Cavalry Target Acquisition and Reconnaissance Platoon had tried to leave the TAA earlier that morning to screen for the Pathfinder insertion mission. At 3:30 A.M., however, one of the platoon's OH-58D Kiowas (tail number 288) crashed near the line of departure (LOD) and burned. Both crew members survived but were hospitalized. The aerial observer had third-degree burns on his back.

After the Kiowa crashed, General Peay decided to delay the Pathfinder mission for at least an hour. Eventually, he chose to launch its mission simultaneously with the 1-101st Aviation's mission to screen FOB Cobra.

In the PZs, the troops began to ready themselves for the thirty-five minute flight into FOB Cobra. They put on their rucksacks, picked up their weapons and other gear, and lumbered up the steps into the Black Hawks. Fifteen combat-equipped soldiers flew in each Black Hawk. Once inside the helicopters, some of the troops sat on their rucksacks, some were wedged into slots between bundles of supplies, and others sat on the metal floors. Dennis Steele, writing in *Army,* said that sitting on the metal floor panels was "a position that completes a connection between the aircraft and the raw nerve that runs from the tailbone to the brain.

169

The nerve sends lightning-quick, unimpeded signals of every shudder, dip and bump the helicopter encounters or creates, along with the incessant throbbing of the engines, straight out the top of the head."[5]

"We planned an 0600 H Hour [6:00 A.M.] (touch down in Iraq) with an 0520 PZ [5:20 A.M. takeoff time]," wrote Colonel Hill later.

> This allowed for the initial insertion to take place at dark, but landing just at daylight. To put the force on the ground required the 66/30 mixture [Black Hawks to Chinooks] to make initial lift plus an additional turn after refueling. Prior to PZ time we began sending out Apaches, OH-58Ds and 1 UH-60, especially configured for night flight and reconnaissance, to check the air route, engage any enemy they might find, insert three teams of Pathfinders with aviation beaconing devices to aid navigation, and take up overwatch of the objective areas. All of this started at H-minus 4 hours. Weather looked good initially, but the fog we had feared materialized at H minus 2 hours . . . and forced us into a two hour weather hold, making H-Hour 0800 [8:00 A.M.]. The last weather report from the Apaches and beacon teams en route to the objective at 0700 [7:00 A.M.] still contained a great deal of fog in it, at about halfway mark, but we made the decision to launch anyway, knowing we were on a tight schedule if we were to get in the initial RRP (a build up that would take all day) and betting that the fog would diminish as the air assault wore on. It was a calculated risk and the fog slowed us down somewhat going in the first time, but caused no further problems with subsequent lifts.[6]

The lead company in the 1st Brigade's air assault was Capt. John Russell's A Company of the 1-327th Infantry. In TAA Campbell, like the rest of the brigade's troops, Russell's men spent the night before the assault camped out—it could hardly be called sleeping—next to their helicopters. "Everyone was a little on edge," Russell remembered after the war. "A lot of us sat up and talked, just trying to get rid of some of the nervousness." Russell did not sleep much that night. "You look around at your soldiers, and you're responsible for them. And you want to bring them back, you want to bring them all back."[7]

General Peay's two-hour delay did not ease the flapping butterflies in the troops' stomachs. The troops realized that the night landing was now impossible and that a daylight landing would make them more vulnerable to enemy small-arms fire, AA, and shoulder-launched rockets. Russell said that the delay "turned the tension up a notch or two."

At revised H-Hour, the scores of helicopters in TAA Campbell—sixty-seven UH-60 Black Hawks, thirty CH-47 Chinooks, and ten UH-1 Hueys—revved up their engines. The rotors churned up a rolling, mushroom-like cloud of sand near each position in the PZ. The flight took off at 7:20 A.M. for FOB Cobra. By 7:27 A.M., the aircraft, flying at 115 knots and only 20 feet off the desert floor, filled a wide lane in the desert sky. To an observer on the ground, it was an unprecedented sight—helicopters in an almost endless chain whirling north toward FOB Cobra area in another rendezvous with destiny, forty-seven years after the first.

To the cramped troops inside the Black Hawks, the flight was a churning, noisy, bumpy ride. If they could have looked out the Plexiglas windows, they would have seen a desolate, barren desert landscape of sand, rocks, and scrub growth—almost literally a "no-man's land." After the benumbing flight, the troops were glad it was over even though, when they touched down in yet another swirl of blowing sand, they were in enemy territory.

For the flight north, Colonel Hill and his staff flew in a command and control (C&C) UH-60 Black Hawk. Also aboard were Lieutenant Colonel Adams, CO of the 5-101st Aviation Battalion and the air mission commander; the U.S. Air Force liaison officer; and Lt. Col. Lynn Hartsell, CO of the 2-320th Field Artillery Regiment and fire support coordinator. The C&C aircraft took off at 7:15 A.M., and, from the air, Colonel Hill coordinated and directed the air assault. His C&C "bird" had multiple radios, permitting him to talk "with all the lifts, the ground, Corps and division Air Force Liaison Team, and with a TACSAT (Tactical Satellite) radio which kept us in contact with division and the objective, in expectation of great distances which a normal FM radio could not reach," Colonel Hill wrote. "The air route, in and out, put all aircraft, especially the Chinook, right on the edge of their fuel capacity. We had calculated a speed of 115 knots, optimum for fuel conservation.

"Additionally, we internally loaded the HMMWVs on the first insertion, instead of slinging them under the Chinooks, to insure: (1) They could land, as dust creates 'brown-out' for the pilots as they hover over the landing area too long; (2) To conserve fuel. Internal loading a HMMWV is no easy task, as there are only three inches of side clearance in the Chinook. The second turn [trip to FOB Cobra] of the Chinooks was normal slinging, as we knew when, by then, we could bring them in safely. . . . Everything went very smoothly on the air assault and in less than three hours, we put in 2050 soldiers, 50 TOWs, two artillery batteries and our Command and Control people and equipment."[8]

Forty-one minutes after A Company took off, the four Black Hawks carrying Russell and fifty-nine of his men landed in Cobra. It was a "cold" LZ. Russell was surprised that his men took no Iraqi fire as they unloaded. He knew from advance intelligence reports that Iraqis were in the area. "I really thought the LZ would be hot. It wasn't," remembered Russell.[9] After landing, the infantrymen gladly "uncramped" and piled out with all their gear, reorganized into units, spread out, and moved on to secure their assigned areas.

By H-Hour, all three companies of the 1-101st Aviation Regiment Battalion, were in contact with Iraqi forces north of the landing zones along MSR Virginia (an east-west route north of FOB Cobra). "The Iraqis used their AAA guns this time," remembered Colonel Garrett, "resulting in an AH-64 having its hydraulics shot out (the crew recovered the aircraft to Cobra). In accordance with the plan, the 1-101st conducted a battle handover to 3-101st, who continued contact with Iraqi forces vic Virginia. 3-101st simultaneously conducted an aerial screen of TF

Citadel, the ground convoy advancing up MSR Newmarket to link up with forces at Cobra."[10]

Immediately after landing, Lt. Col. Gary Bridges's 3-327th Infantry was fired on by Iraqis on the eastern side of FOB Cobra. The AH-64 Apaches, on alert, quickly fired on the enemy bunker. Troops from the 3-327th Infantry then moved in and captured eleven Iraqi soldiers.

Lieutenant Colonel Bryan's 2-229th Aviation—the "day" Apache battalion—air assaulted into FOB Cobra while his support elements made a tactical road march 90 miles into Iraq. When the 2-229th Aviation arrived in FOB Cobra, Bryan immediately set up a "jump TOC." The 2-229th Aviation was responsible for the western sector of the 101st Airborne's zone with priority given to screening MSR Texas north of the French 6th Light Armored Division and the 2d Brigade of the 82d Airborne Division. The MSR Texas—a route along FOB Cobra's western edge—was Iraq's major avenue for reinforcing or withdrawing from Objective White, an area that straddled MSR Texas. Three OH-58 Kiowas and crews from the 2-229th Aviation also flew with the 3-101st Aviation in the morning and afternoon to assist the 3-101st Aviation's mission. And that evening, Bravo Company of the 229th Aviation flew a recon mission up MSR Texas all the way to the Euphrates. Along MSR Virginia, the 2-229th Aviation captured ten EPWs and extracted them with internal UH-60L Black Hawks.

"While Objective White was in the French sector," wrote Colonel Garrett, "it possessed a heavy concentration of Iraqi troops (to include armor forces) only thirty kilometers from FOB Cobra. With the advance of the 6th French Division on the left flank expected to reach Objective White on G+1, there was concern that Iraqi armor would withdraw east along MSR Virginia into the 101st flank." Colonel Cody's 1-101st Aviation had discovered the force just north of MSR Virginia at about H-Hour. It turned out to be the 1st Battalion of the 82d Brigade of Iraq's 49th Infantry Division.

Lt. Col. Frank Hancock's 1-327th Infantry had landed in its zone in FOB Cobra at 8:25 A.M. The lead battalion of the 1st Brigade Task Force, it was the first complete unit of the 101st to land in Iraq. The battalion had moved north in two lifts of twenty-four UH-60 Black Hawks and two lifts of six CH-47 Chinooks. Upon landing in FOB Cobra, the battalion made contact with the Iraqi force, and a sharp firefight began.

"Intelligence reports had stated that there were possibly 30–50 Iraqi soldiers in our area," Colonel Hancock wrote later. "However, an Iraqi infantry battalion (339 Iraqis) was securing the road network next to where the battalion was landing. The enemy (which was on the reverse side of a ridgeline) was being engaged by Apaches [2-229th] and Cobra [3-101st] attack helicopters when we landed.

"Upon landing, I made contact with the Battle Captain from the 3-101st (Cobra Battalion), a CPT Best, and asked that he land and talk to me about how we would coordinate our attack. Upon landing, he said that an Iraqi bunker complex ran about three kilometers in length to our northeast and that there were several heavy machine guns on the positions. During this time, my S-3 (Major

Dempsey) and A Company Commander (CPT Russell) had maneuvered to where they could overlook the bunker complex. Also at this time, one of the Apache helicopters that was supporting us had been shot down. I told CPT Best that I would have the artillery battery (C Battery, 2-320th Artillery) that was in support of us (and which had air assaulted in with us) start firing on the objective. I asked CPT Best to guide in the Close Air Support (CAS) we received and help in calling in the artillery. For the next 1 1/2 hours, we called in the 105mm artillery on the objective, along with two sorties of F-16s and two sorties of A-10s. The Cobras and Apaches continued to fire on the objective during the time we would adjust the artillery and CAS.

"At around 1030 hrs [10:30 A.M.], the first group of Iraqis started to come out of their bunkers. I sent my D Company commander, CPT Gill, along with my scouts to accept the surrender. We initially thought there were perhaps 50 prisoners, but ended up taking 339 prisoners. At about 1045 [10:45 A.M.], the Brigade Commander, Colonel Hill, landed and offered assistance in the form of two UH-1 helicopters in moving some of my forces around. CPT Gill had now under his control the Iraqi Battalion Commander and was receiving the Iraqi surrender. I received the UH-1s at about 1200 hrs [noon] and flew to the bunker site around 1230 hours [12:30 P.M.]. We believed that there were other Iraqis across the highway to our north under the control of the Iraqi Battalion Commander.

"Because of this, I approached the Iraqi commander and told the interpreter, 'Tell this son-of-a-bitch that if he doesn't surrender all his troops, I'll bring back the airplanes and destroy all of his troops.' At this time, I recognized that the Iraqi commander spoke some English as his eyes got big when I used profanity. After some discussion, the Iraqi commander was placed in a HMMWV with the battalion S-3 and we placed some scouts in another HMMWV and proceeded to go north to get the rest of the Iraqis. At this time, all the Cobras which had been supporting us left because of the report of an Iraqi counter-attack. I told the S-3 I would follow in the UH-1 and provide cover with the door guns as we figured since the Iraqis had been hit by Apaches and Cobras, that they wouldn't know that the UH-1 was not an attack helicopter. We travelled about two kilometers and rounded up the last 15 prisoners who were across the road to our north. We brought the 15 prisoners back (10 in the HMMWVs and five in the UH-1) to the bunker site."

After Hancock's men had assembled the EPWs, they marched the 339 prisoners about 4 kilometers south, kept them under guard for about twenty-four hours, and then turned them over to the 101st Airborne's MPs. In addition to the EPWs, Colonel Hancock's men had gathered up some 775 rocket-propelled grenades (RPGs), 600 rifles, four heavy machine guns, four mortars, two antiaircraft pieces, eight tons of ammunition, and $5,000 worth of Iraqi money in the bunker complex.[11]

This firefight took place in the same area that Colonel Hill had originally planned to use as an LZ but changed his mind after early aerial reconnaissance picked up enemy activity. "Had we gone in there," Colonel Hill recalled, "we would have been in a large fight from the onset. The unit turned out to be the division reserve of the unit facing the French in As Salman. The battalion commander later reported he had been prepared to fight, but expected the French in 4 or 5 days and was overwhelmed by the speed and ferocity of our attacks deciding 'he owed Iraq more than Saddam' and chose to save his soldiers, all veterans of the Iran-Iraq War. Later clearing operations of their bunker complex uncovered a huge cache of arms and ammo. . . . "[12]

While Hill and his men were clearing and setting up FOB Cobra, Colonel Cody and his 1-101st Aviation were screening north. One of his AH-64 Apaches (tail number 976) took either small-arms or AAA fire while flying near MSR Virginia. The plane was damaged but managed to return safely to FOB Cobra.

At 10:39 A.M., Colonel Hill reported to General Peay that FOB Cobra was secure. The ninety-six aircraft used to deliver the first lift returned to FOB Cobra with the brigade's second lift by 11:56 A.M. At the same time, Task Force Citadel in a massive convoy of 632 vehicles of all kinds and 2,000 soldiers was rumbling north along dusty MSR Newmarket.

Lieutenant Colonel Broderick, CO of the 426th Supply and Transportation Battalion, had landed in FOB Cobra at H+two minutes with Colonel Hill's assault command post. Broderick orchestrated the buildup of the RRP using twenty-five CH-47 Chinooks. They were able to make three and a half trips to FOB Cobra before dark and to bring in 75,000 gallons of aviation fuel. At H + thirty minutes, Broderick and his men had set up a smaller RRP and rearm pad for FOB Cobra's aircraft, permitting the AH-64 Apaches to return to TAA Campbell and get ready for upcoming operations north of FOB Cobra. In TAA Campbell, Lt. Col. Bob VanAntwerp's 326th Engineer Battalion had built a refueling point that had a 750,000-gallon capacity and could refuel twenty-five helicopters at a time. The Cobra battalions remained in FOB Cobra, providing Colonel Hill's task force a 35-kilometer screen out in front of the RRP.

As soon as the TOW Humvees landed, Hill sent them out ahead of the perimeter to set up a "TOW antitank in-depth screen" 7 to 10 kilometers in front of the infantry. As the 1st Brigade Task Force was consolidating in FOB Cobra, a second AH-64 Apache battalion and the cavalry squadron flew into the FOB. These two battalions refueled and flew north to the Euphrates to begin the 101st's interdiction mission along Highway 8, the major east-west highway that parallels the river.

"Cobra," reported Colonel Hill, "with its infantry positions and TOW screen, turned out to be larger than the entire Ft. Campbell training and cantonment area." Colonel Garrett purposely spread his planes out over a large area to prevent accidents, especially at night, and to present the smallest targets to any incoming artillery or rockets.

At 3:00 P.M. on G-Day, the lead elements of Task Force Citadel, the ground convoy moving north from TAA Campbell, arrived in FOB Cobra. The first serial of the convoy, Team Citadel with 31 vehicles and Task Force David with 184 vehicles, had departed TAA Campbell at 11:25 A.M. Team Oliver, with 218 vehicles, had left at 12:05 P.M.; 2d Brigade's Team Smith, with 199 vehicles, had departed at 2:18 P.M. The 1st Brigade's sergeant major and a team of motorcycle scouts sorted out the vehicles in the convoy as they arrived and distributed them to their assigned locations in FOB Cobra. The final serial in the convoy arrived in FOB Cobra early the next morning.

The 2d Brigade had been the 101st Airborne's reserve in TAA Campbell. On January 25, Colonel Purdom had been released from "working with the 1st Cavalry Division," and General Peay had him prepare plans for offensive operations.

"As we were in the attack phase," Purdom remembered, "there were several scenarios that unfolded. The first plan called for us going to establish FOB Cobra with the 1st Brigade being the lead. One of my battalions was attached to the 1st Brigade to make that offensive, securing the FOB on G-Day. That was the plan. The brigade headquarters and the other battalions we air assaulted in on G-Day at 1330 [1:30 P.M.]. Now, as we're planning this operation, I have other follow-on missions. There were two particular objectives that we planned for. One was an air assault on Objective Strike, which is Tallil Airfield, as well as Objective Gold, which is a supply point farther to the east. It would interdict the lines of communications south of the Euphrates River at An Nasiriyah as we projected combat power back to Basra.

"So I had those two specific missions that I planned for in detail. . . . And it [the plan] vacillated between them. First it was Objective Strike. We would go into Cobra on G-Day and later the 3d Brigade would assault on up to the Euphrates and then as soon as those were done, then we would project an attack to the Tallil Airfield and take that down as the Division would swing back to the east."

After the 1st Brigade Task Force had been air assaulted into FOB Cobra, it was the 2d Brigade's turn to make the trip. Because of poor weather conditions—fog, wind, and rain—Colonel Purdom was not able to move his entire task force into FOB Cobra on G-Day. Ten CH-47 Chinooks with the 2d Brigade's equipment and thirty CH-47 Chinooks with DISCOM gear also had to wait until the next morning. The aviation brigade did manage to bring in seventy sorties of logistics gear on G-Day, and by that night, Purdom had brought in his brigade headquarters, the 3-502d Infantry, 1-320th Field Artillery, and his brigade's combat support and combat service support slices.

As soon as his troops landed, they moved to their assigned areas and began to dig in. The ground was deceptively firm; this was not the sand that they had become accustomed to in CE II. Then came the winter rains, and the foxholes quickly filled with water. "But the troops were very upbeat," said Colonel Purdom later. "The weather was miserable. . . . I had soldiers in foxholes that were knee deep in water. . . . It was very, very cold. . . . The soldiers had trained hard, they had trained well, they were ready for combat if attacked. We had prepared the soldiers for it.

"These soldiers are the best that I can describe. They did everything they were asked to do. They did it better than they were asked to do it and you never heard them complain at all. I can't overplay the strength of those soldiers."[13]

On G-Day, the bad weather caused several aircraft accidents. In addition to the OH-58 Kiowa and the AH-64 Apache damaged early in the day, five other helicopters sustained damage. A UH-60 Black Hawk from the 5-101st Aviation Battalion nearly struck another helicopter while making a hard landing in the pickup zone. The UH-60 Black Hawk suffered major structural damage, but its crew was uninjured. Another UH-60 Black Hawk had to abort its mission when it experienced a stabilizer failure.

The most serious and bizarre incident was actually a series of three accidents, all involving UH-1 Hueys from Lt. Col. Jim Mullen's 6-101st Aviation Battalion. The first UH-1 Huey developed a compression stall and had to make a hard landing. Its skid tore off as the plane flipped upside down and caught on fire. When the pilot of a second UH-1 Huey stopped to assist the first, he also made a hard landing. A third UH-1 Huey made a hard landing as its pilot stopped to assist the first plane, which was now in flames. Personnel on the first helicopter sustained the only injuries. One of its pilots, Lieutenant Pelurame, fractured his elbow. Lieutenant Randell, the 3d Brigade's air defense liaison officer, was flying as door gunner for the flight and suffered a mild concussion and minor cuts. Fortunately, all of the crews were able to walk away from the crashes.

The CH-47 Chinooks were not without their problems. On three separate occasions, when the crews cut their sling loads, they damaged some equipment. One was a RATT (radio teletype) Rig communications van, another was a Humvee carrying most of 1st Brigade's computer equipment, and the third was a pallet of class V (ammunition) supplies. All the loads were destroyed.

By the end of G-Day, FOB Cobra was established. Its assembly involved the largest helicopter-borne air assault ever conducted in a single day. Maj. Daniel F. Grigson, the 101st Airborne's public affairs officer, called the air assault a "bold and bodacious action."

To set up FOB Cobra—a wide area of 200 square kilometers in Iraq's desert—the UH-60 Black Hawks and CH-47 Chinooks had each made the 180-mile round trip three times. On the ground were five forward area refuel points, about forty separate refueling stations, and 200,000 gallons of fuel. Some 370 helicopters, counting all of the assault and recon aircraft transport, made 1,046 sorties on G-Day.

To support the massive number of aircraft that carried the 101st Aviation's soldiers to the Euphrates, Lieutenant Colonel VanAntwerp's 326th Engineer Battalion had expanded the rapid refuel point in TAA Campbell. In addition, VanAntwerp's Task Force Grader worked through the night of February 24 to improve the surface of MSR Newmarket.

By the end of G-Day, most of the 1st, 2d, and 101st Aviation brigades were deployed in FOB Cobra. Support elements from the Division Support Command went about their tasks of readying the refuel points. Attack helicopters from the 101st Airborne were operating in the Euphrates River Valley. The enemy bunkers to the north of Cobra had been knocked out. The troops had consolidated their positions, dug in where necessary, and prepared to support the main effort of the division toward the Euphrates.

FOB Cobra was ready to support the 101st Aviation's northward thrust to cut off Iraqis escaping along Highway 8. While not included specifically in its mission, it could also place the division in a tactical alignment to threaten Baghdad itself.

Back in TAA Campbell, Col. Bob Clark's 3d Brigade, the Rakkasans, readied itself for the launch to the Euphrates—the most combat-oriented phase of the division's air assault into Iraq.[14]

AH-1 Cobra of 2d Squadron, 17th Cavalry, screens forward of the division in the Euphrates River Valley.

16 | On to the Euphrates

By the morning of G+1, February 25, General Peay was ready to attack. He had established FOB Cobra with the largest and longest helicopter-borne air assault in military history. Now, using FOB Cobra as a springboard and support base, he could "attack, interdict, block and defeat enemy forces operating in and through AO Eagle (read Highway 8) and, on orders, conduct attacks to the east (read toward the Republican Guard and other units retreating westward from the Kuwait area and north of Basra) to assist in the defeat of the RGFC Forces."[1] It was now time to catapult the Rakkasans into the division's main combat effort.

Col. Robert T. Clark was the commander of the Rakkasans, the 3d Brigade of the 187th Infantry. He had assumed command of the brigade on November 7, 1990, from Col. John McDonald while the brigade was in the covering force role in Camp Eagle II. After the war, when an interviewer asked Colonel Clark about assuming command at the brigade level in a wartime situation, he replied that "it was . . . pre-programmed. . . . [I took command] in the sand in the covering force area near the brigade command post. A very austere change of command . . . [with] just . . . company commanders and first sergeants, brigade staff, and battalion commanders and staffs."[2] A conventional change of command at Fort Campbell would have involved the entire three-thousand-man brigade lined up on the review field with the attendant ceremonies: the band "sounding off" and marching in front of the brigade; officers and colors marching "front and center"; the adjutant publishing the orders; the brigade sergeant major passing the brigade's colors from one commander to the next; the incoming and outgoing commanders speaking to the troops; and finally the entire command passing in review.

The 3d Brigade was known as "the Rakkasans" because its three infantry battalions were successors to the 187th Glider Infantry Regiment that fought valiantly in the Philippines during World War II. In those days, the regiment was one of

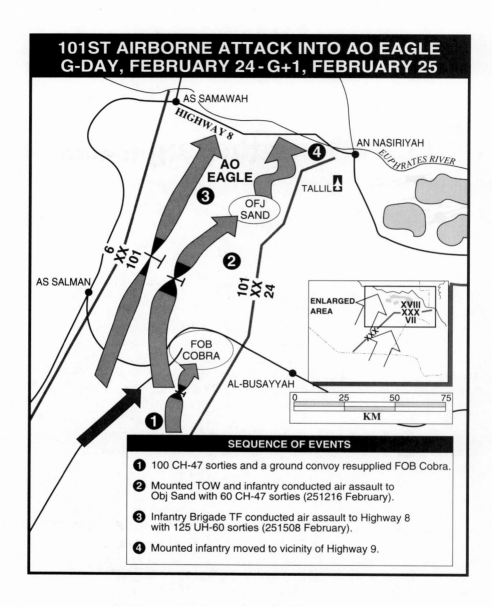

101ST AIRBORNE ATTACK INTO AO EAGLE
G-DAY, FEBRUARY 24 - G+1, FEBRUARY 25

SEQUENCE OF EVENTS

① 100 CH-47 sorties and a ground convoy resupplied FOB Cobra.

② Mounted TOW and infantry conducted air assault to Obj Sand with 60 CH-47 sorties (251216 February).

③ Infantry Brigade TF conducted air assault to Highway 8 with 125 UH-60 sorties (251508 February).

④ Mounted infantry moved to vicinity of Highway 9.

two glider regiments in the 11th Airborne Division. They were small regiments with only two infantry battalions each.

During the Korean War, the 187th Airborne Regimental Combat Team (RCT)—by now a separate parachute RCT of three infantry battalions, an artillery battalion, and support companies—made two combat jumps. The first was at Sukchon-Sunchon in North Korea on October 20, 1950, and the second at Munsan-Ni, South Korea, on March 23, 1951. Between its three tours in Korea during the Korean War, the 187th RCT was home-based in Japan, with its major units at Beppu and Kumamoto on Kyushu. It was in that environment that the RCT was tagged with the name "Rakkasans," or falling umbrellas in Japanese.[3]

AO Eagle, the target area of operations for the 3d Brigade, was 155 miles north of TAA Campbell, 85 miles northeast of FOB Cobra, and 145 miles southeast of Baghdad. It bordered both sides of the east-west Highway 8 from As Samawah in the west to Basra in the east. General Peay's plan called for the Rakkasans to air assault all three infantry battalions into three LZs in AO Eagle—just south of the Euphrates and near the town of Al Khidr—the night of February 25. This air assault would jump the Rakkasans in a couple of hours over as much terrain as an armored or mechanized division could move in a day or more.

The planning for the Rakkasans' air assault had been in the formative stage for months. "After extensive study, COL Clark and the division planners eventually settled on an area roughly equidistant from As Samawah and An Nasiriyah, just to the south and southwest of a small city named Al Khidr," Costello wrote. "A bridge over a major canal on the west and an overpass over the Iraqi State Railway in the east offered two superb places to cut the highway, and the area was far enough away from any major cities to enable us to engage in major combat operations without the constraints of a major civilian populace. A major pipeline traversed the area from the southeast to the northwest, with a major pumping station that posed an obvious objective at the southeastern corner of what was named Area of Operation Eagle."[4]

Colonel Clark planned the operation as follows. After the battalions landed, he would send Lt. Col. Andy Berdy and his 2-187th Infantry to the right flank as the brigade's main effort. Their mission would be to cut the Baghdad-Basra railroad intersection and engage forces coming from the east. The 2d Battalion would be supported by the 1st Battalion to its rear and would also be facing "east against expected Iraqi forces and seizing what we had determined to be key terrain within AO Eagle, the Darraji Pump Station along the pipelines leading from the Rumaila fields to refineries in As Samawah," wrote Lt. Col. Peter C. Kinney, the brigade S-3. "Darraji offered a small airstrip that would benefit logistic buildup for future operations and save helicopter wear and tear in the sand. 1st Bat [Battalion] was commanded by LTC Hank Kinnison. . . .

"3d Bat would be on 2d's left flank facing west up Highway 8 toward Baghdad and engaged primarily Iraqi logistic traffic bound for Kuwait. 3d Bat was commanded by LTC Tom Greco who commanded TF Rakkasan, all the wheeled assets of the Brigade coming into LZ Sand on CH-47s. Sand was 40 km shy of the Euphrates due to the range limitation of the CH-47 vice UH-60. Tom's XO, Major Jerry Balzack, fought the 3d Bat for its first 24 hours on Highway 8 till the linkup with TF Rakkasan."[5]

The aviation brigade would help prepare the battlefield prior to the air assault of the 3d Brigade. In the actual operation, the 2-229th Aviation and the 2-17th Cavalry conducted an aerial recon of the area from 1:30 P.M. to 6:00 P.M. on G-Day, February 24. Next, the 1-101st Aviation and one company from the 2-229th AATK conducted a recon in AO Eagle's zone from FOB Cobra all the way to the Euphrates. This second mission lasted throughout the night. The recon missions located the main supply route, pinpointed the 3d Brigade's landing zone, located the road into AO Eagle, and looked for any enemy positions. Neither mission reported any enemy contact.

"Another mission planned for the night of G+1 was cancelled before it got under way," wrote Colonel Garrett. "Two AH-64 companies from 1-101 were scheduled to conduct an attack on the Tallil airfield, a heavily defended target. With the weather deteriorated to such low visibilities, the Apaches would have been unable to achieve any kind of stand-off capability, and the mission was scrubbed for the night." (But on the morning of G+3, Col. Ted Reid's 197th Brigade of the 24th Division attacked a logistics base just outside Tallil airfield and captured 1,290 Iraqi soldiers and civilians. The 197th Brigade destroyed bunkers, ammunitions stores, and other hardware. By nightfall, it was mopping up the remnants of the Iraqis on Tallil.)[6]

Colonel Clark also wanted to know the terrain in the area of AO Eagle; therefore, he needed ground reconnaissance. On G-Day, he inserted his scouts and four long-range surveillance detachment (LRSD) teams to gather information for the assault. To get even more detailed information on the LZ area, that afternoon he sent 1st Lt. Jerry Biller of 3-187th Infantry and his scout platoon into LZ Sand, 40 kilometers south of AO Eagle. LZ Sand would be the LZ for the heavy-lift CH-47 Chinooks that lacked the range to make a full round trip to AO Eagle on one tank of fuel.

In the rain, Biller's "Team Jerry" air assaulted into LZ Sand and quickly unloaded its gear, including motorcycles, from the helicopters. Biller's mission was to mark an LZ for the CH-47 Chinooks and to check the trafficability of the ground route, Route 41A, that led up to AO Eagle. (Route 41A was not an Iraqi route designation; an unknown division staffer with a sense of humor dubbed it 41A after the highway that runs past Fort Campbell in Kentucky.)

It continued to rain throughout the day, quickly turning the ground into a quagmire of thick, clinging, clayey mud. Several of Team Jerry's motorcycles got stuck, and off-road vehicular traffic was virtually impossible. Biller recognized the futility of trying to set up LZ Sand in that area. This sharp and decisive lieutenant took the initiative and moved the LZ 10 kilometers west. Later on the night of G-Day, the skies cleared, the wind picked up, and the temperature dropped to near freezing.

The LRSD teams described the LZ in AO Eagle as a series of rolling hills pockmarked with shallow wadis and pools of standing water. Their accounts also emphasized that the area was full of mud. They reported that their helicopters sank a foot into the muck when they tried to set down.[7]

After the war, Clark recalled his reactions while he was still waiting for the launch in TAA Campbell's pickup zone. "As I looked out over it for as far as the eye could see," he said, "there were helicopters, soldiers and equipment sling-loaded, prepackaged, ready to go. Mind boggling sight. No way you could capture it on camera or film. . . . [W]hen I described it to my Dad, . . . a World War II veteran, he said he had the same feeling when he looked out on the English Channel."[8]

The division's original plan was to launch the Rakkasan Brigade Team/Task Force into AO Eagle during the hours of darkness on the night of February 25. Nighttime, reasoned General Peay, "gives us more protection from any possible air defense that . . . [the Iraqis] might have."[9]

On the morning of G+1, Colonel Clark got a call from General Peay. As he remembers it, General Peay said, " 'The weather forecast for tonight is bad. You need either to make the call to go early in daylight to beat the weather, or wait.' I opted to go early."

The air assault of the 3d Brigade out of TAA Campbell was basically done in two huge lifts. The first lift was the "heavy" element of Task Force Rakkasan, or essentially the wheeled vehicles of the brigade. TF Rakkasan was composed of two artillery batteries from the 3d of the 320th Artillery Battalion, three antitank companies, two mounted rifle companies, and four engineer vehicles. Colonel Clark gave command of TF Rakkasan to Lt. Col. Tom Greco, CO of 3-187th Infantry. TF Rakkasan's first elements—four CH-47 Chinooks, each carrying two TOW Humvees—left TAA Campbell at 11:00 A.M. on G+1 and began landing at 12:16 P.M. Three more elements delivered six TOW vehicles from the 1-187th Infantry. The rest of the task force followed into LZ Sand over the next six hours. General Peay remembered that "it was a long assault 'on the deck' at full speed to avoid the [Iraqis'] air defenses. Soldiers and equipment were crammed into helicopters like sardines."

During that time, First Lieutenant Smith and his platoon from D Company of the 3-187th Infantry left LZ Sand and reconnoitered Route 41A to Checkpoint (CP) 25. At the checkpoint, the platoon captured twelve Iraqis and two vehicles. One of the vehicles was a tank and pump unit that was used to refuel Iraqi vehicles moving up 41A.

Colonel Clark had split his command into two major elements and sent the "heavy" ones into LZ Sand in sixty heavy-lift CH-47 sorties, because, he said, "it was the timing thing. Their mission [TF Rakkasan] was just to go in but not progress towards the Euphrates until the infantry was on the ground. They [TF Rakkasan] went in after the area had been reconnoitered in the air by Apaches and Cobras so that we were assured they'd be going into a relatively benign envi-

ronment. We just didn't have legs with the aircraft, fueling, refueling requirements to bring them all the way in . . . we got them as close as we could."[10]

Lt. Col. Tom Costello, CO of the 3-320th Field Artillery Regiment, remembered his final hours in TAA Campbell before he and his two batteries in TF
Rakkasan flew to LZ Sand.

"On Sunday morning, the 24th, we could see the dust from the 1st Brigade's
lift, from the PZ we would be using the next day, into FOB Cobra. It sounds trite,
but grim determination is the best phrase I can use to describe the atmosphere in
the TOC. (I was scared, but tried not to show it. I imagine everyone else was as
scared as I was. Grim determination is a good cover for fear.) . . .

"By late afternoon [of G-Day], 1st Brigade's lift was completed, and we were
able to go into PZ posture. We positioned and rigged the loads, gave some last
minute instructions, and settled in for a few hours' sleep. Our lifts began the next
morning, and would be an all day affair. As each CH-47 completed its first turn
and refueled, it returned for another load. B Battery would be going in the first
lift, and C Battery and the TOC with the second lift. So we knew it would be early
afternoon, at best, before we went. As the day wore on, the weather forecast wors-
ened, and we learned that the plan was changing. Colonel Clark and General Peay
made the decision to go early with the light elements, and have Task Force
Rakkasan link up as early as possible. The scouts that were inserted on Sunday, to
recon the route from LZ Sand into AO Eagle, gave a dubious report: the road on
the map did in fact exist on the ground and was OK ' . . . except in a few places,
where (they) think the vehicles can get through.' Hmmm.

"Our turn finally came, and we loaded into the Chinook for the hour-plus
flight. We took off in sunshine, and flew into gray skies as we went North. We
crossed the border into Iraq almost immediately, and it looked no different from
Saudi Arabia. Not sure what I was expecting. About half-way into the flight we
passed over FOB Cobra, and were reassured to see that it was already a significant U.S. presence. The skies got darker as we went along, and we landed in a
drizzle, to be met by CPT Jim Waring, who was now my assistant S-3. We got into
position on the ground as we had planned and rehearsed. . . . ."

Colonel Costello then met Colonel Greco, who briefed him on the situation on
the ground. Greco had decided to send ahead to AO Eagle the first of three TF
Rakkasan's serials. Greco put his S-3, Maj. Carlos R. Glover, in charge and tasked
him with finding out if Route 41A was passable and with reporting back as he
moved ahead.[11]

Just as Glover and the first serial were about to leave, Greco got word from
Colonel Clark, who was on the ground in AO Eagle, to stay put for the night. The
trafficability in the AO was terrible, he said. With the ground elements barely able
to move, Clark had grave doubts about any vehicle's ability to operate up there.

Glover and his serial had just moved out. Glover sent back route reports as he
moved forward. At 10:00 P.M. on G+1, Glover and Capt. Michael W. Dejarnette,
CO of D Company of the 3-187th Infantry, one of the antitank companies that

had come in with TF Rakkasan, linked together along Route 41A and moved on to AO Eagle.

Colonel Clark flew in the command and control plane for the TF Rakkasan launch. After he determined that there were no significant problems, he flew back to TAA Campbell and briefed the commanders of his infantry battalions on the ground.

At 3:00 P.M., he flew out again in the C&C "bird" for the infantry elements' flight. The first wave of about one thousand soldiers rode north in some sixty-six UH-60 Black Hawks.

"We launched the infantry at 1500 [3:00 P.M.]," Colonel Clark remembered, "and although it was hot and the sun was shining at TAA Campbell, by the time we got deep into Iraq, cloud cover was low, it was raining and very windy, and we went in on final [end of flight approach] into the Euphrates. It was relatively dark, raining pretty hard, visibility was pretty low." The flight time was about an hour and seventeen minutes; the distance, 150 miles. The LZs in AO Eagle were dubbed Chester, Festus, and Crockett.[12]

Maj. Steve Chester, the 3d Brigade's S-5, was in the third UH-60 Black Hawk of the first serial into LZ Chester. After the war, Chester recalled in some detail his flight from TAA Campbell to AO Eagle.

"For any combat air assault the seats are removed from the aircraft and the troops are terribly laden . . . ," he wrote. "I think that the required load list, coupled with a combat load of rations and ammunition, and the extras that many troops carried against all directives and common sense, resulted in personal loads that went beyond reason. Several of the people required the assistance of two others to ruck up and get off the ground. I really felt for the people with M-60s or Dragons. You can also imagine what this did to foot mobility at the far end.

"I carried my share of the common gear, 2 fragmentation and 2 smoke grenades, 100 rounds for my 9mm, a combat lifesaver kit, sleeping bag, ground roll, wet weather suit, poncho, 1 change of clothes, a hygiene kit and a small radio. One thing I've always found is that the thirst for information is almost overpowering when you are in the middle of something and isolated from the big picture. The BBC [British Broadcasting] and VOA [Voice of America] broadcasts were a godsend, even if not always accurate. 'Baghdad Betty' had been bombed off the air before I got there. Even with the spare load I was carrying, I was at about 80-pound load, so I would guess that some of the loads went to 150 pounds."

His account of the hour-and-a-quarter-long flight from TAA Campbell to AO Eagle describes a scene that was repeated in each of the Black Hawks carrying the infantrymen to AO Eagle.

"Our lift of 66 birds took off, if I remember correctly," he wrote, "at 1500 [3:00 P.M.] on the 25th. I spent the flight with a knee in one kidney, a rifle muzzle in the other, and a large air assault trooper on my skinny lap, gas mask squarely pressed into my bladder for the entire hour and 45 minute flight. No one seemed frightened, but a couple of the younger kids seemed a little tense. It amazed me at that point how young they looked. The only thing that was universally felt was a strong

185

desire to get out of that UH-60. We flew a low-altitude, high-speed profile that took us over FOB Cobra in a large flock. It was nice to see the guys at Cobra waving flags at us as we flew over. The whole flight, the weather got worse, and I spent most of the time mentally preparing for the wonderful feeling of cold water running down my neck. I *hate* that. One minute out, the troops locked and loaded and the doors were opened in an icy blast of wind and rain. The standard chorus came up from every throat—'Oh, shit!' The landing was every bit as pleasant as expected—rain, high winds, 40 degree temperature and a quagmire of some of the most tenaciously clinging mud I've ever seen in my life. We had several people who fell and suffered sprained legs and backs.

"As an aside, we landed virtually on top of some Iraqi in his car. He took off running, falling several times. He left his car running, windows open and lights on. We left it that way, figuring he'd get himself in trouble with a full tank of gas."

After landing, Chester and the command group started to slog their way to the CP location, some 4 miles from the LZ. But the mud was so thick and the weather so abominable, that Colonel Clark halted them. The staff bunkered down in "an incredibly fetid drainage ditch" until daylight. "Actually," Chester wrote, "we had a fair vantage point to watch the troops cut the MSR, with the resulting fireballs from trucks being ambushed, providing the fireworks. We resumed our trek until midday the next morning, when one of the aviation battalion commanders happened by in his UH-60 and shuttled us to our link-up point with the ground convoy. He was a very popular man at that point."[13]

Sgt. Steven Edwards, a squad leader from the 1st Platoon of B Company of the 2-187th Infantry and his squad rode in the fourth UH-60 Black Hawk to land in AO Eagle. About five minutes from touchdown, the pilot signaled Edwards, who, in turn, alerted his squad. Later Edwards said that the five-minute warning was time to start "getting your head together. Then he gave us one minute. You open the door and you start getting that scary feeling—and I have to admit that I was pretty scared."[14]

Lieutenant Colonel Berdy's 2-187th Infantry was the first battalion to land. It landed just short of Battle Position Abilene, where Berdy and his troops dismounted in the muck and mud. Later, he admitted that his first thought was, I'm 42 years old and I'm too old to be doing this stuff.[15]

Staff Sgt. Sean M. O'Brian was the squad leader of the 1st Squad of 1st Platoon of C Company of the 1-187th Infantry. He and his squad loaded up in a drizzle late on the afternoon of G+1. He carried a heavy load: two Claymore mines, two 60mm mortar rounds, two hand grenades, three smoke grenades, two star clusters, ten magazines of 5.56 ball ammo, six quarts of water, nine MREs, a poncho and liner, pen and paper, 50 [empty] sandbags, extra socks, an IV (intravenous fluid) set, and other first aid supplies. He also managed to cram into his rucksack a few toilet articles and three cartons of cigarettes. He also carried a mission-oriented protective posture (MOPP) suit, load-bearing equipment, a protective vest, a kevlar helmet, and his individual weapon. Consequently, the UH-60 Black Hawk carrying O'Brian and his squad was so overloaded with men, fuel, and equipment that the pilot had to use a rolling takeoff to gain the necessary airspeed to lift off.

Spc. Johnny W. Hall was a member of O'Brian's squad. "We were in the air about one and a half hours, but it seemed longer," he remembered. "We had the whole time to think about it. I was scared. I was thinking what would happen if my friends got shot. How would I react? What would happen if I got shot? Would I keep my cool? I started looking around at everybody; they all had straight faces, trying not to show they were scared. . . . I closed my eyes for a couple of seconds and prayed."

"Everything was going through my head," said Sgt. Jose W. Lourido after the war, "whether I'd come back or not, and since I'm a team leader, I was thinking about how I was going to do things. Some of the squad looked out of the windows for a while, but nobody said anything. I put my head down, and when I looked up, everybody else had his head down, just waiting."

At the end of the flight, the UH-60 Black Hawks began their descent. The heavy rains that had been pounding the landing zone turned what had been hard clay into a slippery, greasy surface.

"We landed flat, and we seemed to slide forever," said Staff Sgt. O'Brian. "The bird on one side slid by us as we slowed to a stop, and the bird on the other side slid by. I was waiting for the next bird to slide into us."

"The landing was the wildest ride I've ever been on," remembered Pfc. Kevin E. Bosworth. "We landed at almost full speed. At the time, it was scary. Now I think about it as fun, but I still wouldn't want to land like that again."

"It was wild—thick, packed clay, fish-tailing," said Sgt. Mark H. Schlindler. "I was thinking, 'Oh, boy, gotta have faith in the pilot.' Then, suddenly, we were throwing stuff out so the bird could get off the ground." And as each trooper jumped or slid out of the UH-60 Black Hawk, he found himself ankle-deep in the muck.

Conditions in AO Eagle were, in a word, lousy. "The weather conditions were abysmal," said Colonel Clark later. "We had mud up to our knees, soldiers were carrying very heavy rucksacks, mobility was very hampered. . . . You talk about a mobility problem. Things were a little tense that first night."

On their arrival, Lieutenant Colonel Kinnison and his 1-187th Infantry were to secure Objective Boston—a pump station and airstrip. Sergeant O'Brian's UH-60 Black Hawk landed about 1,000 meters from Objective Boston. In about fifteen minutes, C Company reached the compound. A team from the company breached the perimeter, and the company scrambled through the hole in the fence. About twenty buildings of various sorts were scattered inside the pump station compound. C Company moved carefully through the area, alternating between covering and clearing teams. They searched each building carefully but found no Iraqis. Apparently, the buildings had been abandoned only minutes before the helicopters landed. In one, dinner was still on the table. According to one report, about thirty to fifty people had been there, and judging from the uniforms found, the men had been in the Iraqi militia. All they left were papers, some ammo, and the omnipresent pictures of Saddam.

Shortly before dusk, O'Brian's men heard a burst of automatic weapons' fire from a bunker complex outside the compound. He and his squad got the mission to clear the bunkers. Lieutenant Colonel Kinnison later said, "As an infantryman, I can't think of anything I would rather do less than going into a bunker."

"I was scared, no other way to put it, scared for me and my guys," O'Brian admitted later. "It was raining, foggy, a moonless night." But he and his squad got on with the task of clearing the bunkers to make sure that A Company, moving toward the airfield, did not get caught passing through their own lines. Sergeant O'Brian and his men put on night vision goggles and used laser-sighting devices to clear the bunkers, moving from one to the next very carefully. They cleared ten of them.

"We could tell what was going on outside," said O'Brian later. "But the worst part—when we were most vulnerable—was working our way inside the bunkers. It was very close quarters. It took 30–45 minutes to complete the job, but it seemed to take forever. We never did find the guys who were shooting. We were disappointed about that on one hand and relieved on the other." When they finished, Objective Boston was secure.[16]

"I think one of the most remarkable facets of the fight on the Euphrates," wrote Colonel Kinney, "was the fact that Colonel Clark only got half of his brigade on the ground for the first 24 hours because weather prevented the planned turn-around of the 66 UH-60s for the 2d lift into AO Eagle. What that amounted to was a brigade of only 6 companies supported by 81mm mortars and a few ground mounted TOWs for the first 24 hours of combat. Those six companies carried the fight till the night of G plus 2 when TF Rakkasan arrived with our artillery from 3-320th FA, our mounted TOWs, and the engineer demo [demolition materials] required to cut Hwy 8.

"I don't believe the Iraqis ever figured us out till too late. We took some small arms fire from local militia just off the Landing Zones in the 3d Bat sector but they were brushed away quickly and never bothered us again. 1st Bat surprised the forces in the Darraji Pump Station who ran when they heard the thunder of so many helo's, leaving their warm supper on the table inside the pump station; negligible contact there. The real story was on Hwy 8 where C/3/187th on the left and B/2/187th on the right, separated by about 8 kms, began a busy three days ambushing Iraqi trucks. . . . Every vehicle shot by 2d Bat contained contraband stolen from Kuwaiti homes. TV sets, VCRs, bicycles, tea sets, silverware, and women's and children's clothing seemed to be Iraqi looters' priorities. It was clear the second day that we weren't facing a beaten army, but a bunch of thieves."[17]

If the Iraqis had had an armored force of tanks and armored personnel carriers in the area, they could have devastated the lightly equipped Rakkasans along Highway 8. Nonetheless, the lightly equipped Rakkasans were still able to destroy

Iraqi vehicles on the highway that night. In a firefight in Engagement Area Yankee, B Company of the 2-187th Infantry killed two Iraqis and wounded seventeen. B Company evacuated the wounded to the battalion aid station.

That night of G+2, February 26, the second lift of the Rakkasan light infantry elements, which had flown up to FOB Cobra the day before, arrived in AO Eagle. Thus, Colonel Clark then had enough infantrymen to raise his strength to two thousand two hundred men.

TF Rakkasan, starting at early light on G+2, began moving north along Route 41A toward AO Eagle. By 2:00 P.M., Colonels Greco and Costello and the lead elements of the task force closed in AO Eagle. The trip had not been easy. Colonel Costello described it.

"At about 0300 [3:00 A.M. on G+2], I was called to a meeting at Greco's CP at which we discussed plans for the morning. He had arranged, via TACSAT [tactical satellite], for the Chinooks to return, after dropping off at Cobra, and lift the remaining elements of TF Rakkasan into the AO, thus bypassing the road. At first light, we assumed PZ posture again, but the winds and visibility precluded aircraft operations. Glover's element had still not closed on Eagle, although it was getting close now. The light elements of the brigade were up there with no heavy weapons, and only their mortars for fire support. They had not been heavily engaged as yet, but we knew that Highway 8 would be a key withdrawal route for the Iraqi forces; for all we knew, the entire Republican Guard could be on its way up the road, and there were no TOWs, artillery, or, due to the weather, attack helicopters to stop them. In fact, the demolition materials intended for use in cutting the highway were still with us. It was time to get up there.

"We reconfigured the loads (again) for ground movement, and Greco headed out with the second serial; the third serial, under me, followed a few minutes later. The wind continued to howl, reducing visibility to a few hundred meters for most of the trip. We followed the second serial, making reasonably good time, and seeing very little. We passed a Bedouin encampment, but they seemed to show little interest in us, so we showed little interest in them. We made the trip fairly uneventfully in the end, covering the distance in about six hours, and encountering no problems negotiating the route with the howitzers, notwithstanding their heavy loads. We closed in AO Eagle about 1500 [3:00 P.M.], and CPT Joe Connor immediately began to reconnoiter for a position for his C Battery. CPT Jim Mathis [B Battery commander] had occupied the only paved road inside AO Eagle, a pipeline service road that ran from the northwest to the southwest, leading to the pumping station that 1-187th had taken the night before (Objective Boston). Our plan had been for both batteries to occupy south of the pipeline, to have that obstacle between them and the bad guys, but the terrain prohibited doing so, and they both wound up on the north side. The pipeline was the buried above ground type, so it wasn't much of an obstacle as an elevated one would have been, and there were a couple of crossing sites available, so the risk was acceptable—particularly since there was no real choice."[18]

By the evening of G+2, the 3d Brigade was astride Highway 8 and deployed in a defensive configuration to block any Iraqi traffic moving either east to reinforce the Iraqis near the Kuwaiti border or west to escape the attacks by the coalition forces in the east. As one writer in *Triumph Without Victory* put it, "As Iraqi military convoys attempted to crash through the American roadblocks, they were fired upon by soldiers from Clark's 3d Brigade of the 101st Airborne. Most deadly were the wire-guided TOW missiles fired from launchers mounted on Humvees. Seeing the carnage, some Iraqi soldiers turned their vehicles around and fled. General Binford Peay's soldiers had seized and secured Highway 8. Nothing would move on the road without his permission."[19]

In FOB Cobra, the 1st Brigade continued to improve the division's posture. "First Brigade TF cleared MSR Virginia in zone and Logbase Oscar, planned to be a vital XVIII Airborne Corps supply point," wrote the division historian. "The 'Always First' Brigade TF also conducted a linkup with the 197th Infantry Brigade on the 24th ID (M) on MSR Virginia near the division's eastern boundary. The linkup with the 82d Airborne Division on our western border was delayed because the 82d was stuck in the backlog of traffic in the French 6th Light Armored Division sector."

Meanwhile, the 2d Brigade continued to deploy into FOB Cobra from TAA Campbell. Colonel Purdom made plans for his combat mission. His choice hung between an attack to the northeast into either Objective Strike (the Tallil airfield) or Objective Gold, southeast of Strike. "Early indications," wrote the historian, "had suggested Second Brigade would be going into Objective Gold, but messages from Corps on the night of the 25th indicated an assault into Objective Strike. Colonel Bolt, the division chief of staff, informed the division staff that a move into Gold would probably come only after the 24th Division had already taken Gold.

"Further events obviated the need for either of these missions. On the 26th of February, XVIII Airborne Corps notified the division that the Corps' operations were being reoriented from a northern thrust to a flanking move to the east in order to cut off the enemy's escape routes north of Basra. The division was instructed to plan to posture south of the 24th Infantry Division's Objective Orange in order to further interdict Iraqi escape routes."[20]

General Peay had moved his assault command post to FOB Cobra on G-Day. With his battle staff there, he made adjustments to the change of plans dictated by General Luck at XVIII Airborne Corps. In keeping with the corps's new plan to attack east, General Peay decided to establish a new forward operating base, FOB Viper, to the east of FOB Cobra as a base for attacks to the northeast. He directed Colonels Purdom and Garrett to be ready to move the 2d Brigade and two aviation attack battalions to FOB Viper. The 2d Brigade's objective, FOB Viper, was named Objective Tim.

To assist General Peay in this assault to the east, General Luck reassigned to his operational control the 12th Aviation Brigade, commanded by Col. Emmitt Gibson from V Corps, Europe, and also attached the 5-8th Field Artillery.

General Peay remembered that he "had not seen Gibson since the covering force days when his aviation brigade had been OPCON to the 101st. It was great getting them back working with the Division because they were very professional."[21]

The 101st Airborne was ready to continue the attack to the east as part of the wide envelopment Schwarzkopf and his planners had mapped out. Desert Storm was roaring to a climax.

An Iraqi storage facility partially destroyed in AO Eagle, Euphrates River Valley, February 1991.

17 | Storm Blowout

By the night of G+1, February 25, General Schwarzkopf was well beyond just a simple Hail Mary plan. And with the way things were going in Iraq, he was probably counting his blessings. That evening, ARCENT evaluated its units' achievements in meeting their objectives.

The 101st Airborne's 3d Brigade Task Force straddled Iraq's main highway, Highway 8, a virtual lifeline between Kuwait and Baghdad. The 1st and 2d Brigades worked in FOB Cobra to improve its utility as a major operating base. In addition, outside FOB Cobra, the 1st Brigade had cleared MSR Virginia in zone and Logbase Oscar, a proposed, vital supply point for XVIII Airborne Corps's future operations in the sector.

Colonel Purdom had moved his 2d Brigade headquarters, 3-502d Infantry, 1-320th Field Artillery, and his support and combat service slices (elements of support units) into FOB Cobra on G-Day. Lt. Col. James Donald, CO of 1-502d Infantry, had also moved his battalion into FOB Cobra and reported to the 1st Brigade's commander Colonel Hill.

East of the 101st Airborne, advance elements of the 24th Infantry Division (Mechanized) arrived about 70 miles southeast of FOB Cobra. Col. Ted Reid's 197th Brigade of the 24th Infantry Division had made it halfway to the Euphrates River and just east of FOB Cobra when it linked up with the 1st Brigade along MSR Virginia, near the 101st Airborne's eastern boundary. Farther east, on the 24th Division's right, was the 3d Armored Cavalry Regiment.

"It was just like a parade," said Lt. Col. B. J. Craddock, a battalion commander in the 24th. "The only problem was the weather. We faced, in my opinion, the worst weather we had the whole time we were over there, what with the sandstorm followed by the rainstorm." And the roads that the commanders had selected from maps before moving into Iraq turned out to be nothing more than muddy "goat trails," or quagmires of muck.[1]

The 101st Airborne's linkup with the 82d Airborne Division to the west of FOB Cobra was delayed because the 82d Airborne was stuck in the traffic backlog in the

193

French 6th Light Armored Division's sector. But by the end of G+1, both the 82d Airborne and the French 6th Armored were in the vicinity of the As Salman airfield to the west of FOB Cobra and along the west flank of XVIII Airborne Corps's sector.

Lt. Col. Joe Chesley and his 2-502d Infantry Battalion were relieved of a corps reserve mission at 6:50 P.M. on G+2 and alerted to move at 8:34 P.M. to FOB Cobra, where they would rejoin the 2d Brigade. But the poor weather conditions that night prevented the move, and the battalion had to stay in TAA Campbell until February 27.

The wintery weather was especially significant to the 101st, dependent as it was on reasonably decent flying weather. But even in the bad weather, DISCOM was able to fly 110 CH-47 Chinook sorties into FOB Cobra on February 25 before the weather shut down further logistics' flights.

"The weather factored heavily on operations for both air and ground forces on G+1," wrote Colonel Garrett.

With rain, haze, and low ceilings throughout the day, the plan to air assault 3d Brigade to the Euphrates with two turns under NVGs [night vision goggles] was in jeopardy. The decision was made to air assault 3d Brigade to the Euphrates on the afternoon of G+1, 25 February. Two turns of the UH-60 task force under the control of 4-101 [4th Battalion, 101st Aviation Regiment] accomplished the task with the last serials arriving back to COBRA under NVGs in extremely poor weather. 3d Brigade reported heavy traffic during the initial hours following the air assault landing, and 1-101 [1st Battalion, 101st Aviation Regiment] responded by destroying several cargo vehicles, including one with an AAA gun in tow. By 2200 hours [10:00 P.M], the weather had deteriorated to where AH-64 crews reported less than 1/8th of a mile visibility with FLIR. Nonetheless, by that time 3d Brigade was entrenched astride Highway 8 to the southwest of As Samawah.[2]

By the morning of G+2, the weather grew even worse. The wind was up to 25 knots with gusts to 40 knots throughout the day. Lt. Col. Bill Bryan, CO of the 2-229th Aviation Regiment, remembered that "poor visibility on the 25th, and a fierce 'Shamal' [sandstorm] on the 26th, limited the battalion's operations." And these conditions grounded the remainder of the 101st Airborne's aircraft. Colonel Garrett said that "the resultant dust made it impossible to see across the tent, and aviation operations were virtually non-existent throughout the day."

On February 26, the weather had so deteriorated that the CH-47 Chinooks from DISCOM could not get through to continue the logistics buildup of FOB Cobra and were placed on a "weather hold." Truck convoys, however, continued to roll up MSR Newmarket through the rain and mud. By that afternoon, FOB Cobra had 14,000 gallons of water and a fully operational rapid refuel point in place. FOB Cobra reminded the troops of "great big 7-11 stores."

After the war, General Peay said, quite simply and forcibly, "Logistics was clearly a major factor in winning the war." He highly praised his DISCOM officers who were responsible for much of the success of FOB Cobra's rapid buildup and for the general logistics success of the entire operation. He observed that two men in particular—Lt. Col. John Broderick, the CO of the 426th Supply and Transportation Battalion, and Maj. Mark Dille, the division's transportation officer—developed new schemes and techniques to solve any problems as they developed. He noted their tirelessness, ingenuity, and determination to make the operation a success. And of Lt. Col. Tom Shrodzki, the division logistics officer, Peay declared that "he was a hero throughout the whole thing."

General Peay also lauded highly some of his officers who did the "dirty work" of moving troops and of keeping abreast of the constant changes in plans and locations. Brig. Gen. Ronald Adams, his ADC-S (assistant division commander for support), and his chief of staff, Col. Joe Bolt, did yeoman service, he said in an interview. From the division's main CP at TAA Campbell, they were the key planners "in rolling the division up," keeping the logistics on the move, sorting out convoys, figuring out the impact of new missions from corps, and converting them into detailed plans for subordinate commanders. Colonel Bolt "was a hard-nosed, tough Chief of Staff," Peay said, "but under that tough veneer, he loved people, he was smart, a professional soldier, and well-qualified to handle the details of the tactical plans that the division had to change so often."[3]

By the night of G+2, the coalition forces along the entire front had moved north into Iraq with unexpected speed. Because of this success, which required General Luck to issue the 101st Airborne new orders and missions, General Peay was forced to make rapid, almost immediate changes in his plans. He had to remain flexible. And to do so, he used the division's aerial assets to move brigades rapidly and decentralized command and control. He reorganized these command and control elements into four major units: a jump command post of seven staffers, an assault CP of forty men, a main CP of about two hundred, and a rear echelon composed of the rest of the division staff.

Using two UH-60 Black Hawks and two CH-47s Chinooks on G-Day, General Peay had moved his jump CP from TAA Campbell to FOB Cobra with the 1st Brigade's lead elements. His scaled-down jump CP, which could be set up any place in less than an hour, included simply several small tents, a couple of command vehicles, a communications node, and a small infantry security element. With basic FM radios, he could talk to corps and all of his subordinate commanders and control the air assault and improved high-frequency radio (IHFR) for his intelligence and logistics updates.

The main command post remained at TAA Campbell under Chief of Staff Bolt, basically to push logistics forward and to work out the details of mission changes. The division rear, under General Adams, also stayed at TAA Campbell.

On G+1 and G+2, the main CP remained at TAA Campbell but was prepared to move to FOB Cobra and then, on order, on to Objective Strike or Gold by ground convoy, which could be set up in less than three and a half hours. General Peay, throughout the operation, used a command and control UH-IH or his jump CP and moved frequently to avoid setting up a target. Because of the CP's mobility, he could go where the action required him. He also insisted that the forces and facilities in FOB Cobra spread out because of the threat of a Scud, gas, or chemical attack. When his ADC, General Shelton, moved to a new locale, he also moved first with the assault CP.[4]

*　　*　　*

The choice of a 2d Brigade assault into either Objective Strike or Gold still hung in the balance on G+1. Early plans had the 2d Brigade air assaulting into Gold, but on the evening of February 25, a message from General Luck at corps suggested preparing for an assault into Strike, the Tallil airfield. "Colonel Bolt," wrote the division historian, "informed the division staff that a move into Gold would probably come only after the 24th Infantry Division had already taken Gold."[5]

On February 26, General Luck notified General Peay that the entire coalition force was reorienting toward the east "in order to cut off the enemy's escape routes north of Basra." The division's new direction of attack, Luck told Peay, was north of the 24th Division "to further interdict Iraqi escape routes." This move required the 101st to slide under the 24th—a "by-the-right-flank" move in old infantry drill maneuvers—and then directly over the 24th Division for an attack to the east.

General Peay had no qualms about attacking the Iraqis aggressively. After Lt. Col. Frank Hancock and his 1-327th Infantry troopers had captured the bulk of the 1st Battalion of the 82d Brigade of Iraq's 49th Infantry Division on G-Day, General Peay got up at 2:30 A.M., went back to TAA Campbell, and interviewed some of the prisoners. He said that they were outfitted in reasonably good uniforms and that they were hungry but not starving. Moreover, almost to a man they did not want to fight for Saddam. This revelation led him to believe that the Iraqis would not fight for extended periods and that he could take risks and "stretch" his division. Peay felt that one of his most important tasks during the war was this correct reading of the Iraqis' military mind. This understanding made him willing to attack and take some risks when, under other circumstances, he might have been more cautious.[6]

Thus, after he received General Luck's new battle plan, General Peay quickly adjusted his scheme of maneuver. He decided to establish a new forward operating base 93 miles due east of FOB Cobra called FOB Viper from which he could launch helicopter attacks to the northeast. The area around FOB Viper had initially been secured by the 3d Armored Cavalry Regiment but was now vacant. He ordered Colonel Purdom and his 2d Brigade to prepare to move. Their target in FOB Viper was Objective Tim. In support, he ordered Colonel Garrett to send four attack helicopter battalions to FOB Viper, where they would attack the Iraqi columns escaping north from Kuwait. By this time, General Luck had also sent to General Peay the 12th Aviation Brigade and the 5-8th Field Artillery.

According to Lieutenant Colonel Cody, General Peay "called an 'audible' [changed the plan] at Cobra and rather than attack Tallil, air assaulted the 2d Brigade and the Aviation Brigade into Viper and conducted a classic pursuit of the trapped and retreating Iraqi forces along the Euphrates River in the vicinity of Basra."

The rains finally stopped on February 26, but the sandstorm blew on unabated. Cody said that "all during the 26th of February, the winds picked up and a heavy 'shamal' dust storm made air/ground operations impossible. 1-101st had C Company forward of Cobra at LZ Sand supporting 3d Brigade, and we had just sent the Battalion XO, CPT Howard Killian, forward to LZ Sand with a convoy of fuel and ammo HEMTTs in preparation for our attack into Objective Strike

(Tallil). It took Killian and his convoy over 4 1/2 hours to get to LZ Sand only to have to return when 2d Brigade's mission changed."[7]

In an interview after the war, General Peay said that the sandstorms on G+1 and G+2 were unlike any storms he had ever seen. In the previous six months, "we had been through shamals but never anything like this. These troopers flew in and around it. They were enormously proficient aviators. It is almost miraculous to think that we covered the kind of distances we did in this war that went so fast when the sand storm was so thick that even you and I [sitting across a table] could not see each other. . . ."

At 8:30 A.M. on February 27, G+3, Colonel Purdom launched his 2d Brigade 93 miles east from FOB Cobra to FOB Viper. His first helicopters started landing unopposed in FOB Viper about an hour later. He used 55 CH-47 Chinook and 120 UH-60 Black Hawk sorties. For the assault, Colonel Purdom had regained control of his 1-502d Infantry and assumed attachment of the 3-327th Infantry from the 1st Brigade. As a trade-off, General Peay attached to the 1st Brigade Purdom's 2-502d Infantry, which was still waiting in TAA Campbell for the weather to clear before moving to FOB Cobra.

"The air assault into Viper went relatively smoothly," wrote Lieutenant Colonel Cody, "when you consider all of the moving parts Division and Aviation Brigade had to juggle. At the end of the day on the 27th, the division had the 1st Brigade at Cobra, the 3d at AO Eagle, 2d Brigade and most of the Aviation Brigade at Viper as well as the attack assets chopped [transferred] to 3d Brigade. Initially, when we arrived at Viper, a squadron of the 3d Armored Cavalry Regiment was still in place awaiting release from their regimental commander (Col. Doug Starr) because of a 'friendly fire' incident that happened early that morning with some engineer vehicles from the 1st Armored Division. It was obvious that the 3d ACR had fought a tough battle the night before against some Iraqi mech forces. We flew over several burning Iraqi vehicles. We coordinated with Lieutenant Colonel Dailey's squadron so we knew where they were moving out to and what the enemy situation was north and northeast of their position."[8]

For artillery support on FOB Viper, Colonel Purdom had the eighteen 105mm howitzers from his direct support battalion, Lt. Col. Harlan Lawson's 1-320th Field Artillery (FA) Battalion, and eight 155mm howitzers from C Battery of the 5-8th FA Battalion.

Unbeknownst to General Peay or Colonel Purdom, large areas of FOB Viper were covered by unactivated mines. General Peay's assault CP was actually in a minefield. Later, he acknowledged that it was extremely fortunate that no one from the 2d Brigade or the assault CP was injured in the landings or in moving around the area.

Meanwhile, up with the 3d Brigade deployed along the Euphrates, traffic along Highway 8 was almost at a standstill by G+2.

"The night of 26–27 Feb passed quietly for us," wrote Lieutenant Colonel Costello about activities in the 3d Brigade's sector in AO Eagle. "There was some small arms activity along the road, but no artillery business. The weather was better now, sunny and warm, and we had some attack helicopters up with us, giving us an added feeling of security. One of the aircraft, while on patrol during the day, took small arms fire from the town of Al Khidr, making a precautionary landing outside our lines, and causing a good deal of excitement. At about 1500 [3:00 P.M.], Colonel Clark called for a brigade command and staff meeting, our first since we had come into the area. This was the first time I had seen LTC Hank Kinnison and Andy Berdy, the 1st and 2d battalion commanders, since we had conducted the air assault, and it was good to see them well. The brigade S-2 [intelligence officer] gave us a situation brief, and, for me at least, the first update I had had. It was evident that things were going very, very well. The marines and coalition forces were on the outskirts of Kuwait City, and the VII Corps was turning on the flanks of the Republican Guard. Colonel Clark cautioned against carelessness and told the infantry battalion commanders that he wanted more use of artillery (truly a gifted soldier!). His intent was to create a big signature, to discourage anyone from messing with us. After the brigade meeting, I walked back to the TOC and had a BC [battery commander] and staff call of my own to pass on the data I had collected at the brigade meeting."[9]

Maj. Steve Chester, S-5 of the 3d Brigade, had joined up with the brigade's S-4 and a rifle platoon. Together, they cleared a village along Highway 8 for the site of the JLAB (joint logistics assault base—the 3d Brigade's combat trains, or those vehicles that carry their own supplies). For his own operation, Chester moved into a cinderblock building that was surrounded by a block wall. With a large central room and four large rooms to the side, the place was supposedly being built as the home and office of the local Ba'ath functionary. Chester called the building the Alamo because of "our light armament, isolated position, and a Texas flag that Major [Michael L.] Oates insisted on hanging up all over the place," he wrote later. At the Alamo, Chester processed EPWs, refugees, and stragglers.

"The first two days in the Alamo," he wrote, "I processed about 57 prisoners for shipment to the rear. There were several interesting vignettes prior to a decision to turn loose prisoners unless it appeared they had intelligence value or might appear on the gray or black lists of 'wanted men.' I was thrilled when I got word that one of the people I sent back was on the list. He was a major who had tried to run a road block on the MSR and got shot in the shoulder for his trouble. He was big, well fed, surly and the other prisoners wanted nothing to do with him. He had on new British desert camo and an intelligence beret. We sort of put the obvious together and sent him back special delivery. The only time he tamed down was when the morphine reacted with the water he was drinking and he puked all over everything. Later that day, the contents of his vehicle came in—several thousand dollars in Syrian, Iraqi, and Jordanian currency, thumbscrews, and some very sophisticated civilian brick-type commo [hand-held radio], as well as a new Browning Hi-Power. He apparently was one of the nastier elements to high-tail it.

"In general, the prisoners that came in were filthy, half-starved, ill-trained, illiterate, and wanted nothing to do with Saddam's war. In spite of the propaganda they had been subjected to, most had no qualms about being captured and several expressed hopes they could stay in Saudi Arabia. . . . The prisoners scarfed up MREs at a tremendous rate and cared not if pork were involved. A common comment was that they appreciated how accurate the U.S. bombing was, since the Brits and French were a little less discriminating and had hit a fair number of civilian targets. I had never heard of anyone thanking someone for bombing their nation before. As a group, the POWs were very cooperative and eager to talk. They were starved for news and said they could be shot for listening to a radio, one reason being the mistaken belief we could home in on a receiver. Actually, based on their reports, they could be shot for about anything. They were all amazed at how well we treated them and that we let them keep harmless personal effects.

"One of the battalions brought in a guy about 50 who had polio and was retarded— he had been drafted and made a cook. . . . He was in such sad shape that he had to be carried around. Several of them came in wounded and were pathetically grateful for medical treatment given by Dr. [Montie] Hess's people. One guy that came through, about 18, collapsed crying when an Apache flew over. We found out from others that he had been gunned by AH-64s and it made quite an impression on him. They seemed to fear the Apache more than any other system, B-52s included, and credited it with supernatural capabilities. The next day, a group was brought in and I noticed, passingly, that one [prisoner] seemed fairly small. A few minutes later, one of the 311th MI guys came in and told me the little guy was crying and resisting a strip search. I told him to take one of the more gentle interpreters we had out and check to see how old the prisoner was. I developed a suspicion we had caught a young one. That was confirmed when the kid told them he had turned 14 that week and had been press-ganged into the army two weeks earlier. He had no training, no equipment and was scared senseless. They got the kid calmed down . . . the only thing the kid wanted was to go home to his mother. . . . We found some civilian clothes, gave him some food and pointed him in the direction of Ad Diwaniyah and his mother.

"The MI guys more or less adopted a 15-year old who came in with the last batch of prisoners we shipped. There was a delay in airlift in getting them out, due to a dispute with the aviators over who was to guard what and who had to clean the Iraqi puke out of the aircraft. At any rate, the kid was tame and wandered around wrapped in a blanket the medics gave him. The MI guys named him 'ET' after the Spielberg movie and more or less gave him the run of the place. I brought that to a screaming halt when I came back to my area and found him camped on my sleeping bag within reach of a stack of weapons and grenades that had been captured that day—and eating *my* MREs. The little fool picked up a bandoleer with grenades all over it and gave me an 'Is this what you're looking for?' expression and he held it out. I may not have eaten an MRE that day, but I did eat some 311th MI posterior. The local version of 'McHale's Navy' and Fuji came to a quick halt and 'ET' found that pets were best kept in cages.[10]"

By the evening of G+3, the 3d Brigade's blockade of Highway 8 was in full force. Lt. Col. Peter C. Kinney had been the brigade's S-3 on the operation. "I think the two most dramatic moments for me were on G+3 when in the morning I overflew Hwy 8 with the commander of 3-101 Attack Aviation [3d Battalion, 101st Aviation Regiment], LTC Mark Kern, and viewed the devastation wrought by the two infantry battalions and later that night when we brought two batteries from 3-320 FA [3d Battalion, 320th Field Artillery Regiment] to bear on some trucks skirting our kill zones," wrote Kinney.

"The scene on Hwy 8 was right out of a movie as we hovered east above the Iraqi dead. Their bodies had been removed from the GAZ-66 command cars they were driving, laid on the ground with arms and legs crossed signifying that they had been searched. Farther ahead was a burning Mercedes truck towing an antiaircraft gun with the crew's bodies hanging out the doors. A squad from 2d Bat was on line advancing to search with their rifles at the ready, bayonets fixed. The highway bridge over the railroad had been cut and in 3d Bat's sector our engineers from C/326 had blown an enormous crater adjacent to a culvert, effectively cutting Hwy 8 in two places. All of this destruction had been wrought by very disciplined, well trained light infantry.

"The artillery made its mark that night. If there was any thought in the local Iraqi commander's head of counterattacking our airhead, it probably ended that night when the King of Battle spoke. 2d Bat's S-3 called me late that night and reported that two Iraqi trucks had bypassed the roadblocks and were following the railroad embankment cross country. His TOW gunners had them only briefly in their thermal sights and couldn't get a shot as they ducked along behind the embankment and over irrigation dikes next to the Euphrates. The brigade FSO [fire support officer] did a great job computing the movement of the targets. . . . Minutes later 60 rounds of 105mm HE/VT [high-explosive/variable time] caught their two trucks as the valley echoed and reechoed with their concussion and the flashes of impact illuminated the whole AO. We were literally jumping up and down in our holes and cheering that display of raw power. I was never so impressed with the power of the U.S. Army or as proud to be one of her soldiers as I was on the 27th of February 1991.

"As for the Iraqi soldiers we faced on Hwy 8, I feel pity for them now—I didn't then. They never knew what hit them and were never smart enough to warn others of our presence until after the cease-fire. We encountered few officers, mostly NCOs from Republican Guard units who told us that their officers had abandoned them by helicopter on the 20th of February and told the troops to find their way home the best they could. Leadership as befits a bunch of thieves. Of the POWs that were taken, most were genuinely surprised that as soon as we'd shoot them [with medical shots, that is], they'd be MEDEVACed to our rear and/or fed. All the POWs were very cooperative, even friendly, once they knew we weren't going to treat them to the same standard they probably would have given us. . . . In the words of the battalion commander of the 841st Infantry who surrendered to the 1st Bat: 'You Americans don't fight fair.' Fair to him as a veteran of the Iran-Iraq war was mowing down Iranian children in his minefields. What we did to them was beyond their comprehension."[11]

With Highway 8 cut off, the Iraqis leaving Kuwait could move only on a road due north out of Basra. To interdict that road, General Peay set up Engagement Area (EA) Thomas about 120 miles northeast of FOB Viper. The four attack helicopter battalions that General Peay had based at FOB Viper could then launch against the Iraqi armored and motorized forces trying to escape the pressure of the coalition forces driving them north.

Colonel Garrett wrote later that "TF HEMMT, a support convoy consisting primarily of FARP assets for the attack battalions, would also leave the morning of the 27th. This mission change was a direct result of the success of 3d Brigade's establishment of a blocking position on Highway 8. Intelligence showed that the Iraqi withdrawal which was channeled both north through Basra and west up Highway 8 suddenly turned exclusively to the northern route as word spread amongst the Iraqis that the U.S. had cut off the western escape route. The turning of the Iraqi Army created an impossible bottleneck at the few surviving bridges crossing the Euphrates, resulting in a classic kill box to be exploited by the Allied forces."[12]

Lieutenant Colonel Bryan's 2-229th Aviation Regiment was one of the attack helicopter battalions ordered to move from FOB Cobra to FOB Viper. As he recalled,

> About 1600 [4:00 P.M.] on the 26th we were ordered to move. . . . The two attack battalions, 1-101st and the 2-229th, were warned that we were going to move out of Cobra and move to the east to another airfield which was tagged as FOB Viper. The airfield was about 200 kilometers east and it was southeast of the big air base of Tallil, about 75 kilometers southeast of Tallil.
>
> Viper was an Iraqi airfield, a very clandestine type of thing that is an improved dirt strip. It covered a large area and had a tower off to the side . . . obviously an alternate air strip. There was nothing permanently stationed there, but it was an alternate recovery field that they had done an extremely good job of selecting. All they had were some dirt roads and they had a very usable dirt strip and a tower down in the corner and it was a great facility, clandestine facility. I don't think anybody knew it was there. It was not on any of the maps or anything. We were told to move to Viper the following morning and so, from 1600 [4:00 P.M.] on we were in the prepare-to-move stage. At 0600 [6:00 A.M. on G+3] the battalion wheels moved. They departed on a convoy we estimated was going to take until 1800 [6:00 P.M.] because of the distance, the route they were going to take, went through some areas that had been hit with DPICM (dual-purpose improved conventional munition) which later became a problem.

Bryan's wheeled support elements started out on a hard-surfaced road, but the last quarter of its route was unimproved. The route from FOB Cobra to FOB Viper went through the XVIII Airborne Corps's area to the VII Corps's area. "A lot of the area had been objectives that VII Corps had seized, a lot of the towns along the road," Bryan remembered. "They had fired cluster munitions in there. Vehicles would get stuck when they would get on these unimproved roads. . . . In the process of everybody getting out and stomping around trying to push this vehicle out, this guy stepped on a cluster munition. Fortunately, he wasn't seriously hurt. . . . Keeping track of DPICM-dudded areas was complicated by the fact that one Corps moved into another Corps area."

The aircraft of 2-229th Aviation Regiment closed into FOB Viper at about noon. With the aircraft was a jump FARP, moved in by CH-47 Chinooks and a security force. "We had the combat power on the ground," said Bryan, "and we had fuel and ammunition on the ground and wheels were still en route."[13]

The 101st was ready to swing its mobility and aerial firepower advantage to the east against the retreating Iraqi forces.

101st Airborne MP during live-fire exercises just prior to Desert Storm.

18 | The Battle of the Causeway

By the evening of G+2, the coalition forces were attacking forcibly with almost Stateside, maneuver-like speed across the entire Iraqi front—from the 1st Marine Division near Kuwait City in the east to the French 6th Light Armored Division more than 200 miles to the west.

"As I studied the lines on the battle map," wrote General Schwarzkopf, "I felt confident that this war was going to end very soon. Central Command's Army corps were now moving inexorably east, like the piston in an enormous cider press. We were driving the enemy into the pocket across the Euphrates from Basra, which our Air Force had begun referring to matter-of-factly as the 'kill box.' "

"You guys are doing a great job," said General Schwarzkopf to Gen. Gary Luck on February 26. "Now I want to make sure you understand your mission from here on out. It is to inflict maximum destruction, maximum destruction, on the Iraqi military machine. You are to destroy all war-fighting equipment. Do not just pass it on the battlefield. We don't want the Iraqis coming at us again five years from now."[1]

General Peay had a plan ready to support General Schwarzkopf's intent. Early on the morning of G+4, he intended to exploit the theater attack to the east by flying the 1st Brigade from FOB Cobra, refueling the aircraft at FOB Viper, and then air assaulting into EA Thomas, north of Basra, to block the Republican Guard and other forces attempting to retreat from Basra. General Peay called it "blocking the back door." He also planned to move the division's main command post from TAA Campbell to either FOB Cobra or FOB Viper.

The coalition forces were now definitely in the "exploitation and pursuit" phase of the campaign. Its objective centered on removing Iraq's offensive potential and destroying its capability for large-scale mechanized movement. With Iraqi forces escaping to the north, clearly their escape routes had to be cut and their mechanized forces destroyed.

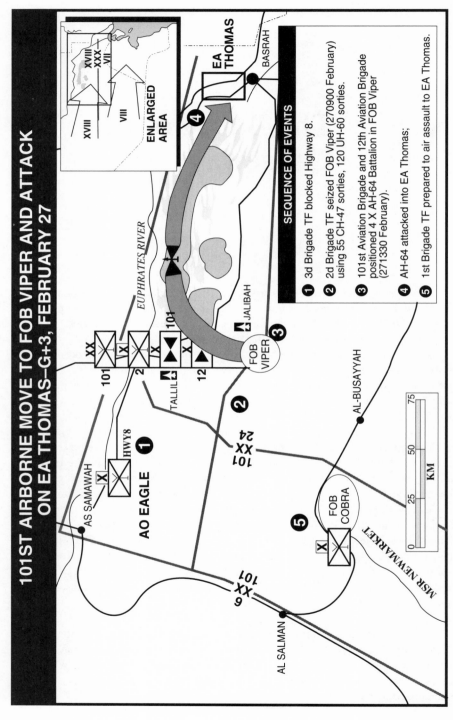

101ST AIRBORNE MOVE TO FOB VIPER AND ATTACK ON EA THOMAS–G+3, FEBRUARY 27

ENLARGED AREA

XVIII
XXX
VII

VIII

EA THOMAS

BASRAH

EUPHRATES RIVER

JALIBAH

FOB VIPER

AS SAMAWAH

HWY 8

AO EAGLE

TALLIL

101

2

101

12

XX 101

24

XX 101

6

AL SALMAN

AL-BUSAYYAH

FOB COBRA

MSR NEWMARKET

KM

0   25   50   75

SEQUENCE OF EVENTS

1. 3d Brigade TF blocked Highway 8.

2. 2d Brigade TF seized FOB Viper (270900 February) using 55 CH-47 sorties, 120 UH-60 sorties.

3. 101st Aviation Brigade and 12th Aviation Brigade positioned 4 X AH-64 Battalion in FOB Viper (271330 February).

4. AH-64 attacked into EA Thomas;

5. 1st Brigade TF prepared to air assault to EA Thomas.

204

Of the three main routes out of the KTO, two had been blasted by the U.S. Navy and Air Force. Damaged and burning vehicles blocked almost all motor vehicle traffic on the roads. Only the causeway over the Euphrates was still usable. The air strikes had also blown up many vehicles on the causeway, causing a bottleneck; however, reconnaissance proved that several thousand more vehicles were inching forward and waiting to snake their way through the litter—a veritable trash pile of trucks and military vehicles. Around the causeway, smoke from those burning vehicles and Kuwait's oil well fires reduced visibility to 1,000 meters.

General Luck ordered the aviation units under his command—the 101st Aviation Brigade and the 12th Aviation Brigade—to cut this final escape route of the Iraqi mechanized forces. Three AH-64 Apache battalions—the 2-229th Aviation, the 1-101st Aviation, and the 1-24th Infantry, and the cavalry squadrons of the 101st Airborne and 24th Infantry took part in the battle.

At about 10:00 A.M. on February 27, G+3, General Shelton received a frago from the 101st Airborne's main CP that he had a new mission from corps: use the 12th and the 101st Aviation brigades to attack the traffic trying to escape north out of Basra. At this time, General Peay was forward with the 3d Brigade in AO Eagle but stayed in close touch with General Shelton via radio. General Shelton immediately contacted Colonels Garrett and Gibson and told them to meet him at his jump CP at FOB Viper.

By midday, four advanced attack helicopter battalions had moved up to FOB Viper. Two were from the 12th Aviation Brigade: Lt. Col. Tony Jones and his 3-227th AAH and Lt. Col. Randy Tieszen and his 5-6th Cavalry. The other two were Lieutenant Colonel Bryan and his 2-229th Aviation and Lieutenant Colonel Cody and his 1-101st AAH Battalion—the battalion that fired the first shots of the air war. With the jump FARP brought in that morning by Lt. Col. Frankie Wilmoth's 7-101st Aviation Battalion, the 2-229th Aviation and 1-101st Aviation were ready to bomb and strafe the bottleneck in an aerial fight that eventually became known as the "Battle at the Causeway."

By G+1, the jump CPs' crews had become so proficient and the communications so good, that General Peay rethought the need to move the main CP up to FOB Cobra. General Shelton's operations officer, Lt. Col. Keith Huber, and his team were "pros at the business," according to General Shelton. "Keith Huber was a meticulous individual and a great officer."

When General Shelton flew into FOB Viper on G+3, the division's jump CP consisted of two UH-60 Black Hawks with the necessary radios to link up with General Luck at the XVIII Airborne Corps's tactical CP, the division's assault CP at FOB Cobra, the division's main CP in TAA Campbell with its even more extensive communications, and the subordinate commands of the 101st Airborne. Throughout the campaign, General Shelton had fine-tuned the jump CP and rehearsed its movement and setup, day and night. As soon as the helicopters landed, the crews raced to set up the four outside antennas to maximize the range of the console inside the UH-60

Black Hawks, extended the headsets and handsets, attached some generators, and covered the interior with blackout curtains so that the assault CP could operate day or night. Then the crew set up a small tent outside the door of the UH-60 Black Hawks, unfolded a couple of tables, hung some maps inside the tent, and brought in the extended headsets and handsets. The assault CP was in business.

Also that morning, the remainder of the division's tactical CP had left FOB Cobra but got caught up in heavy traffic along the main supply routes outside FOB Cobra. It would not arrive at FOB Viper until about 2:00 A.M., February 28.

Garrett and Gibson arrived at FOB Viper about noon on February 27. As soon as they got there, General Shelton stretched out a large map in the sand outside the jump CP. The three officers knelt in the sand and planned the attack. Using the maps that each of them carried, they assigned boundaries between units and routes through the 24th Division area and decided on distinct control measures to separate safely the several helicopter assault teams. That completed, General Shelton would coordinate with XVIII Airborne Corps so that all the corps's units—the 24th Infantry, 82d Airborne, and 3d Armored Cavalry Regiment (ARC)—would know where they were supposed to fly. General Shelton told Garrett and Gibson that the attack would have a time "window" from 2:00 P.M. to 5:00 P.M. when the air force would stay out of the area. At 5:00 P.M., the air force would take over. When Colonel Gibson expressed his concern that his AH-64 Apaches did not have enough fuel and ammo, General Shelton assured him that there were sufficient supplies at FOB Viper or on the way.[2]

It was now 12:30 P.M. General Shelton asked Garrett and Gibson if they could be ready on time. They both assured him that they had alerted their units earlier and could make that afternoon's deadline. General Peay had told General Shelton to give the aviation brigade commanders "their heads [freedom to use their initiative], to put a line on a map to separate them and to give them mission-type orders."

Shortly thereafter, at about 1:30 P.M., using the maps that they had prepared that morning, General Shelton and Colonel Garrett briefed the commanders on the plan. Colonel Garrett pointed out EA Thomas on the map and instructed the AH-64 Apache commanders to launch their attacks that afternoon. Colonel Garrett then outlined the sequence of the assault. He told the commanders to move out from FOB Viper, fly due north, pick up the Euphrates, and fly due east along the river—a distance of about 50 kilometers—to the causeway, which went north and then turned back to the west toward Baghdad. The causeway was at the northern end of a vast swamp, the Hawr Al Hammar, and at the eastern end of the Euphrates, where it intersects the Tigris. "Intercept or do a flanking attack on the Republican Guard forces that are attempting to flee north and escape," Garrett told them.

"The aviation brigade mission," wrote Colonel Garrett, "was to conduct deep attacks on withdrawing Iraqi forces in the vicinity of a causeway which crossed the Euphrates. The first AH-64 company from 1-101st departed Viper at 1430 hours [2:30 P.M.] and encountered numerous targets en route to the target and in the target area, with most of the traffic on the causeway having already been engaged by the Air Force. A second AH-64 company from 2-229th launched to conduct a battle handover with 1-101st and continue the attack."[3]

*   *   *

By that afternoon, the burning oil wells created a smoke screen and reduced visibility considerably. The smoke also blocked out the sun and darkened the target area.

A little after noon, "Cpt. Doug Gabram, B CO Commander, 1-101st," wrote Lieutenant Colonel Cody, "gave Colonel Garrett and me a detailed SITREP [situation report] as to the enemy situation along the causeway, the lowering visibility, and an account of the USAF pilot's (Lt. Andrews) radio call, on 'Guard' frequency, right after . . . [he] was shot down. Andrews was the downed pilot that the SAR [search and rescue] UH-60 from 2-229th went in to rescue. Basically Gabram reported to COL Garrett that it was chaotic along the causeway and in the reeds along the Euphrates . . . Iraqis were waving 'white flags' while others were engaging our aircraft; due to the very low visibility (fog/oil/smoke) our engagement ranges were down to 1,000–500 meters against a trapped enemy."[4]

The intelligence data on the Iraqi forces near the causeway was, obviously, rather scant. Colonel Bryan said that "all the enemy info we had was, the enemy is on the causeway. The causeway is your objective and there is a main highway which comes down and parallels the Euphrates, runs down by Tallil and heads over to Basra. The only graphic measure that we had was the word that friendly forces are south of that highway, anything north of the highway is the enemy. . . . We also knew that on the south end of the causeway, there was a big built-up area, a citadel-type of affair . . . about 3–4 kilometers square."

On the afternoon of G+3, Bryan and his team left FOB Viper. His description of the helicopter air attack is typical of the other three assault helicopter battalions in the battle.

"About 1515 [3:15 P.M.] we took off and I had set the three companies to cycle up in 30-minute intervals, to maintain constant pressure up here," he remembered. "We departed with five Apaches, three 58s and one Black Hawk for command and control. That was Charley Company plus my bird. I had a 19th Apache that was the commander's aircraft and I flew from the front seat on an Apache the whole time. . . . I did it because, until there is another, until the Comanche or another platform comes along, the only thing where the commander can be where he needs to be is in the front seat of an Apache . . . 58s can't keep up. Black Hawks don't have FLIR, don't have all the target acquisition, so in my mind it is kind of clear where the commander needs to be.

"The Black Hawk was the battalion S-3, the command and control bird, and was also our SAR (search and rescue). We arrived on station up there at approximately 1545 [3:45 P.M.]. I had set it up at 30-minute intervals because I expected it would take about 30 minutes to rotate off station. We went up across the highway, hit the Euphrates, headed east. The Euphrates then opened up into a very large marsh area probably 15 kilometers wide and 30–40 kilometers long. It was like flying back in time because of the resemblance to Vietnam. There were water buffalo up there, there were some type of Iraqi native people that live in long pontoon, cigar-type boats, pushing along in the water with these long poles. There were actually people [on boats] that were tied up out in the middle of the lake, living. You could see the smoke coming out of these thatched huts that were floating on these boats. . . . It was really like the twilight zone, flying back in time. It was bizarre.

"We continued to fly, and along the way we were strobed by a variety of different systems. APRs [radar warning receivers] are keying, never got locked on or anything, but a lot of different systems [were] in the area and we were flying pretty low over the water. We encountered two hazards en route to this thing. Number one was bugs. I don't know what they were. By the time we got to the causeway, most of our windshields were pretty well obscured just by bugs. . . . The other hazard we had were waterfowl. We hit two of them. . . . We had blood and guts all on the side of the nacelle. . . . We took one on the wing . . . it physically damaged the air frame . . . like somebody hit it with a sledge hammer. . . . A couple of guys took them in their windscreens."

At the start of the flight, the weather conditions were good. It was partly cloudy, but there was still plenty of sunshine. The temperature was in the 65-degree to 75-degree range, and the wind was calm. This pleasant atmospheric condition changed as the helicopters flew into the area near the causeway.

"It was like going into darkness," Bryan said. "There were just so many oil fires there from the burning oil wells north of Basra and Kuwait. Plus, the vehicles that had already been destroyed were burning. As we approached the causeway, we had to go from Day TV to FLIR to be able to see. We reduced air speed and came in and flew into the northern edge of this citadel complex and that was just an incredible array of hardware and positions. Concrete bunkers of huge proportions . . . 50 meters wide by 100 meters long that you could drive vehicles into. We personally overflew probably half a dozen assorted anti-aircraft positions that had been abandoned, but they were still loaded, with weapons in there. Soldiers, groups of soldiers everywhere waving white flags. It was bizarre. We continued in, and the deeper we went the worse the visibility became. Finally, at the point where we moved up to where we could see the causeway, the visibility was probably less than 300 meters and it was just pure black smoke."[5]

Bryan and his Charley Company were not the only assault helicopter units in the causeway fight at that time. To his south was a company from 1-101st AAH. Across the swamp, about 20 kilometers to the north, were units from the 12th Aviation Brigade, the 5-6th Cavalry and the 3-227th AAH.

Near the causeway, some Iraqi soldiers fired small arms at Bryan's helicopters, but the Iraqis quickly ducked back down. An SA-6, about 600 meters to 700 meters to his front, "strobes and then locks on to us," Bryan remembers, "Capt. Wiggins picked him up," Bryan said, "and shot him with a 30mm. We are still not sure if he actually launched or this engagement caused the launch, but an SA-6 came off of the rail and kind of went straight up in the air and then just kind of spun straight down and landed right in front of us. We continued to hose him down, but his radars, they were still active so we finished him off with a 30mm."

When Bryan and his team arrived at the battle site, he called it "hammer time. It was hammer time and we were launching everything we had—2.75s, Hellfires, and 30mm depending on the target and the range."

The causeway actually had four lanes jammed with a number of burning vehicles. Bryan and his team shot up a number of other vehicles and then moved back to the citadel. When they arrived, the causeway was still passable, but after all four battalions attacked, it was blocked.

The citadel area was jammed full of military equipment. "It was like the rear security point for traffic, people heading south into Basra," Bryan said. "I don't know what it was. Bunkers, vehicles, hardware, anti-aircraft, you name it . . . I would say upwards of two thousand vehicles in that whole complex. . . . Again we came back to the south and we began to hit targets on the causeway or the highway leading to the causeway, but we also then started servicing targets on the other side of the causeway. Some of those reached out to 2500–3000 kilometers and that was about as far as we could see through the smoke with the FLIR. But we could see that far and we did do some Hellfire engagements out there."

Bryan and his team stayed on station for about thirty minutes, by which time they had expended almost all of their ammunition. B Company of the 2-229th Aviation relieved C Company in place and continued the fight slightly to the south. B Company, said Bryan, "found the same target-rich environment. They found BM-21s . . . they took them out with a 30mm. BM-21s, BMPs [Russian tracked APC], a lot of BRDMs [Russian LAV]. For whatever reason, we never saw tanks. My theory is that when they were fleeing, they were getting into vehicles that would move quicker. And we knew from the get-go that a lot of their tanks had mechanical problems."

The coalition ground forces on the afternoon of G+3 were still about 75 kilometers from the causeway area. Certainly a huge number of trucks, lightly armored Iraqi vehicles, and stolen Kuwaiti cars, trucks, and buses could have escaped to the north if the helicopters had not closed the gap.

"This was purely a helicopter fight," said Bryan. "In my mind, first of all, the Air Force had nothing they could fly and fight in 300 meter visibility and there is no other piece of equipment that can fly that distance, that fast, and certainly it would have taken an armored division a day to get there. So this was clearly a classical, armed-helicopter mission especially with the FLIR system. Get in there and fight in obscurance with reduced visibility. This was basically in the daytime. So, we got up there, there are fires everywhere, there are fires in front of us and most of them are burning vehicles, some of them are actual oil wells, but it is dark, occasionally you will see a flame through the smoke and then the obscurance will come in again, but the fires are all in front of us and everybody is pretty much servicing targets. There were enough of them out there. They were hovering over this citadel complex, bunkers, vehicles. At one point I looked down on the right side of me was a 57mm that I could spit on and on the left side was a 23mm."[6]

Among the vehicles and other military hardware destroyed in the "battle of the causeway" were fourteen Iraqi APCs, eight BM-21 multiple rocket launchers, four M-16 helicopters, fifty-six trucks, and two SA-6 radars. They also damaged one of the few surviving major bridges across the Euphrates.

With the end of that battle, the war was almost over for the assault helicopters of the 101st Airborne and the attached 2-229th Aviation—almost, but not quite.

CH-47 crew chief observing from door gunner's window somewhere over Saudi Arabia.

19 | The SAR Incident

During the four days of the ground war, the 101st Airborne's helicopters, attached and assigned, flew thousands of sorties in Iraq in weather conditions that were at best only marginal and often abominable. Violent, record-breaking sandstorms, burning oil wells and Iraqi vehicles, vast temperature fluctuations, and rain did ground some flights from time to time. Iraqi antiaircraft systems and ground fires did hit a helicopter every now and then and shot some of them down.

For the most part, though, the young fliers of the 101st Aviation Brigade, 2-229th Aviation Regiment, and the 12th Aviation Brigade, supporting the air assaults of the 101st Airborne Division (Air Assault), flew on, day and night. They accomplished their history-making missions, using their skills, instruments, discipline, high morale, and good fortune. The first fatalities in helicopters assigned or attached to the 101st did not occur until the last day of the ground war.

On February 27, somewhere between 3:00 P.M. and 4:00 P.M., according to General Shelton, "the Air Force received over their channels a 'Mayday' report that an F-16 [Fighting Falcon] pilot had been shot down in the vicinity of Basra. The Air Force asked for a rescue mission. Corps had also picked up the report." At the time, the 2-229th Aviation was operating in the general area around the causeway.[1]

Maj. Rhonda Cornum, a flight medical officer with the 2-229th Aviation Regiment, wrote later that "we were not performing a CSAR mission at that time. We were simply moving our TOC [Tactical Operations Center] to a more forward area. Our convoy of trucks was a day behind. I always moved with the headquarters."[2]

Division headquarters radioed Colonel Garrett at FOB Viper that an F-16 had been shot down and that the pilot had ejected in the vicinity of the causeway. Colonel Garrett passed the coordinates and what information he had to Lieutenant Colonel Bryan. All that Colonel Garrett knew was that the pilot was from the 363d Tactical Fighter Wing (TFW), had a broken leg, and was supposed to be somewhere in the area over which the 2-229th Aviation had been fighting near the causeway.

Bryan immediately established contact with an AWACS and launched his CSAR mission shortly prior to 4:00 P.M. He sent a UH-60 Black Hawk, accompanied by two AH-64 Apaches, to find and extract the downed pilot. Now–Lieutenant Colonel Cornum wrote later that "we did not have a dedicated SAR UH-60. All three of them [UH-60s] were equipped with litters and a chest of medical supplies. On all of our attack missions, we had a UH-60 in trail, so that should we need to extract a downed pilot (or as usually occurred, pick up prisoners), the UH-60, Pathfinders and a medical person would be immediately available."[3] En route, the

211

AWACS vectored the team to the last known location of the downed pilot—south of the causeway and over terrain later known to be held by an RGFC division.

"Actually," wrote Cornum, "the original coordinates we were given were in error. AWACS gave us the correct coordinates en route, and we were following their directions. The actual problem was that although a corridor had been cleared by Marine F-18s, AWACS did not vector us through the cleared corridor. I know this to be true, as a marine CPT got the DFC (Distinguished Flying Cross) for performing this clearance mission. And HE happened to be the NEXT exchange officer in my husband's F-15 wing, and we attended his award ceremony!"[4]

Near this area, two aircraft were hit with "murderous AAA fire from what was probably the 'Al Faw' Division of the Iraqi Republican Guard," said Bryan.[5] "The UH-60L was shot down and crashed within the enemy defensive positions." Only the first of the two AH-64s was hit," wrote Lieutenant Colonel Cornum, "and it was hit extensively. The second aircraft was unscathed."[6]

Colonel Garrett wrote that "the UH-60 was last reported to have hit the ground at 130 knots and disintegrated. The two AH-64s returned to Viper, and eight soldiers on board the UH-60 were thought to have died in the crash."[7]

One of the eight personnel aboard the UH-60 Black Hawk on the rescue mission was Maj. Rhonda Cornum. "Major Rhonda Cornum, a friend," wrote Lieutenant Colonel Cody after the war, "was the flight surgeon for the 2-229th AHB [Attack Helicopter Battalion]. She was shot down in a UH-60 while on a CSAR mission to pick up an F-16 pilot, Capt. Bill Andrews, who was shot down along Highway 8. Cornum was riding in the back of the UH-60 Black Hawk with 2 AH-64s as escorts. The UH-60 got shot down—five killed, with Cornum, Stamaris, and Dunlap survived." Later he added that "all of our troops in the 1-101st had great respect for her . . . she was colocated with us back at King Fahd and she really took good care of all of the troops' medical problems.

"I was there when Colonel Garrett passed the mission to the S-3 of the 229th, and I believe with the information the Aviation Brigade had at the time, the mission was a correct one . . . even if Aviation Brigade had Gabram's subsequent SITREP, there was no way to predict the AAA activity that the UH-60 and its two Apaches ran into.[8]

"Major Cornum [was in the] UH-60 just before it left Viper" according to General Shelton. "It was a customary thing for her to do. She was an extremely capable, concerned and conscientious flight surgeon and she felt that when a rescue was being attempted, she should be with it." Lieutenant Colonel Cornum said that "what our S-3 actually did was ensure that I was on the aircraft prior to assigning that mission. I had in fact been on the aircraft all day, the only last minute addition was SGT Dunlap. In addition, I had been on numerous missions prior to this one, and have my Army flight records to document over 23 combat hours. They assigned our aircraft because there was a doctor on board [Major Cornum], and they knew the downed pilot was injured. Not only that, but the fact that a medical officer or medical NCO would be on every CSAR (i.e., every UH-60 following the Apaches) was written in the medical annex of the 2d-229th war plan which had obviously been submitted to and approved by the 101st command structure."[9]

The irony was that the downed F-16 pilot was actually in an area controlled by the 24th Infantry Division—not in the 101st Airborne's sector. In the crash of the UH-

60, "five soldiers, CWO4 Philip Garvey, CWO3 Robert Godfrey, SSG William Butts, SGT Roger Brelinski, and SGT Patbouvier Ortiz died in the crash. . . . Three other soldiers were taken prisoner by the Iraqis," wrote the 101st Division historian.[10]

When the antiaircraft fire slammed into the UH-60 Black Hawk, Major Cornum was crouched on the floor and knew that the helicopter was about to crash. Later she said that at the time she thought, Well, I wonder if this is the end. It was a great life.

In the crash, she was knocked unconscious. Later she awoke in the desert with both arms broken, 40 ruptured ligaments in one knee, and a bullet in her shoulder, and she was surrounded by Iraqi soldiers. At that moment, Major Cornum, thirty-seven, became the second female POW of Desert Storm.

The day after the crash, the 24th Infantry Division (Mechanized) arrived at the scene. Inside a bunker near the crash site, a trooper found the personal gear of three of the crew members, and the 101st Airborne realized that some were still alive. "I was not known to be captured 'til seen on TV," wrote Lieutenant Colonel Cornum. "The International Red Cross called the U.S. with my name, when we were with them."

On the first day of her capture, she was in the back of an Iraqi truck with another U.S. soldier. "As a fellow American prisoner watched helplessly," wrote Elizabeth Gleick and Cindy Dampier in *People* magazine on August 10, 1992, "a guard unzipped Cornum's flight suit and attempted to rape her. When she screamed in pain as he jostled her broken arms, he resorted to manual penetration. Cornum, focused on her survival, told herself, 'Rhonda, nobody ever dies from pain, and you're not gonna.' "

"I was vaginally, rectally and manually violated," she told a Presidential Commission on the Assignment of Women in the Armed Forces at a hearing on June 8, 1992. "It was not life threatening. I'd have much rather they not displace my broken arm."

After a painful truck ride to Baghdad, she spent four days in a hospital, maintaining a spirit of bravery through her inner strength. Later, when the cease-fire took effect, she and other prisoners were moved to a hotel, where they were met by the International Red Cross and then returned to U.S. lines.

She was, fortunately, returned to the American side after just one week's captivity. When she got off the plane that brought her back to the coalition side, she walked down the steps with both arms in slings. General Schwarzkopf was there to meet her. When she saw him, she quipped, "I normally salute four-star generals."

Lieutenant Colonel Cornum is married to Maj. Kory Cornum, U.S. Air Force, a flight surgeon whom she met at the Uniformed Services University medical school in 1982. Both Rhonda and her husband served in the Gulf War. After she was released, she had a reunion with him aboard the *Mercy,* a navy hospital ship in the gulf. She plans to stay in the military as long as she can, whether or not combat positions are opened to women. "When my eyeballs go to crap and I can't bend my knees enough to get in an airplane, I'll probably quit flying," she said. "But until then, well, I don't see much changing."[11]

Meanwhile, recovering the bodies of the five men killed in the SAR UH-60 crash had to be delayed because of a dust storm on February 28. "On 1 March," according to Lieutenant Colonel Bryan, "a combat search and rescue mission was

213

executed to locate and retrieve the downed UH-60L crew, at which time five bodies were recovered. . . . Direct coordination was conducted with the 24th ID (Mech) to provide security and artillery fires in support of the mission."

General Shelton had high praise for the aviators who flew the causeway mission. On the evening of G+3, General Shelton went to the 101st Aviation Brigade's CP at FOB Viper to look at the gun camera films so that he could have some idea of the terrain in the area along the major highway north of Basra. The 101st Airborne still planned to launch a large air assault force there the next day. The film portrayed "a scene hard to describe," he said later. "It looked like a burned out village or a futuristic nuclear holocaust. Some vehicles were still flowing out of Basra and it was hard to tell if they were military or civilian." The more he viewed the films, the more he was impressed with the discipline of the pilots who had to make split-second decisions to fire. Was the target civilian or military?

"The front seat guy talked to the back seat guy and they had to decide whether or not to fire a Hellfire or 30mm on what could be civilian vehicles," he said later. "In one case, the pilots saw a truck carrying a load of cargo. The pilots discussed it on the spot. One was for and one against. The one 'for' won. After the attack, the truck blew up with a cloud of smoke soaring two hundred feet into the air. They had made the correct decision. The pilots were very compassionate, concerned, professional, competent and disciplined."[12]

The 101st Airborne had one more mission—to assist the 24th Infantry with AH-64 Apache air support in its area. The helicopters were launched at 4:30 A.M. on G+4, but with the announcement of the cease-fire, they were recalled to FOB Viper by 7:00 A.M.

General Schwarzkopf called General Powell on the evening of February 27, G+3. "Here's what I propose," he said. "I want the Air Force to keep bombing those convoys backed up at the Euphrates where the bridges are blown. I want to continue the ground attack tomorrow; drive to the sea and totally destroy everything in our path. That's the way we wrote the plan for Desert Storm, and on one more day we'll be done."[13]

But that one more day of combat was not to come.

Both President Bush and General Powell had secure red telephones directly connected to CENTCOM headquarters, 7,000 miles away. No dialing was necessary; they just had to pick up the phone, and it rang in Schwarzkopf's office. General Powell and Schwarzkopf spoke at least once a day during the six months of Desert Shield and Desert Storm; but the president had been reluctant to use his direct line to Schwarzkopf, saying that it was neither necessary nor proper to keep close tabs on the commander in the field.

During the day on G+4, however, the White House staff had been directly in touch with the CENTCOM commander. Bush was under pressure from the Arab members of the coalition, particularly Egypt and Saudi Arabia, to end the conflict. And in the United States, his administration was beginning to come under heavy criticism for the seemingly wanton destruction along the "Highway of Death"—the road out of Kuwait littered with thousands of wrecked Iraqi vehicles—whose scenes were repeatedly telecast to millions of concerned and deeply interested Americans.

On February 27, General Schwarzkopf held a press conference. He pointed out that it was not the coalition forces' intent to destroy Iraq. "When we were here," he said, pointing to the position of the 3d Brigade of the 101st Airborne in AO Eagle along Highway 8, "we were 150 miles from Bagdad. If it had been our intention to take Iraq, to overrun the country, we could have done it unopposed for all intents and purposes."

In actuality, earlier in the war, to give Schwarzkopf as many alternatives as possible, Gary Luck and his XVIII Airborne Corps staff had discussed informally a plan to attack Baghdad with the 82d Airborne, the 101st Airborne, the 24th Infantry, and the 3d ACR. They suggested dropping the 82d Airborne by parachute on one side of Baghdad, air assaulting the 101st Airborne to another, and attacking the heavy armored and other defenses of the city with the 24th Infantry and the 3d ACR. The XVIII Airborne Corps staff had even tried, unsuccessfully, to find the jump aircraft for the 82d Airborne's attack.

Generals Powell and Schwarzkopf had additional phone conversations on February 27th in which General Powell relayed to General Schwarzkopf the gist of the discussions going on in the Oval Office. Aides to the president wanted a cease-fire at 8:00 A.M., February 28, but, thinking no doubt about a "Hundred-Hour War," they suggested terminating hostilities at 5:00 A.M. and announcing a cease-fire at 8:00 A.M. When General Powell relayed that information to him, General Schwarzkopf replied, "I don't have any problem with it. Our objective was the destruction of the enemy forces, and for all intents and purposes, we've accomplished that objective. I'll check with my commanders, but unless they've hit some snag I don't know about, we can stop."[14]

Schwarzkopf called his major commanders. He told Gen. Chuck Horner to keep reloading his bombers but to make sure that they'd be able to stop at 5:00 A.M. Gen. John Yeosock, the army component commander, was told, "Until five o'clock it's business as usual. I encourage you to do as much damage as you can with your Apaches right up till then."

Then, he wrote, "I called Admiral [Stan] Arthur, General [Walt] Boomer, and Major General Wayne Downing, who was running the U.S. special operations deep behind enemy lines. Nobody seemed surprised that a cease-fire might be declared.

"A few hours later Powell called to confirm: 'We'll cease offensive operations, but there's been a change. The President will make his announcement at nine o'clock, but we won't actually stop until midnight (Washington time). That makes it a hundred-hour war.' I had to hand it to them: they really knew how to package an historic event.

"President Bush and Secretary Cheney each came on the line to offer congratulations. Finally Powell came back on and said, 'Okay, that's it. Cease fire at eight o'clock local tomorrow morning.' "[15]

In a televised address from the White House on the evening of February 27, 1991, President Bush announced, "Kuwait is liberated. Iraq's Army is defeated. Our military objectives are met. . . . [This] is a time of pride in our troops. . . . And soon we will open wide our arms to welcome back home to America our magnificent fighting forces."

215

Soldiers from 801st Maintenance Battalion redeploy from TAA Campbell to Camp Eagle II by C-130 after the ground offensive.

20 | Cease-fire

Through CENTCOM the word went out: Cease-fire at 5:00 A.M. local time.

Up in AO Eagle, the night of February 27, the Rakkasans continued their blockade of Highway 8. In his battalion TOC, Lieutenant Colonel Costello was waiting for the arrival of his XO, Maj. Bob Randle, and Task Force Randle, which included the remaining ground combat elements of the 3d Brigade. That night, Costello's artillery batteries launched a series of fire missions against Iraqi convoys on the highway.

"After the first couple of missions," he wrote, "things settled down for a while, and I went out to my vehicle to stretch out for a couple of hours before departing for the linkup with TF Randle. I had only been there for a few minutes when Dennis Murphy came out to see me. He had just gotten a call over the landline from MAJ [Carlos] Rodriguez in the brigade TOC. They had monitored a message over the TACSAT net, indicating a cease-fire would begin at 0500 [5:00 A.M.] local time. We looked at each other in a certain amount of disbelief, and I asked him: 'Do you suppose that's the end?' His answer was, 'I think so.' We sort of self-consciously shook hands, not quite willing to believe that it was going to be this easy. After that, I was in no mood for rest and went back to the TOC. Someone had his portable SW [shortwave] radio tuned to VOA [Voice of America], and we heard General Schwarzkopf's press briefing. At this point, we still knew very little about what was going on in the rest of the theatre, and listened, riveted, to his every word. We were thrilled when he talked about the forces poised 100 miles from Baghdad, knowing it was us to which he was referring, and were frustrated when he showed his casualty chart, but didn't brief any numbers, not knowing just how big a miracle he referred to.

At about 2300 [11:00 P.M.], I headed off to the rendezvous point, and waited for Bob Randle and his task force. They arrived right on schedule, dead tired, and we split A Battery off to occupy its position. I told CPT Kerry Straight that it was

217

imperative that he occupy and register as quickly as possible, but didn't tell him why. I did not want the battery to come all that way, by ground, after six months of training and waiting, only to not fire a shot. We were able to conduct a registration and fire a check round from each gun just before the cease-fire went into effect.[1]

The 3d Brigade, strung out along Highway 8 in AO Eagle, was faced with a problem unique to the division: the brigade was compelled to handle hundreds of refugees, both before and after the cease-fire.

"The Iraqi refugees were, at the start," wrote Major Chester, "not in too terribly bad shape. For the most part, they were trying to flee the regime. They had no compunction about Americans and were friendly. They did have great difficulty in understanding why we couldn't provide them more assistance. The best we could do was give a quick once over for major medical problems and get them on their way after they had been screened. With the start and subsequent collapse of the rebellion, that all changed drastically. The refugees began to flood out of the various cities retaken by the Republican Guard. Their condition was really pitiful. Starvation was in evidence and they were clearly terrified. We had them show up from areas as diverse as Kurdistan, Baghdad, Basra, and An Nasiriyah. A new surge would appear as each city fell. The proportion of wounded and injured grew to upwards of a third of the total. There were several cases I particularly remember. One little boy came through with a bayonet wound delivered by the RGFC as they retook Karbala. He was about 8, the only survivor of his family and clearly knew he was going to die. The look in his eyes was haunting—profound fear, pain, and lack of hope. The government forces seemed to kill all of the adults and maim the children horribly. Another boy about the same age came through with his genitalia burned beyond recognition. His four-year-old sister had had her eyes gouged out. They were both dying. One man was brought to a check point on a litter, shot through both knees and elbows. He had been forced to watch his wife and daughter being raped to death, his infant son swung against a wall until his head burst and his other child stuck to a pole with a bayonet through his belly. Others came through horribly burned, with fragmentation wounds, shot or terribly tortured.

"Many from Dirvaniyah had been beaten or burned with lengths of reinforcing bars. One man had his eyes, tongue, and ears hacked out and fingers cut off. Most of the wounds were badly infected and I still gag thinking about the smell of rotting injuries.

"The Kuwaiti refugees also ran the gamut from the fat cats and collaborators trying to sneak home to burned, tortured prisoners. Once the rebellion was in full swing, the resistance began to bring us Kuwaitis they sprang from prisons in droves. Thousands of Kuwaitis had been hauled to Iraq as prisoners or hostages. One group of air force people broke out of a prison and hijacked a bus to go south. They had all been imprisoned and tortured for the duration and bore terrible scars. The resistance brought in one group that had been in an underground facility and the entrance blasted shut. The resistance took a week to dig them out and were still trying to locate another group similarly treated. The litany of stories was incredible, and the Kuwaitis ecstatic. They universally ate themselves sick. . . .

"In general, when we identified Kuwaitis, we brought them back to the school-house in 'Chesterville' [compound in 3d Brigade area along Highway 8] while I arranged transport. . . . The Kuwaitis were shifted to division, then to a corps processing center of KKMC where they were handed off to the Saudis and Kuwaitis. We ran into real problems, since there were different levels of Kuwaiti citizenship, and Kuwait started its own version of ethnic cleansing.

"At the schoolhouse, we normally put the refugees up over night with a couple of CA [Civil Affairs] guys to play nursemaid. It drove them nuts, because the Kuwaitis would jabber and sing all night and talk endlessly between bouts of the runs from the MREs. All of us endured hundreds of hugs and kisses.

"I pulled schoolhouse duty once and left it to the CA guys after that. We had a family of Kuwaitis come in with a group. They had been famous actors in that part of the world and were taken as political prisoners. Though the kids didn't know it, their father had been executed and all of them tortured while the others watched. The mother was attractive, as was the daughter 15, and son, 12. I spent some time talking with them. . . . When we finally got them all settled down, I crawled under my poncho liner for some well deserved rest. The boy came over and squeezed in between one of the CA guys and me and crashed, in short order snatching both poncho liners. The next day, his mother said that it was the first night in six months he had not spent the night screaming and crying, and until they flew, he clung to the CA guy, holding his hand. It was that sort of thing, coupled with all of the work with the other refugees, that made me really feel good about what I was doing, amid all the frustration. I was one of the few who could build something amid the destruction.

"The other half of the Kuwaiti equation was the 'questionables' who showed up heading home. One guy drove up in a Mercedes, sleek, fat, and imperious. He claimed to be coming back from Iran, a crock, I'm sure. He tried to lord it over us and was bitching the whole time he was there. We had to fly him out, but the consensus was we all would like to have strangled him. Several of that sorry bunch showed up, claiming to be great patriots. They certainly didn't fall into the same category as those who had such torture as a coke bottle up the rectum or electrodes to the testicles performed on them."

After the cease-fire, the Rakkasans stayed in position along Highway 8 and continued to man their defenses and handle refugees. With the cease-fire, those Iraqis opposed to Saddam's brutal dictatorship started a rebellion. Major Chester was in a position to witness its beginning and aftermath.

"Essentially, the entire Euphrates valley and Kurdistan rose up just before the cease-fire. Iraq is an artificial entity, like all of the Middle Eastern countries, comprised of Shiites, Sunnis, Kurds, Christians. . . . Saddam's dictatorship had its power base in one Sunni tribe. The Shiite majority is dispossessed, and the Kurds persecuted. For three decades of secular control, the traditional emirate tribal leadership still existed in the shadows. Once all of the opposition felt Saddam's chips were down, they rose, only to be flushed out of the cities they had taken and exterminated. . . .

"As the rebellion occurred, the official U.S. policy was one of noninvolvement. . . . We were told 'Hands off.' This decision was in deference to the Saudis. . . . The Saudis had, and have, a dread fear of Shiite radicalism and decided that 'the devil they knew' was preferable to the devil they didn't know. . . . Even among the radical Shiite factions in Iraq, there is no desire for a theocracy or interest in allying with Iran. Hatred of the Persians runs too deep. The Shiite revolutionaries ran around with posters of an Iranian mullah, but this simply was a rallying point for their movement, since the mullah was the spiritual leader of that sect. All the revolutionaries wanted was to be free of Saddam and left alone. All of the leaders I spoke to seemed to want an elected national assembly under the leadership of a committee of the 16 traditional tribal leaders. Granted there would have been a period of chaos, but I think we missed a chance to create a stable country.

"As the rebellion grew, the leadership came repeatedly to our area to beg help and armed bands appeared constantly around the area. At one point, I was holding meetings with 13 of the 16 emirs, who wanted military, medical, and food assistance. They were upset, to say the least, when we told them we couldn't help. Higher headquarters refused to send anyone more qualified or higher ranking to deal with these people, though I now know that the requests I sent up got as far as ARCENT. The best I could do was keep sending up messages explaining the situation, and tell the rebels, 'I can't help, but I will tell my superiors.'

"After a few days, that didn't wash. The rebels brought Kuwaitis to us constantly, and sought antitank weapons, medical supplies and food. All the while, they would plead, 'Don't you understand? We want our freedom, like your revolution.' The rebels took out a good deal of hate on government officials in areas they took, exercising brutality on a scale that matched the government's, proudly carrying around body parts of officials they had killed. They took extra care in their treatment of the Muhaberatt, or secret police, they caught. One rebel proudly told me it took five days for one guy who ran the prison in An Najaf to die.

"The surviving RGFC troops were turned on the rebellion by Saddam after the cease-fire, and my job grew more difficult as the survivors fled in our direction. . . . Daily I met with groups who told of entire populations massacred. Casualties typically ran into the tens of thousands and every conventional weapon was used against the rebels. . . . The Iraqis made heavy use of WP and other flame weapons against the rebels. I saw plenty of evidence of that. When the rebellion completely collapsed in mid-March, we saw a lot of people who had cast their lot with the uprising trying to flee with nowhere to go. Again, I felt in a hopeless situation. All I could do was point them south. Several Iraqi Army units also switched sides, donning green armbands to signify which side they were on. We had several close calls after the cease-fire as these guys approached the perimeter, but we got the word down to squad level that these guys 'were on our side,' uniform notwith-standing. . . .

"The bottom line was that the 3d Brigade was dropped into a sea of chaos for a month."[2]

Maj. Gen. J. H. B. Peay III leads the 101st Airborne in the New York City victory parade.

21 | The Road Home

To the troopers of the 101st Airborne Division (Air Assault), who had been away from Fort Campbell for upwards of five months, the CEASE-FIRE (spelled in capital letters in their minds) meant one thing: HOME (and that was spelled in technicolor and neon lights). Home meant spouses, children, girlfriends, daily showers, clean uniforms, home-cooked meals, temperate climates, an occasional beer, a full night's uninterrupted sleep, a car, and ladies in American-style clothes. It meant an end to rain and sandstorms, torrid temperatures, MREs, daily consumption of gallons of water in plastic bottles, mud-filled holes, dust, Saudi non-waterproof tents, sand dunes, sandbags, camels, sheep, Bedouins, chemical warfare threats, Scud alerts, box latrines, slit trenches, hand-washed clothes in buckets or basins, irregular mail, long lines at rare telephones, scant goodies at mobile PXs, Iraqi soldiers with black mustaches, and noisy, bumpy flights in crammed helicopters. It meant, most of all, that going home—the "real world," the land of the big PX—was a definite possibility. But when?

"It always takes a lot longer to clean up than you think," said Lieutenant Colonel Kinnison, CO of 1-187th Infantry. "We got some more time here in this wonderful country sucking sand."

With the cease-fire, the division staff rapidly changed its posture and thinking. Offensive planning gave way to the defensive and then to withdrawal—pulling the division back from its forward locations, moving it to Camp Eagle II, and then redeploying it to the States.

Up on the Euphrates, the Rakkasans had to go into "idle" if not "reverse." "Our planning had already progressed to three possible follow-on objectives," remembered Major Chester. "North to just outside Baghdad, east to a bridge and choke point on the Tigris and southeast to seal the area north of Basra. Any of these would have caused some fierce fighting." The cease-fire halted that thinking and planning.[1]

After the cease-fire, "it was really a matter of waiting" for the Rakkasans along Highway 8, wrote Lieutenant Colonel Costello. "The cease-fire held, of course, and the POWs were returned on schedule. We were careful not to get too optimistic, knowing full well what the Iraqis were capable of and not trusting them for a minute. We were hard pressed to believe that they would be so thoroughly beaten so quickly and could not believe our good fortune in their failure to employ chemicals. There were a couple of false alarms and intel reports of imminent, surprise chemical attacks over the ensuing few days, but things remained peaceful."[2]

At FOB Viper on the day of the cease-fire, "we showed videotapes to General Shelton of some of our engagements," wrote Lieutenant Colonel Cody later, "to include the destruction of the SA-6 site. Colonel Garrett and Bill Bryan were working [over the] details on the recovery of the UH-60 and its crew and passengers. The mood around Viper was one of mixed emotions on the 28th. . . . We were all glad the fighting was over, but those of us in Aviation Brigade were saddened at the loss of life in the 2-229th. Colonel Garrett came to our TOC early in the morning and gave a moving 'thank you and well done' talk to our guys on duty. General Peay came by on 1 March to talk to me, my company commanders, and my staff. I can remember how we were all impressed with General Peay's detailed knowledge of the events over the past three days . . . down to Attack Company battles and missions. General Peay asked why we (the division) were successful from Cobra thru Viper. . . . We all answered it was teamwork.

"I think it is important to note that Generals Peay, Shelton, and Adams had forged together a solid team during the early months of Desert Shield. They were blessed with great young infantry commanders like Greco, Berdy, Kinnison, Benjamin, Donald, Hancock, Thomas and Bridges; artillery commanders like Lawson, Hartsell, and Costello; aviation commanders like Curran, Johnson, Adams, Brophy, Bryan, Wilmoth, and Hamlin; as well as VanAntwerp (Engineers), [Lt. Col. John] Carden, [Lt. Col. John] Broderick (DISCOM) . . . most of these lieutenant colonels had served consecutive tours in the division as XOs and S-3s together and I believe we all understood and trusted each other, understood the tactics, techniques, and procedures of 'Air Assault' and we all thoroughly understood the battle plan that Peay, Shelton, Adams, Bolt, Garrett and Hess had come up with.

"Brigade-sized air assaults are complex and potentially dangerous in peacetime. To pull one off in war and achieve full mission success you have to have the right combat mix, precision timing and navigation by pilots, flexible and redundant C[3]I and responsive logistics. By the time the division had secured Highway 8 along the Euphrates in AO Eagle, General Peay had a seasoned team that he could call to the line of scrimmage and call 'audibles' and move the division down the 'field' much like [Joe] Montana ran the [San Francisco] 49ers thru [sic] their 2-minute drills. From my perspective, that is what impressed me the most about the events of 26–27 February 91 and that is what makes the 101st such a powerful division . . . its ability to rapidly project combat power, over great distances, uninhibited by terrain."[3]

On March 12, the 3d Brigade actually packed up and moved out of AO Eagle and flew back to FOB Cobra. But the next day, General Peay received orders from General Luck to send the 3d Brigade back to the Euphrates area "to maintain a presence of force in support of the cease-fire negotiations." While the 3-187th Infantry remained at FOB Cobra, two battalions of the brigade—1-187th Infantry and 2-187th Infantry—helicoptered back to Eagle, spread out, and resumed their defensive positions. The Rakkasans had been gone only overnight, but when they returned to the same buildings they had left—the water purification plant and the electrical power plant—they found them completely trashed by the people in the area. Twelve days later, on March 24, the 2d Armored Cavalry Regiment rumbled into AO Eagle with their tanks and APCs and occupied the defensive positions created by the 3d Brigade.

Between March 25 and March 27, the Rakkasans moved their soldiers, vehicles, and equipment from AO Eagle back to the airport at Rafha. From Rafha, the 3d Brigade took C-130s back to KFIA and CE II. From March 28 to April 5, the 3d Brigade cleaned equipment and vehicles and prepared for deployment back to the real Campbell—Fort Campbell, Kentucky.

In FOB Viper, after the cease-fire, the 2d Brigade continued to collect and destroy enemy equipment. The remainder of the 2d Brigade flew in to FOB Viper from FOB Cobra, and the brigade's main body arrived with its vehicles overland.[4] In FOB Cobra, the 1st Brigade conducted defensive operations and prepared to move back to Camp Eagle II.

The first 101st Airborne troops to return home were 905 men from the 2d Brigade who, on March 6, flew out of FOB Viper to TAA Campbell. Two days later, they boarded commercial aircraft in Dhahran and flew to Fort Campbell via Frankfurt, Germany, and JFK International Airport in New York. The movement of those first troops was almost a spur-of-the-moment operation.

"Very hushed up, very hurried," remembered Colonel Purdom, the 2d Brigade commander.

> There were three flights from Frankfurt into JFK and the first indication I had [of the reception in the United States] was at JFK when basically the aircraft were met, as we taxied down the runway, by fire trucks, by police cars, sirens. We got into JFK International Airport and everybody was clapping and applauding, what have you. Then when we came back to Ft. Campbell, there's 1,000 people out there on the tarmac and the bands are playing and the flags are waving. It was an emotional experience that was very uplifting. The soldiers were glad to be home. Basically, that welcome was given to every aircraft that came in.
>
> We felt it from the cards and letters. We did not have CNN over there or the news media. The only thing that we had was BBC, Voice of America and then they would set up airborne stations where they could. What we were hearing

were the 0600 [6:00 A.M.] briefings at 1800 [6:00 P.M.]. From cards and letters we were told they'd never seen such 'pro-country behind you' attitude. You read that, but you can't really appreciate it until you get back here . . . very grateful for the job that was done and the overwhelming public, global, statewide, national support for the young persons . . . emotionally uplifting, to say the least.[5]

On March 4, the 2d Brigade received orders to move the rest of the brigade by air and ground from FOB Viper to TAA Campbell. The next day the movement began. Later, at TAA Campbell, the priorities for all of the division's units were accountability and equipment maintenance, checking to make certain that all equipment was present or accurately written off, and cleaning and reconditioning all gear—to extremely high sanitary and operational standards.

Another group of soldiers from the 2d Brigade arrived at Fort Campbell on March 31, Easter Sunday. Four commercial flights delivered 1,527 soldiers from 1-320th Field Artillery and another battalion of the 2d Brigade. This was the largest 101st Airborne contingent so far to come home from Saudi Arabia.

Meanwhile in Saudi Arabia, the troops found themselves working hard. General Peay said that in theater after the cease-fire, the division "cleared the war zone, washed vehicles, checked gear, and went through innumerable customs inspections. There were some real troop irritants . . . but the troops performed professionally because they were going home."[6]

Following the cease-fire, the 101st Aviation Brigade remained in position in FOB Cobra until it began redeploying to CE II on March 11. It closed in CE II on March 29. The redeployment route was the reverse of the routes used to deploy to TAA Campbell on 17 January, wrote Colonel Garrett. "The task of cleaning equipment and preparing stateside redeployment was accomplished at Camp Eagle II and then flown or driven to the port of Ad Dammam for loading onto ships. The first personnel from the brigade began redeployment to Fort Campbell on 2 April with the brigade closing on 15 April 91. The brigade's equipment was shipped to the port of Jacksonville FL from where the brigade off-loaded, reassembled, and flew all aircraft to Ft. Campbell. Aviation operations at Jacksonville port were conducted from 1 May to 15 June 1991. Vehicles and containers were off-loaded and rail-loaded to Ft. Campbell."[7]

The 101st's Division Support Command was the power behind the division's combat elements while they were deployed over such a vast area in Southwest Asia during the combat phase. In fact, the 101st's last element in Iraq, a convoy for DISCOM, returned to Saudi Arabia at 12:35 A.M. on March 25.

The 426th Supply and Transportation Battalion, commanded by Lt. Col. John Broderick, deployed its 812 troops, issued nearly 4 million gallons of Jet-A-1 fuel and 10 million meals, purified more than 500,000 gallons of water, and passed out an unknown quantity of bottled water. The 426th Supply also executed more than 500 sling loads while the 53d Quartermaster airdropped 300 short tons of supplies to the troops in the forward areas. The men in D Company drove their trucks nearly 95,000 miles during the ground war alone. The 63d and 761st Chemical companies performed numerous decon and smoke training missions.

The 101st's Corps Support Group was commanded by Col. Roy E. Beauchamp. It supplied services and support to the division all the way from Ad Dammam to the Euphrates and back home again. "The Support Group," said General Peay, "was always within earshot and gave us superb logistics backup."

"Operation Desert Shield/Storm brought about many inventions, innovations and firsts in the support field," wrote Col. Stuart W. Gerald, the 101st's DISCOM commander.

> The sling loads of 10,000-gallon fuel bags with 200 gallons of fuel revolutionized the concept of fuel support in the air assault environment. The 101st Personnel Service Company developed a totally automated casualty reporting system that eliminated over 70% of the keystrokes needed to prepare a casualty report. Medical personnel became instantly familiar with rarely seen ailments like camel spider and sand viper bites as well as their share of scorpion stings, dysentery and heat injuries. The threat of Scud missiles or the Iraqi Air Force delivering chemical warheads put an emphasis on chemical survivability and made it one of the primary training objectives.
>
> The Division Support Command returned to CE II and prepared to redeploy to Campbell. Soldiers redeployed to CE II by convoy and C-130. Each battalion cleaned and packed equipment with untold deliberance [sic]. The Division Comptroller developed a plan for cleaning vehicles prior to redeployment. The Facility Engineers coordinated with the Bechtel contractors to construct a large vehicle wash point in addition to the small one they had built already.[8]

Cleaning and steaming the vehicles and equipment went on twenty-four hours a day. The inspections were "white glove standards," said General Peay after the war. "It was very difficult and time-consuming work but the troops worked hard because they were going home. To keep up the morale of the troops who were working so hard, the division moved in hamburger stands and other conveniences at the wash-up sites."[9]

A rear detachment was established to clear CE II and supervise the DISCOM's loading and shipping. The DISCOM began redeploying on March 29, and the majority of the personnel had returned by April 15. A DISCOM memo said: "Redeployment of equipment was a major undertaking both in Saudi Arabia and at Fort Campbell. The equipment was moved by sea to the port of Jacksonville. Once in Jacksonville, the equipment was off-loaded and placed on trains or line haul trucks to be transported to Fort Campbell. MCC [Movement Control Center] and DTO [division transportation officer] tracked the arrival of equipment and notified units for pick up. Reserve units handled the actual loading and unloading of vehicles. Military containers were transported with the equipment. Much of the division's MTOE items were placed in civilian containers and shipped by the civilian contractor."[10]

In late March, General Schwarzkopf made a visit to the 101st Airborne at CE II as it prepared to redeploy. General Peay assembled all the battalion and brigade commanders, sergeants major, and the division staff in a room in the water treatment plant that he had used as division headquarters. "It was crowded," Lieutenant Colonel Cody remembered. After being briefed on the division's combat operations, General Schwarzkopf made a speech to the assembled 101st commanders.[11]

Lieutenant Colonel Riccardelli, CO of the 311th Military Intelligence Battalion, was also present at the briefing. Later, he reminisced about the occasion: General Schwarzkopf "is a dynamic figure . . . bigger than life. As he listened to our briefing of combat operations, he said that when he spoke to the world about the 'thunder and lightning' of the coalition forces' ground attack on the Iraqi Army, the tanks of the divisions and aircraft were the thunder of Desert Storm and the 101st was the lightning in the Storm."[12]

After General Schwarzkopf's talk to the division's senior officers and NCOs, General Peay led him to the center of the tent city at CE II, where the bulk of the division had lined up. After brief ceremonies, General Schwarzkopf pinned medals on six troopers who had earned combat citations.

The bulk of the 101st Airborne returned to Fort Campbell Army Airfield on civilian aircraft between April 3 and 15, 1991. Every flight landing at Fort Campbell was met by Ms. Carol South, secretary for the Association of the U.S. Army, and Mrs. T. C. Freeman, the wife of a colonel who had retired in the Fort Campbell area. They helped the unmarried soldiers find telephones and assisted them in any way they could while the married soldiers spent twenty minutes in a hangar with their families. Then, with a National Guard band playing, all the troops moved to buses for a ride to their troop area. There they turned in their weapons, gas masks, and other issued equipment and got ready for two weeks' leave. Those who had left their cars at Fort Campbell made their way to the parking lot and tried to start them after eight months.[13]

A contingent under General Adams, the assistant division commander for support (ADC/S), had remained at CE II to move the division's equipment to the port. Thus, the last 101st Airborne soldier to leave Saudi Arabia departed on May 1, 1991.

At 2:10 P.M. on April 13, General Peay and some four hundred 101st troopers arrived at Fort Campbell Army Airfield aboard a Boeing 747. The return of the colors marked the symbolic return of the 101st Airborne to Fort Campbell.

"A joyful crowd of family members and guests cheered the desert-weary troops as they stepped off the plane," wrote Bettina Tilson of the *Leaf-Chronicle*. "The sea of colorful homemade banners, flags, and balloons were in sharp contrast to the 'chocolate chip' brown desert uniforms of the soldiers as the two groups stood facing one another, anxious for the ceremony to end so they could be reunited."

Among those welcoming the troops home were Gen. Edwin H. Burba, Jr., the commander in chief of Forces Command; Senators Jim Sasser and Wendell J. Ford; and many local officials.

"Last August upon our rapid deployment, I wrote you that the Eagle was in full flight," General Peay told the crowd. "Today the Eagle has officially returned to his nest as represented by these splendid soldiers and the division colors. . . . The soldiers of the 101st returned desert-hardened, broader, wiser and more mature." He mentioned that more than 1,000 sorties were flown by his 270 helicopters during the massive, history-making air assault into Iraq.[14]

In a postwar interview with Peay—now a four-star general and the Army's vice chief of staff—he said that he felt the greatest successes of the 101st were, first, an "ability to gain operational positioning and to go deep and cut the Iraqi line of communications at the Euphrates. It bothered the enemy psychologically that the division could go so far so fast and so deep." Coupled with that was the division's rapid move into FOB Viper and launching the four attack helicopter battalions on the bottleneck at the causeway north of Basra. A second success, he said, was the ability to "operate the division in a covering role during the first six months of the campaign in an area the size of the state of Montana."

One of his disappointments was that the division was not called upon to exploit its deep penetration of Iraq and air assault near Baghdad.

He felt that his major accomplishments were twofold. The first was the establishment of Camp Eagle II during the covering force mission. Camp Eagle II was designed and developed so that it could maintain people in Saudi Arabia's harsh environment. It was a far superior camp to some of the others established by American units in Saudi Arabia, and the division spent almost eight months in and out of it.

His other major accomplishment, he felt, was his ability to read the intelligence correctly, to know the enemy, and to know how much risk to take. He got a gut feel for the enemy by interviewing the first EPWs captured and deciding that the bulk of the Iraqis did not want to fight. "This allowed the division to take increasing risks," he said later, "and project itself in three days over distances from Tennessee to Boston."

General Peay was proud of his soldiers. He saw their morale reflected in the manner in which they saluted proudly and gave the 101st's slogan, "Air Assault," as they did so. "They made history just like the great veterans and alumni of this division who marched before them," he said after the war.[15]

The air assault concept, developed and nurtured over the years by some of the U.S. Army's top tacticians, was put to the test in Desert Storm. The 101st's bold, deep, rapid flights into the enemy's rear proved the concept's validity. Given the chance, the division could have done more. It was loaded and ready. And, as Saddam discovered, lightning can strike unexpectedly anywhere in a vast area.

Appendix

Gulf Lingo

All wars spawn a plethora of euphemisms, abbreviations, and expressions. The Gulf War was no exception. The "sandspeak" included the following definitions, some old, some new.

Baghdad Betty	Iraqi female disk jockey who became a favorite among the troops
BCD	Big chicken dinner, or bad conduct discharge
BCDs	Birth control devices, or another term for BCGs
BCGs	Birth control glasses, or unsightly military glasses
Big Red	The desert sun
BMOs	Black moving objects, or Saudi women, heavily veiled and dressed in traditional black *abayeh,* an outer garment worn by men and women—black for women; black, brown, or white for men
Bob	Bedouins and any Iraqi; also used as an adjective to describe Saudi property—*Bob* car and *Bob* clothes, for example
Bolo Badge	Purple Heart; more specifically, one gained in a foolhardy fashion and awarded posthumously. Also used as a verb, as in "If you messed up this bad, you *boloed* too much."
Bone domes	Helmets
Bovine scatology	Not widely used but known as CINCENT's euphemism for BS
Buff	Big ugly fat fellow, or a B-52. As the soldiers used to say, the B-52 is "the most accurate weapon we have—its bombs always hit the ground."

Camel meat	An unappetizing entree
CNX	Pronounced "Cank," it's short for the verb to cancel, as in "waiting for the war to be *canked.*"
Cold, cold smoked the bitch	Pilot's report of shooting down an Iraqi plane
Desert Shield	Anything that protects a soldier from the blowing sand
Diver	The nickname for CNN's Charles Jaco for his Olympic-quality dives off camera during Scud alerts
Dog him out	To chide or find fault with
Echelons beyond reality	Command decisions
Emerald City	King Khalid Military City
Eskon Village	Quarters for troops stationed in Riyadh. The term was used by soldiers as a derogatory expression for a marble-floored paradise.
Face-shot	Air-to-air missile fired on an enemy aircraft, also called "in the lips."
Fast movers	High-performance jet aircraft
Frogfoot	An Iraqi attack plane. It is the North Atlantic Treaty Organization's designation for Soviet A-10-like aircraft.
Furballs	Air-to-air combat
Get your gut right	To eat. Soldiers also used to say "take it in the face."
Golden BBs	Iraqi antiaircraft artillery; usually referred to derisively by U.S. pilots.
Good grab	Any delectable Bedouin culinary treat
Good to go	Ready to perform admirably
Grease	Food
Hajji hose	Mystical hose located in every latrine
Heat tab, Nature's	The hot desert sun
Homers	Iraqi leaders. Apparently, the term was derived from Homer Simpson, the father in the TV situation comedy *The Simpsons.*
Hoo-ah	Also, *U-rah! Ooh rah!* Widely used yell to express approval.
Humma	Et cetera
JIB rat	A trooper or correspondent sitting out the war at Dhahran International Hotel's Joint Information Bureau
Joe	Any U.S. soldier
Johnny Weissmuller shower	A frontline shower so cold it induces a Tarzan-like yell
KSA	Kingdom of Saudi Arabia
Little Hollywood	The back veranda of the Dhahran International Hotel where four major U.S. networks set up a stage

	for their live shots. Blue cabana domes completed the stage.
MOPP, To go	To go from one of the four stages of MOPP. *MOPP4* is full anti–nuclear-biological-chemical warfare gear: rubber gloves and boots, charcoal-lined pants and jacket, and the ever-present gas mask.
Morality Police	Muslims who keep other Muslims in line spiritually, reportedly, by stoning or beating them
Mother of all. . .	Derived from Saddam's prewar, boastful statement that his troops would defeat the coalition in the "Mother of All Battles," the troops used the term as a descriptive phrase in many contexts, as in "I have the *mother of all* backaches."
MORE	Meals, organizational, ready to eat. Off-the-shelf items introduced by the army to supplement the existing supply of field rations.
MREs	These meals were also known as *meals, rejected by everyone* or *meals, rejected by Ethiopians*.
Ninja women	Arab women in their *abeyahs*
Nittenoid	Petty detail or one who is obsessed with petty details
Nuclear coffee	A mixture of a half cup of hot water and the instant coffee, cocoa, cream, and sugar from an accessory packet in the MRE
Patriot baiters	TV correspondents in Little Hollywood during Scud alerts
Pogue	Anyone who got there after you did
Prayer Patrol	Saudi sound trucks that wander through the city streets and announce prayers five times daily
PUNTS	A British term for people of utterly no tactical significance
Q-8	Kuwait
Quick-turn burn	Also *hot turn*, it refers to reloading and refueling an F/A-18 fighter in five minutes for a quick return for yet another sortie during the days of the multiple air strikes.
Rambo rag	Bandanna
Ree	Meal, ready to eat
Rumint	Intelligence derived from rumors
Rumor control	The official source of rumors
Sammy	Saddam (means "bumper" in Arabic) Hussein
Sand-biter	Any trooper who wasn't a pogue or pilot
Saudi champagne	Sprite or 7-Up and apple juice
Scud	A verb meaning to give someone a big bashing
Scud-a-vision	CNN

Scud Bowl	Also known as King Abdul Aziz Naval Air Station, it was a rarely used soccer stadium north of Port Al Jubayl. The U.S. Marines used it as an OV-10 Bronco and AV-8B Harrier base. (They called it "Paradise," said one marine, until officers and pogues moved in and started putting up signs reading "Officers' Head" or "Pogues' Head.")
Scud buster	Patriot missile
Scudded	Drunk. (One trooper said, "Ain't no such thing in Saudi Arabia.")
Scudinavia	Israeli name for the area in western Iraq from which the Iraqis launched Scuds toward Israel
Scud magnet	Dhahran
Scud stud	Arthur Kent, the handsome television newsman who had great appeal to the females in the States
Snake	AH-1F Cobra attack helicopter
Spammed	Also, *jiffed;* a British term for having been given an unpleasant task
Spot	Also, *Fido;* an average name for a pet scorpion
Spud	Another term for a Scud
Squiggles	Arabic writing, especially on highway signs, as in "only 20 kilometers to *Squiggles.*"
Ts	Tray pack rations
Target-rich environment	Iraq and Kuwait
Tango uniform	Out of action, unable to perform
Tragic kingdom	Saudi Arabia
T,R, double E	"A way to weed out the pogues from the dust-biters," reported one marine. "A dust-biter would ask a pogue if he ever set up a T, R, double E—referring to an antenna—and the pogue would almost always say 'Yes.' Then the hard-charger would reply, 'Stick to pushing papers—there aren't any trees in the desert.'"
Tree head	Special Forces soldier
Weenie	Any individual farther to the rear than the speaker
Woofing	Also, *woof-woof*, or talking without saying anything
Zoom bag	Flight suit

Notes

1. The U.S. Path to Battle

1. Ann McDaniel, "This Will Not Stand," *Newsweek*, Commemorative Edition (Spring/Summer 1991), p. 49.
2. Bob Woodward, *The Commanders* (New York: Simon & Schuster, 1991), p. 206.
3. Editors of *Time, Desert Storm: The War in the Persian Gulf* (New York: Time-Warner Publishing, Inc., 1991), p. 19.
4. Ibid., pp. 20–21.
5. Tom Mathews, "The Path to War," *Newsweek*, Commemorative Edition (Spring/Summer 1991), p. 36.
6. Woodward, *The Commanders*, p. 213.
7. Editors of *Time, Desert Storm*, p. 15.
8. Mathews, "The Path to War," pp. 35–36.
9. Editors of *U.S. News and World Report, Triumph Without Victory* (New York: Times Books, Random House, 1992), pp. 17–18.
10. Editors of *Time, Desert Storm*, p. 19.
11. Editors of *U.S. News, Triumph Without Victory*, p. 19.
12. Mathews, "The Path to War," p. 36.

2. Iraq's Invasion of Kuwait

1. Walter Lang was a Virginia Military Institute (VMI) classmate of Gen. J. H. Binford Peay III, commanding general of the 101st Airborne Division (Air Assault).
2. Woodward, *The Commanders*, pp. 216–17.
3. Ibid., pp. 204–17.
4. Mathews, "The Path to War," p. 38.
5. Woodward, The Commanders, pp. 219–21.
6. Mathews, "The Path to War," p. 38.

3. A Line in the Sand

1. Woodward, *The Commanders*, p. 222.
2. Personal knowledge. Lt. Gen. Tom Kelly was a tank battalion commander in the 1st Infantry Division when I was the division commander.
3. Woodward, *The Commanders*, pp. 225.
4. Ibid.

5. Ibid., pp. 225–29.
6. Mathews, "The Path to War," p. 38.
7. Editors of *Time, Desert Storm*, p. 22.
8. Editors of *U.S. News, Triumph Without Victory*, pp. 61–64.
9. Woodward, *The Commanders*, pp. 242–45.
10. Editors of *U.S. News, Triumph Without Victory*, pp. 67–69.
11. Woodward, *The Commanders*, 267–73.
12. Mathews, "The Path to War," p. 42.

4. Fort Campbell: Summer 1990

1. Personal knowledge and Sean D. Naylor, "Flight of Eagles," *Army Times*, July 22, 1991, p. 8.
2. Personal interview with Lt. Gen. Henry H. ("Hugh") Shelton, Fort Bragg, N.C., August 30, 1991.
3. Editors of *U.S. News, Triumph Without Victory*, pp. 28–29.
4. Tom Donnelly, "From the Top," *Army Times*, February 24, 1992, p. 8.
5. Gen. J. H. Binford Peay Interview, *Army Times*, April 15, 1992, unpublished.
6. Cornelius Ryan, *A Bridge Too Far* (New York: Simon & Schuster, 1974), pp. 187–90.
7. Gerard M. Devlin, *Paratrooper* (New York: St. Martin's Press, 1979), pp. 528–31.
8. Personal interview with Col. James Bradin, July 14, 1993.
9. Lt. Gen. Jack V. Mackmull, letter to author, July 18, 1993.
10. *101st Airborne Division: U.S. Airborne 50th Anniversary Book* (Paducah, Ky.: Turner Publishing Co., 1990), pp. 217–18.
11. Gen. J. H. Binford Peay's comments on the draft manuscript for *The Lightning in the Storm*, July 11, 1993.
12. Col. William J. Bolt, "Command Report: 101st Airborne Division (Air Assault) for Operation Desert Shield and Desert Storm, 2 August 1990 through 1 May 1991," dated July 1, 1991, pp. B1–B3.

5. Reassembly and Preparations at Fort Campbell

1. Personal interview with Brigadier General Shelton.
2. *North to the Euphrates: 101st Airborne Division (in) Operations Desert Shield and Desert Storm* (Clarksville, Tenn.: Tennessee-Kentucky Chapter of the Association of the U.S. Army [AUSA], 1991), p. 18.
3. Col. Tom Hill Interview, *Army Times*, April 15, 1992, unpublished.
4. Sean D. Naylor, "Flight of Eagles," *Army Times*, July 22, 1992, p. 8.
5. Personal interview with General Shelton.
6. General Peay Interview, *Army Times*.
7. Naylor, "Flight of Eagles," p. 8.
8. Personal interview with General Shelton.
9. Ibid.
10. Personal interview with Maj. Gen. Edison E. Scholes, Fort Bragg, N.C., November 4, 1992.
11. Donnelly, "From the Top," p. 11.
12. Personal interview with General Shelton.
13. Ibid.
14. General Peay's comments on draft manuscript.

6. Deployment from Fort Campbell

1. Cpt. Ida M. McGrath, Desert Shield manuscript, August 7, 1990, to January 15, 1991, undated, p. 1.
2. Ibid., p. 7.
3. Colonel Hill Interview, *Army Times*.
4. McGrath, Desert Shield manuscript, p. 8.
5. Naylor, "Flight of Eagles," p. 10.

6. Bolt, "Command Report," p. 6.
7. Lt. Col. William W. Bryan, Memo for Record, Subject: Operations Desert Shield and Desert Storm After-Action Report, 2-229th Attack Helicopter Regiment (AHR), July 19, 1991, pp. 1–2.
8. Bolt, "Command Report," p. 3.
9. McGrath, Desert Shield manuscript, p. 13.
10. Ibid., p. 12.
11. Unsigned letter from unidentified soldier of the 101st Division.

7. Camp Eagle II

1. Personal interview with General Shelton.
2. Ibid.
3. Bolt, "Command Report," p. 6.
4. *North to the Euphrates*, pp. 24–28.
5. Ibid., p. 26.
6. McGrath, Desert Shield manuscript.
7. Ibid., p. 7.
8. Colonel Hill Interview, *Army Times*.
9. Lt. Col. Russell E. Adams, Memo to the Commander of 101st Aviation Regiment, November 1, 1991.
10. *North to the Euphrates*, p. 26.
11. McGrath, Desert Shield manuscript, Part B, p. 5.
12. *North to the Euphrates*, p. 26.

8. Tactical Operations

1. McGrath, Desert Shield manuscript, pp. 20–21.
2. Personal interviews with General Peay at Fort Bragg, N.C., July 7, 1993, and General Shelton.
3. General Peay's biographical sketch, which he sent to me.
4. G-3 Staff Document, "Air Assault Division and Brigade Operations Manual," August 1988.
5. Col. Thomas W. Garrett Interview, *Army Times*, April 15, 1992, unpublished.
6. Donnelly, "From the Top," p. 24.

9. Covering Force

1. Mathews, "The Path to War," p. 38.
2. Editors of *U.S. News, Triumph Without Victory*, p. 40.
3. Woodward, *The Commanders*, pp. 248–49.
4. Naylor, "Flight of Eagles," p. 10.
5. Bolt, "Command Report," p. 13.
6. Lt. Gen. Gary Luck's biographical sketch, which was sent to me by his office.
7. Bolt, "Command Report," p. 12.
8. General Peay Interview, *Army Times*.
9. Col. Emmitt Gibson, letter to author, August 22, 1993.
10. Naylor, "Flight of Eagles," p. 10.
11. *North to the Euphrates*, p. 34.
12. Colonel Hill Interview, *Army Times*.
13. General Peay Interview, *Army Times*.
14. Bolt, "Command Report," p. 11.
15. Ibid., pp. 18–20.
16. Ibid., p. 15.
17. Naylor, "Flight of Eagles," p. 10.
18. *North to the Euphrates*, p. 44.
19. Ibid.

20. Naylor, "Flight of Eagles," p. 11.
21. Personal interview with General Peay, July 7, 1993.
22. *North to the Euphrates*, pp. 44–45.
23. Naylor, "Flight of Eagles," p. 11.
24. Ibid.
25. Col. Robert Clark Interview, *Army Times*, April 15, 1992, unpublished.
26. Personal interview with General Peay, July 7, 1993.
27. Woodward, *The Commanders*, p. 343.
28. Bolt, "Command Report," p. 17.
29. General Peay Interview, *Army Times*.
30. Colonel Hill Interview, *Army Times*.

10. Leaning Forward

1. Editors of *U.S. News, Triumph Without Victory*, pp. 36–39.
2. Mathews, "The Path to War," pp. 41–42.
3. Telephone conversation with Gen. George Crist, September 22, 1992.
4. Tom Donnelly, "The Generals' War," *Army Times*, March 2, 1992, p. 12.
5. Woodward, *The Commanders*, pp. 304–309.
6. Donnelly, "The Generals' War."
7. Mathews, "The Path to War," pp. 45–46.
8. Donnelly, "From the Top," p. 24.
9. Woodward, *The Commanders*, p. 369.
10. Donnelly, "The Generals' War," p. 12.
11. Ibid., p. 15.
12. Woodward, *The Commanders*, p. 335.
13. Ibid., p. 324.
14. Ibid., p. 362.
15. Editors of *U.S. News, Triumph Without Victory*, pp. 203–205.
16. Woodward, *The Commanders*, p. 361.
17. *Special Report: The U.S. Army in Desert Storm* (Arlington, Va.: AUSA, 1991), p. 9.

11. Shift to the Offensive

1. Woodward, *The Commanders*, pp. 347–48.
2. Personal interview with Lt. Col. Terry Peck, Fort Bragg, N.C., November 4, 1992.
3. Gen. H. Norman Schwarzkopf, *It Doesn't Take a Hero* (New York: Bantam Books, 1992), p. 354.
4. Lt. Gen. William G. Pagonis and Michael D. Krause, "Operational Logistics and the Gulf War" (Arlington, Va.: Institute of Land Warfare, AUSA, 1992), p. 8.
5. Telephone conversation with Maj. Gen. LeRoy Suddath, retired, September 17, 1992.
6. Schwarzkopf, *It Doesn't Take a Hero*, p. 422.
7. Personal interview with General Peay, July 7, 1993.
8. Lt. Col. Terry Peck, letter to author, October 27, 1992.
9. Ibid.
10. Pagonis and Krause, "Operational Logistics," p. 9.
11. Personal interview with General Peay, July 7, 1993.
12. Bolt, "Command Report," p. 19.
13. General Peay Interview, *Army Times*.
14. Naylor, "Flight of Eagles," p. 11.
15. Bolt, "Command Report," pp. 20–21.
16. Naylor, "Flight of Eagles," p. 11.
17. General Peay Interview, *Army Times*.
18. Lt. Gen. Henry Shelton, letter to author, October 10, 1992.
19. Colonel Clark Interview, *Army Times*.

20. Col. Tom Purdom Interview, *Army Times*, April 15, 1992, unpublished.
21. Ibid.
22. Editors of *Time, Desert Storm*, p. 34.

12. The First Shots of the War

Lt. Col. Richard A. Cody, the commander of the 1st Battalion of the 101st Aviation Regiment during Desert Shield and Desert Storm, reviewed this chapter in its entirety. All of his comments and corrections have been included.

1. 1st Lt. Thomas R. Drew, letter to author, October 18, 1992.
2. Colonel Clark Interview, *Army Times*.
3. Rob Dollar, untitled article, *North to the Euphrates: 101st Airborne Division (in) Operations Desert Shield and Desert Storm* (Clarksville, Tenn.: Tennessee-Kentucky Chapter of AUSA, 1991), p. 58.
4. Richard Mackenzie, "Apache Attack," *Air Force Magazine* (October 1991): 3.
5. Kyle Davis, "Commander Cody and the 1-101st: Out with a Bang," *Apache* (October 1991):4–5.
6. Dollar, untitled, *North to the Euphrates*, p. 58.
7. Mackenzie, "Apache Attack," p. 4.
8. Lt. Col. Richard A. Cody, letter to author, November 19, 1992.
9. Bettina Tilson, "It Begins," *Leaf-Chronicle Supplement*, Clarksville, Tenn., January 16, 1992, p. 2.
10. Lt. Col. Richard A. Cody's review and comments on this chapter, October 12, 1992.
11. Mackenzie, "Apache Attack," p. 4.
12. Drew, letter to author.
13. Cody's comments on this chapter.
14. Tilson, "It Begins," p. 2.
15. Drew, letter to author.
16. Mackenzie, "Apache Attack," p. 4.
17. Ibid.
18. Drew, letter to author.
19. Mackenzie, "Apache Attack," p. 4.
20. Cody's comments on draft manuscript.
21. Lt. Col. Richard A. Cody, "Task Force Normandy," *Defense Helicopter* (Spring Supplement 1992): 9.
22. Mackenzie, "Apache Attack," p. 3.
23. Ibid.
24. Drew, letter to author.
25. Ibid.
26. Cody's comments on draft manuscript.
27. Drew, letter to author.
28. Cody's comments on draft manuscript.
29. Drew, letter to author.
30. Naylor, "Flight of Eagles," p. 11.
31. Drew, letter to author.
32. Naylor, "Flight of Eagles," p. 11.
33. Drew, letter to author.
34. Cody, "Task Force Normandy," p. 11.
35. Drew, letter to author.
36. Dollar, untitled, *North to the Euphrates*, p. 58.
37. Drew, letter to author.
38. Tilson, "It Begins," p. 2.
39. Mackenzie, "Apache Attack," p. 7.

40. Ibid., p. 8.
41. Ibid.
42. Naylor, "Flight of Eagles," p. 12.
43. Mackenzie, "Apache Attack," p. 8.
44. Drew, letter to author.
45. Cody, "Task Force Normandy," p. 11.
46. Dollar, untitled, *North to the Euphrates*, p. 58.
47. Tilson, "It Begins," p. 2.

13. The Move Northwest

1. Editors of *Time, Desert Storm*, p. 63.
2. Lt. Col. Thomas J. Costello, letter to author, February 23, 1992.
3. Lt. Gen. Henry H. Shelton, letter to author, November 22, 1992.
4. Costello, letter to author.
5. Ibid.
6. Pagonis and Krause, "Operational Logistics," pp. 9–10.
7. XVIII Airborne Corps Staff, "Repositioning of XVIII Airborne Corps," Fort Bragg, N.C., undated.
8. Col. Stuart W. Gerald, Memo, Subject: DISCOM Desert Shield/Desert Storm Historical Summary, May 30, 1991.
9. Bolt, "Command Report," p. 28.
10. Costello, letter to author.
11. Bolt, "Command Report," p. 29.
12. General Shelton, letter to author, November 22, 1992.
13. Bolt, "Command Report," p. 30.
14. Costello, letter to author.

14. TAA Campbell to FOB Cobra

1. Pagonis and Krause, "Operational Logistics," pp. 10–11.
2. Bolt, "Command Report," pp. 31–32.
3. Costello, letter to author.
4. Bolt, "Command Report," pp. 33–34.
5. Maj. Steve Chester, letter to author, March 19, 1993.
6. Lt. Col. John Hamlin Interview, *Army Times*, April 15, 1992, unpublished.
7. Col. Thomas W. Garrett, Memo for Commander, 101st Airborne Division, Subject: Executive Summary—Operation Desert Shield/Desert Storm, June 10, 1991, p. 6.
8. Ibid.
9. Bryan, Memo for Record, 2-229th AHR.
10. Garrett, Memo for Commander, p. 7.
11. Lieutenant Colonel Hamlin Interview, *Army Times*.
12. Bolt, "Command Report," p. 39.
13. Ibid., p. 37.
14. Garrett, Memo for Commander, pp. 7–8.
15. Ibid., p. 8.
16. Bolt, "Command Report," p. 43.
17. Lt. Col. Richard F. Riccardelli, speech to 736th Tank Battalion, Nashville, Tenn., September 12, 1991.
18. Lieutenant Colonel Hamlin Interview, *Army Times*.
19. Naylor, "Flight of Eagles," p. 12.
20. General Peay Interview, *Army Times*.
21. Naylor, "Flight of Eagles," p. 12.

15.   The Launch into FOB Cobra

1. Lieutenant Colonel Hamlin Interview, *Army Times*.
2. Bolt, "Command Report," pp. 49–50.
3. Col. Tom Hill, commander, 1st Brigade, 101st Airborne Division, Memo for Record, "1st Brigade Assault on FOB Cobra," Camp Eagle II, Saudi Arabia, March 2, 1991, p. 1.
4. Ibid., p. 2.
5. Dennis Steele, "150 Miles into Iraq: The 101st Strikes Deep," *Army* (August 1991): 30.
6. Hill, Memo for Record, p. 2.
7. Naylor, "Flight of Eagles," p. 14.
8. Hill, Memo for Record, p. 2.
9. Naylor, "Flight of Eagles," p. 14.
10. Garrett, Memo for Commander, p. 9.
11. Lt. Col. Frank Hancock, Narrative of 1-327th Infantry in Desert Shield/Desert Storm, Fort Campbell, Ky., undated, p. 4.
12. Hill, Memo for Record, p. 3.
13. Colonel Purdom Interview, *Army Times*.
14. Bolt, "Command Report," p. 51.

16.   On to the Euphrates

1. Peay's comments on draft manuscript.
2. Colonel Clark interview, *Army Times*.
3. Personal knowledge. I commanded the 674th Airborne Field Artillery Battalion of the 187th Airborne Regimental Combat Team in Korea and Japan from 1953 to 1954.
4. Costello, letter to author.
5. Lt. Col. Peter C. Kinney, letter to author, April 11, 1993.
6. Editors of *U.S. News, Triumph Without Victory*, pp. 376–77.
7. Bolt, "Command Report," p. 52.
8. Colonel Clark interview, *Army Times*.
9. Personal interview with General Peay, July 7, 1993.
10. Ibid.
11. Costello, letter to author.
12. Colonel Clark Interview, *Army Times*.
13. Chester, letter to author.
14. Naylor, "Flight of Eagles," p. 14.
15. Ibid.
16. Steele, "150 Miles into Iraq," p. 34.
17. Kinney, letter to author.
18. Costello, letter to author.
19. Editors of *U.S. News, Triumph Without Victory*, p. 328.
20. Bolt, "Command Report," p. 55.
21. Peay's comments on draft manuscript, p. 309.

17.   Storm Blowout

1. Editors of *U.S. News, Triumph Without Victory*, pp. 349–50.
2. Garrett, Memo for Commander, p. 10.
3. Personal interview with General Peay, July 7, 1993.
4. Ibid.
5. Bolt, "Command Report," p. 55.
6. Personal interview with General Peay, July 7, 1993.
7. Cody, letter to author, August 10, 1993.
8. Ibid.
9. Costello, letter to author.

10. Chester, letter to author.
11. Kinney, letter to author.
12. Garrett, Memo for Commander, p. 11.
13. Lt. Col. William W. Bryan, documented interview: "Aviation in Desert Shield/Desert Storm, Attack Helicopters," section on the "Battle of the Causeway," undated, p. 77.

18. The Battle of the Causeway

1. Schwarzkopf, *It Doesn't Take a Hero*, p. 466.
2. Tape from Lt. Gen. Hugh Shelton, August 3, 1993.
3. Garrett, Memo for Commander.
4. Cody, letter to author.
5. Bryan, interview re: "Battle of the Causeway."
6. Ibid.

19. The SAR Incident

1. Shelton, letter to author.
2. Lt. Col. Rhonda Cornum, letter to author, October 23, 1993.
3. Ibid.
4. Ibid.
5. Bryan, interview re: "Battle of the Causeway."
6. Cornum, letter to author.
7. Garrett, Memo for Commander.
8. Cody, letter to author.
9. Cornum, letter to author.
10. Bolt, "Command Report," pp. 58–59.
11. "Combat Ready," *People* (August 10, 1992): 91–92.
12. Shelton, letter to author.
13. Schwarzkopf, *It Doesn't Take a Hero*, pp. 468–69.
14. Ibid., p. 470.
15. Ibid., pp. 470–71.

20. Cease-fire

1. Costello, letter to author.
2. Chester, letter to author.

21. The Road Home

1. Chester, letter to author.
2. Costello, letter to author.
3. Cody, letter to author.
4. Bolt, "Command Report," pp. 57–58.
5. Colonel Purdom Interview, *Army Times*.
6. Personal interview with General Peay, July 7, 1993.
7. Garrett, Memo for Commander.
8. Col. Stuart W. Gerald, Memo, Subject: DISCOM Desert Shield/Desert Storm Historical Summary, May 30, 1991.
9. Personal interview with General Peay, July 7, 1993.
10. Gerald, Memo, DISCOM Historical Summary, p. 6.
11. Riccardelli, speech.
12. Personal interview with General Peay, July 7, 1993.
13. Tilson, "It Begins," p. 1.
14. Personal interview with General Peay, July 7, 1993.
15. Ibid.

Sources

Army Times Interviews

In April 1992 at Fort Campbell, Kentucky, Sean D. Naylor, an *Army Times* staff writer, interviewed a number of officers of the 101st Airborne Division who had served with the division in the Gulf War. Tom Donnelly, the editor of *Army Times* at that time, generously sent me, for use in this book, copies of the tapes and transcripts of some of the interviews. Following are the officers whose interviews I used:

Berdy, Lt. Col. Andy, commander of the 2d Battalion, 187th Infantry Regiment.

Clark, Col. Robert T., commander of the 3d Brigade, 101st Airborne Division.

Garrett, Col. Thomas W., commander of the Aviation Brigade, 101st Airborne Division.

Hamlin, Lt. Col. John L., commander of the 2d Squadron, 17th Cavalry Regiment.

Hill, Col. James T. ("Tom"), commander of the 1st Brigade, 101st Airborne Division.

Johnson, Lt. Col. Robert J., commander of the 4th Battalion, 101st Aviation Regiment.

Peay, Maj. Gen. J. H. Binford, III, commanding general of the 101st Airborne Division.

Purdom, Col. Theodore, commander of the 2d Brigade, 101st Airborne Division.

Personal Interviews

Bradin, Col. James. Beaufort, S. C. July 14, 1993.

Peay, Gen. J. H. Binford, III. Fort Bragg, N.C. July 7 and August 16, 1993, and by telephone on August 20, 1993.

Peck, Lt. Col. Terry. Fort Bragg, N.C. November 4, 1992.

Scholes, Maj. Gen. Edison E. Fort Bragg, N.C. November 4, 1992.

Shelton, Lt. Gen. Hugh H. Fort Bragg, N.C. August 30, 1991, and tape, August 3, 1993.

Private Papers, Letters, and Personal Communications

Anderson, CW2 Keith C., unpublished essay, October 3, 1991.

Barnes, Lt. Jim, unpublished essay, October 1, 1991.

Blackburn, CW3 William, unpublished essay, October 10, 1991.

Chambers, Lt. Todd R., unpublished essay, September 30, 1991.

Chester, Maj. Steve, letter to author, March 19, 1993.

Cody, Lt. Col. Richard, CO, 1-101st Aviation Battalion, letters to author, November 12 and November 19, 1992, and August 10, 1993.

Conley, E4 Sean, C Co., 1-187th Infantry, letter to author, undated.

Cornum, Lt. Col. Rhonda, letter to author, October 23, 1993.

Costello, Lt. Col. Thomas J., letter to author, February 23, 1992.

Cottrell, WO1 David E., Jr., unpublished essay, October 12, 1991.

Dingwell, CW2 Gale, unpublished essay, October 13, 1991.

Dinter, Lt. Hienz, unpublished essay, October 1, 1991.

Drew, 1st Lt. Thomas R., letter to author, October, 18, 1992.

Ert, CW2 Van, unpublished essay, "The 100 Hour War," September 30, 1991.

Faircloth, CW3 James C., Jr., unpublished essay, October 12, 1991.

Farina, Lt. Roger, unpublished essay, October 9, 1991.

Gawkins, Lt. Michael, Memo, Subject: Overview of Desert Storm, October 1, 1991.

Gerald, Col. Stuart W., letter to author, July 3, 1991.

Gibson, Col. Emmitt, letter to author, August 22, 1993.

Griffith, Lt. Col. Michael C., letter to author, November 2, 1991.

Hancock, Lt. Col. Frank R., brief summary of battalion's operation, undated.

Harlan, Joe M., unpublished manuscript, "Desert Storm, Saudi Arabia," undated.

Hill, Col. Tom, brief summary of 1st Brigade operation, March 2, 1991.

Kamine, Sgt. Charles A., Jr., unpublished manuscript on Operation Desert Shield/Storm, undated.

Kinney, Lt. Col. Peter C., letter to author, April 11, 1993.

Kitchens, Chaplain Herbert, division chaplain, "More Stories," a series of unpublished anecdotes from the Gulf War written by several of the division's chaplains including Chaplain Bill Hatch, Chaplain Dennis R. Newton, and Chaplain Thomas E. Preston, undated.

Kurtz, CW2 A., unpublished essay, October 3, 1991.

Lippard, 1st Lt. Clifford M., 101st Airborne Division (Air Assault), History for Operation Desert Shield/Desert Storm, July 1, 1991.

Luck, Lt. Gen. Gary E., biographical sketch, undated.

McGrath, Capt. Ida M., unpublished manuscript, "Desert Shield," August 7, 1990, to January 15, 1991, undated.

Mackmull, Lt. Gen. Jack V., letter to author, July 18, 1993, on the origin of the air assault concept.

McNeill, Col. Dan K., two letters to author, November 7, 1990, and January 29, 1991.

Peay, Gen. J. H. Binford, III, letters to author, May 14, June 14, and July 30, 1991; February 27, 1992; and November 27, 1993; also biographical sketch, undated.

Peck, Lt. Col. Terry, letters to author, October 27 and November 27, 1992.

Ramos, WO1 Ramon E., unpublished essay, September 26, 1991.

Riccardelli, Lt. Col. Richard, speech to 736th Tank Battalion in Nashville, Tenn., September 12, 1991; letters to author, August 22, December 3, December 14, and December 27, 1991.

Ryan, 1st Lt. John, unpublished essay, October 1, 1991.

Sadariskis, Lt. Mike, unpublished essay, October 11, 1991.

Scholes, Maj. Gen. Edison, letter to author, April 26, 1991.

Shelton, Lt. Gen. Henry H., letters to author, October 10 and November 22, 1992; and tape, August 3, 1993.

Suchland, Spc. Stuart C., letter to author, undated.

Summers, Maj. K., unpublished essay, October 1, 1991.

Telephone Conversations

Bryan, Lt. Col. William, June 11, 1992.

Cody, Lt. Col. Richard, October 17, 1992.

Crist, Gen. George, September 22, 1992.

Disilvio, Maj. Richard, August 16, 1993; and on an almost daily basis between November 10 and November 30, 1993.

Gibson, Col. Emmitt E., September 3 and October 2, 1993.

Peay, Gen. J. H. Binford, III, August 16 and 20, 1993.

Peck, Lt. Col. Terry, October 22, November 16, and November 17, 1992.

Suddath, Maj. Gen. LeRoy N., Jr., September 17, 1992.

Thomas, Lt. Col. Charles G., January 23, May 6, May 18, May 27, and May 28, 1992.

Military Documents That Provided Many Facts and Background

Adams, Lt. Col. Russ. "History of 5-101st Aviation Regiment in Desert Shield and Storm." November 1, 1991.

Anderson, Col. Randall J. "After-Action Report of 101st Division (AASLT) Artillery in Operation Desert Storm, January–March 1991." January 5, 1991.

Bolt, Col. William J. "Command Report: 101st Airborne Division (Air Assault) for Operations Desert Shield and Desert Storm, 2 August 1990 through 1 May 1991." July 1, 1991.

Bryan, Lt. Col. William W., CO, 2d Battalion, 229th Aviation Regiment. Documented interview: "Aviation in Desert Shield/Desert Storm Attack Helicopters." Undated.

———. Memo for Record, Subject: Operations Desert Shield and Desert Storm After-Action Report, 2-229th Attack Helicopter Regiment. July 19, 1991.

Costello, Lt. Col. Thomas J. "Battalion History: 3d Battalion, 320th Field Artillery Regiment, Operation Desert Shield/Storm." Undated.

DeWitt, Lt. Col. Charles. Memo: "2d Battalion (Air Assault), 44th Air Defense Artillery." Undated.

Dundzila, Capt. Tomas A., preparer. "After-Action Report: 2d Brigade in Operation Desert Shield and Operation Desert Storm." 1991.

Garrett, Col. Thomas W., CO, 101st Aviation Brigade. Memo for Commanding General, 101st Airborne Division. Executive Summary: Operation Desert Shield/Desert Storm. June 10, 1991.

Gerald, Col. Stuart W. Memo, Subject: DISCOM Desert Shield/Desert Storm Historical Summary. May 30, 1991.

G-3 Staff Document. "Air Assault Division and Brigade Operations Manual." August 1988.

Hancock, Lt. Col. Frank R. Narrative of 1-327th Infantry in Desert Shield/Desert Storm, Fort Campbell, Ky. Undated.

Hill, Col. James Thomas. CO, 1st Brigade, 101st Airborne Division (Air Assault). Memo: "Historical Summary of Desert Destiny." June 14, 1991.

———. Memo: "1st Brigade Assault on FOB Cobra." March 2, 1991.

MacDonald, Capt. David L. 326th Medical Battalion. Memo for Assistant Chief of Staff, Civil and Military Affairs, 101st Airborne Division. October 31, 1991.

Nyberg, Lt. Col. James, ed. "Army Focus," June 1991.

Pirozzi, Capt. Thomas L., CO, 53d Quartermaster Detachment (Airdrop Support). Memo, Subject: Unit Historical Summary for Operation Desert Shield/Storm. May 10, 1991.

Riccardelli, Lt. Col. Richard F. 311th Military Intelligence Battalion, Command Narrative Report. June 15, 1991.

Scholes, Maj. Gen. Edison E. XVIII Airborne Corps Staff Paper, "Repositioning of XVIII Airborne Corps." Ft. Bragg, N.C. Undated.

VanAntwerp, Lt. Col. Robert L. 326th Engineer Battalion (Air Assault). Memo for Pratt Museum (Fort Campbell, Ky.): Unit History for Operation Desert Shield/Storm. June 14, 1991.

Magazines and Newspapers That Have Been Quoted from or That Proved Useful for Background

Cody, Lt. Col. Richard A., "Task Force Normandy," *Defence Helicopter* (Spring Supplement, 1992).

Donnelly, Tom. "The Generals' War," *Army Times*, March 2, 1992.

———. "From the Top," *Army Times*, February 24, 1992.

———. "Road to Baghdad," *Army Times*, January 25, 1993.

Editors. "Commander Cody and the 1-101st: Out With a Bang," *Apache*, October 1991.

Editors. *Newsweek.* "America at War," *NEWSWEEK*, Commemorative Edition (Spring/Summer 1991).

Editors. "Wings of Eagles: A Desert Storm Scrapbook," *The Leaf-Chronicle* (Clarksville, Tenn.), January 15, 1992.

Flanagan, Lt. Gen. Edward M., Jr. "Before the Battle," *Army* (November 1991).

Gleick, Elizabeth. "Combat Ready," *People* (August 10, 1992).

Mackenzie, Richard. "*Apache* Attack," *Air Force* (October 1991).

Naylor, Sean D. "Flight of Eagles," *Army Times*, July 22, 1991.

Steele, Dennis. "155 Miles into Iraq: The 101st Strikes Deep," *Army* (August 1991).

Tilson, Bettina. "It Begins." *Leaf-Chronicle Supplement* (Clarksville, Tenn.), January 16, 1992.

Wacker, Bob. "Who Won the Gulf War, Anyway?" *The Retired Officer* (August 1993).

Published Sources from Which Facts or Quotations Have Been Taken

Anderson, Jack, and Dale Van Atta. *Stormin' Norman.* New York: Kensington Publishing Corp., 1991.

Blair, Arthur H. *At War in the Gulf.* College Station, Texas: Texas A&M University Press, 1992.

Charlton, James, ed. *The Military Quotation Book.* New York: St. Martin's Press, 1990.

Devlin, Gerard M. *Paratrooper.* New York: St. Martin's Press, 1979.

Editors of *Time. Desert Storm: The War in the Persian Gulf.* New York: Time Warner Publishing, Inc., 1991.

Editors of *U.S. News & World Report. Triumph Without Victory.* New York: Times Books, Random House, 1992.

Grigson, Maj. Dan. (Concept) *North to the Euphrates.* Clarksville, Tenn.: Tennessee-Kentucky Chapter, Association of the United States Army (AUSA), 1991.

Jones, Col. Robert. *101st Airborne Division: U.S. Airborne, 50th Anniversary Book.* Paducah, Ky.: Turner Publishing Company, 1990.

Pagonis, Lt. Gen. William G. and Michael D. Krause, "Operational Logistics and the Gulf War," Arlington, Va.: Institute of Land Warfare, AUSA, October 1992.

Ryan, Cornelius. *A Bridge Too Far.* New York: Simon & Schuster, 1974.

Schwarzkopf, General H. Norman. *It Doesn't Take a Hero,.* New York: Bantam Books, 1992.

"Special Report: The U.S. Army in Desert Storm," Arlington, Va.: Institute of Land Warfare, AUSA, June 1991.

Woodward, Bob. *The Commanders*,. New York: Simon & Schuster, 1991.

Reviews and Comments

Cody, Lt. Col. Richard. Comments on chapter 13, October 12, 1992.

Gibson, Col. Emmitt E. Review of chapters 18, 19, and 20.

Peay, Gen. J. H. Binford, III. Comments on chapter 16, July 11, 1993, and review of entire manuscript.

Shelton, Lt. Gen. Henry H. Review of first eighteen chapters.

Index

About the Author

After graduating from the United States Military Academy at West Point in January 1943 (the first of the World War II–shortened West Point classes), EDWARD M. FLANAGAN, JR. spent the next thirty-five and a half years in the army, rising from second lieutenant to lieutenant general. In World War II, he commanded a parachute field artillery battery in the 11th Airborne Division in the Philippines; in the Korean War, he commanded the parachute field artillery battalion of the 187th Airborne Infantry Regiment; in the Vietnam War, he was an assistant division commander of the 25th Infantry Division and deputy chief of staff, operations, of the III Marine Amphibious Force. In peacetime, General Flanagan commanded the 3d Armored Division Artillery in Germany in 1964: the JFK Special Warfare Center at Fort Bragg, North Carolina, 1968–1971; the 1st Infantry Division at Fort Riley, Kansas, 1971–1972; and the Sixth U.S. Army, 1975–1978. As a staff officer, he was the comptroller of the army, 1974–1975, and deputy commander of the Eighth Army in Korea, 1974–1975. He retired in Beaufort, South Carolina, in 1978.

General Flanagan attended the full roster of army service schools to include the Army War College. While on the faculty of the Naval War College in Newport, Rhode Island, 1959–1962, he earned an M.A. in political science from Boston University. As a major general in 1970, he attended the army flight school at Fort Rucker, Alabama, where he qualified as a helicopter pilot and army aviator. He is also a master parachutist with one combat jump.

General Flanagan and his wife, Marguerite, have five children. They have lived abroad in Japan, Germany, and Korea. In the United States, the family has moved some nineteen times to keep up with changing army assignments. Currently, the general writes books on military history (this is his eighth).

As Samáwah

IRAQ
SAUDI ARABIA

As Salmán

French Forces

Rafhá'

AIRBORNE

82nd Airborne

AIRBORNE

101st Airborne

XVIII ABN CORPS

3rd Armored
Cavalry Regiment

BREACH

24th Mechanized
Infantry

2nd Armored
Cavalry Regiment

1st Armored   3rd Armored

ARMY CENTRAL
COMMAND

VII CORPS

OPERATION DESERT STORM
24–28 February 1991

Allied Advance, Phase 1

Allied Advance, Phase 2

Allied Advance, Phase 3

Allied Advance, Phase 4

0   60

MILES